Masters and Slaves

Revisioned Essays in Political Philosophy

Michael Palmer

LEXINGTON BOOKS
Lanham • Boulder • New York • Oxford

LEXINGTON BOOKS

Published in the United States of America
by Lexington Books
4720 Boston Way, Lanham, Maryland 20706

12 Hid's Copse Road
Cumnor Hill, Oxford OX2 9JJ, England

British Library Cataloguing in Publication Information Available

Library of Congress Cataloging-in-Publication Data

Palmer, Michael, 1952–
    Masters and slaves : revisioned essays in political philosophy / Michael Palmer.
    p. cm.
    Includes bibliographical references and index.
    ISBN 0-7391-0221-4 (alk. paper) / ISBN 0-7391-0277-X (pbk. : alk. paper)
      1. Political science—History. 2. Political science—Philosophy. I. Title.

JA81 .P28 2001
320'.01—dc21

                                              00-046353

Printed in the United States of America

♾™ The paper used in this publication meets the minimum requirements of American
National Standard for Information Sciences—Permanence of Paper for Printed Library
Materials, ANSI/NISO Z39.48–1992.

To
A and A
AB
BB
CB
C and D

Only good people are free, all wicked people are slaves
– Plutarch

Contents

Preface

The chapters of this book were not, with the exception of chapter 6, originally written to be published in this volume. Their order here nevertheless reveals a coherence in these writings of the past twenty years, which I shall briefly indicate.

I begin with chapters on the ancient philosophers' understanding of mastery and slavery, kingship and tyranny. I examine aspects of Aristotle's *Politics* and Plato's *Republic*. Then I explore Thucydides' presentation, in his *War of the Peloponnesians and the Athenians*, of the controversial career of Alcibiades, who was driven from Athens, with disastrous consequences for both the Athenian democracy and its empire, on the charge that he aspired to tyranny—mastery over his fellow Athenians, indeed all other human beings. I include a review of the most comprehensive contemporary discussion of Thucydides' assessment of Alcibiades' ambitions.

The central chapters make the transition to modern thought by exploring oft-remarked kinship between the ancient thinker Thucydides and the modern thinkers Machiavelli and Hobbes. First, I explore the question of whether Machiavelli and Thucydides are in agreement, as is often alleged, on the question of what constitutes "political virtue." I show that the kinship is more apparent than real. I then present a reading of Machiavelli's modern classic on politics, *The Prince*, to further elucidate the Machiavellian revolution in political philosophy. I critique what I call his "inhuman humanism"—his radical rejection of the transcendent, whether the "Good" or "God"—suggesting that it inevitably leads to understanding human beings as essentially beasts, and that this depreciation of "humanity" leads to so-called "postmodern" thought. Then comes a reading of Machiavelli's classic comedy of domestic life, his *Mandragola*, which demonstrates, among other things, how severely mistaken is the widespread belief that Machiavelli's lessons for princes are not applicable to ordinary citizens. The brief discussion of Hobbesian "realism" and Thucydidean "realism" indicates that alleged kinships between Hobbes and the ancient "realist" are as misleading as those alleged between Machiavelli and Thucydides. In a chapter on Rousseau's *Discourse on the Origin of Inequality among Men*, I show, among other things, how Rousseau tried to recover the insights of the ancient thinkers, but to place them on radically modern foundations.

The final chapters of the book are brief discussions of three twentieth-century "masters" (of admittedly differing degrees of mastery) whose work has most informed my own: Leo Strauss, George Parkin Grant, and Allan Bloom.

There are some arguments that appear in more than one chapter, which redundancies I have allowed to stand, because they are essential in their contexts, and because most readers will consult this book as a collection of discrete essays rather than a single essay, which is appropriate. While some revisions have been made in the chapters that are here reprinted, I can affirm without a trace of irony that no useful purpose would be served by comparing the originals with the reprints. Let me simply say that each of the essays here reprinted is now published as I originally intended it.

Acknowledgments

I owe a special debt of gratitude to Earhart Foundation for several generous research grants I have received over the years: to its president, David B. Kennedy; its secretary and director of program, Antony T. Sullivan; and its trustees. Earhart Foundation has now supported publication of all three of my books, in addition to earlier work that led to them. Without this financial assistance, I have no doubt that these books would not have appeared. Thanks are due also to the journals in which several of the chapters in this volume were originally published for permission to reprint; each of the relevant chapters includes a specific citation and acknowledgment of permission. Special thanks to my friend, James Pontuso, for chapter 7, and to Jeffrey Wilson for invaluable and extensive assistance with the preparation of the entire manuscript for publication, including the index.

Chapter 1

Mastering Slaves or Mastering Science?: An Aristotelian Reprise

The assertion in Aristotle's *Politics*, that there are slaves "by nature," is frequently attributed to his "ethnocentrism," even "racism," under the spell of which he held that non-Greeks were inferior "by nature" to Greeks, and may therefore be justly enslaved. Aristotle's prescriptive teaching on the just society is thus deemed radically flawed because it incorporates a slave class, which we—our vision free of the blinders of the "ancient Greek worldview"—recognize as an unnatural, irrational, and thus radically unjust institution.

I will defend Aristotle against the charge that his political philosophy was historically determined. Among other things, I will demonstrate: Aristotle did not believe Greeks were superior "by nature" to non-Greeks; he defined what a slave "by nature" would be, but knew perfectly well that all extant institutions of slavery were of merely conventional slavery; he was well aware that even the slave class proposed in his *Politics* would consist primarily, if not exclusively, of conventional slaves; and that this does not, in his reasonable judgment, undermine the legitimacy of the "best regime in speech" he proposed. Finally, I will indicate why, in fact, it does not. It goes without saying, nevertheless, I had better say it explicitly: my purpose here is not to advocate institutionalized slavery for the twenty-first century; I wish rather to dispel a reigning prejudice against taking Aristotle's political philosophy seriously.

A "methodological" comment: In reading Aristotle's *Politics*, I proceed on the assumption that his teaching concerning slavery may be simply true. I do so because it is impossible to approach any text without some assumptions, and this particular one is least likely to lead us to discover in the text only what we bring to it. Unless we approach the text with my simple assumption, I believe our modern prejudices will decisively militate against our taking its arguments seriously enough to be open-minded readers. Needless to say, initially approaching

1

Aristotle's teaching with the assumption that it may be true in no way precludes our judging it, upon consideration, false. But in the meantime, we avoid Nietzsche's charge against the "historical" studies of his own day (and not infrequently ours): these "historians" invariably dig up only what they, themselves, have buried.

The Natural Slave

First, I must outline Aristotle's discussion of slavery as it appears in the first book of the *Politics*.[1] In the first chapter, Aristotle states the view that it is erroneous to believe that the rulership of a statesman in a *polis* (political rule of citizens in a city) is the same as that of a monarch over a kingdom, a manager over a household, or a slave-master over a number of slaves (despotic rule). To sustain the legitimacy of the division of ruler and ruled in the *polis*, which must *somehow* be sustained, Aristotle insists that political rule and despotic rule are different in kind, not degree. In the immediate sequel—a discussion of the elements of the household—he speaks (somewhat paradoxically) of two "pairings" that constitute the "first pairing" of those who cannot do without one another: female and male, for the sake of generation, and the "naturally ruling" (neuter gender) and the "naturally ruled" (neuter gender) for the sake of preservation. (The use of the neuter gender renders it ambiguous whether Aristotle is here speaking of relations between human beings, although we tend to assume so.) The pairing of female and male results not from deliberation, but "the natural inclination to leave behind another of the same kind as oneself." As for the other pairing, the "naturally ruling" is whatever is capable of "looking ahead through intelligence (by thinking things through)"; the "naturally ruled" is whatever is capable only of "doing these things." That the naturally ruling should rule despotically, not politically, the naturally ruled is as "natural" for Aristotle as procreation.

In the second chapter, Aristotle observes, in his own name, that females and slaves are distinguished by nature, as are the needs of generation and preservation, but it is characteristic of "barbarians" to fail to distinguish women from slaves; he cites a poet (Euripides) who says it is fitting that Greeks should rule barbarians. This last is *not* Aristotle's own judgment in his own name. Lest I be accused of grasping at straws, it should be remarked that in the discussion of the three best cities known by Aristotle ever to have actually existed (2.9-11), as opposed to "best regimes" that have existed "in speech" only, he names and discusses Carthage, a non-Greek (i.e., barbarian) city of Africa, along with Sparta and Crete; furthermore, the treatment there suggests Carthage may be the best of the three (4.7).[2] Aristotle's judgments are neither racist nor ethnocentric.

It is undeniable that in chapter 2 of book 1 (from which he is usually quoted), Aristotle may appear oblivious to the manifold difficulties of the question of "natural slavery," but in the subsequent chapters (1.3-7), just how problematic the notion is clearly emerges. He forthrightly raises the question whether all human slavery is not merely conventional and therefore unjust. Admittedly, he chooses to deal with this and a number of related questions not so forthrightly, which is not to say deviously: he discusses what sorts of property are essential to a household, and the arts of acquisition.

A household has work to accomplish, and "if one expects the work to be accomplished, the household must be supplied with the proper instruments." A household slave is described as an instrument for living, and living well, a household possession, but with a soul. Such animate possessions could be dispensed with, Aristotle acknowledges, if inanimate possessions could be summoned to accomplish their work:

> Every assistant is as it were a tool that serves for several tools; for if every tool could perform its own work when ordered, or by seeing what to do in advance, like they say of the statues of Daedalus or the tripods of Hephaestus . . . master-craftsmen would have no need of assistants and masters no need of slaves. (1253b-1254a)

(Aristotle thus raises the question concerning technology—concerning which more anon—in the context of his discussion of the question concerning slavery.) A possession, according to Aristotle, is like a part, so the relation of slave to master is like that of part to whole. A slave "by nature" would be "one who is not his own by nature . . . while being a human being, he is a possession."

But it remains an open question for Aristotle whether there exist any human beings who fit this definition; if not, slavery would not exist "by nature"; it would be merely "conventional." And he asks whether it is "better and just" for anyone to serve as a slave, under any circumstances. Better (*beltion*) and just (*dikaion*) are not necessarily synonyms. Could the enslavement of some by others be better but not just? Should there prove to be no slaves "by nature," might it be just but not better to abolish all slavery? Is it not possible that the practical alternatives to slavery might only be worse?

Having raised but not answered the question whether there are any human beings who fit the definition of the slave "by nature," Aristotle turns to a general argument that nature cannot be a *chaos* in which all atoms are equal, but must be a *cosmos* consisting of ruling and ruled elements. He then offers the clearest example he ever provides in the *Politics* of the relation between "naturally ruling" and "naturally ruled," which is that between soul and body in a properly constituted human being. It is to properly constituted beings, not those in a corrupted condition, that we must look to discover what is "natural." And in an uncorrupted human being of the best sort, the soul rules the body "despotically" (like a master rules a slave), and the intellect rules the appetites "politically," or "royally" (with persuasion). This seems crucial for understanding the slave "by nature": a naturally servile human being possesses a soul, but it is ill-constituted, because the soul does not rule the body; consequently, for the proper relation of soul to body to prevail, the servile human being's body requires a ruling soul— the kind of soul that rules the body, and is therefore worthy of ruling slaves.[3] Would that nature very often achieved her intention (according to Aristotle) of giving the "naturally free" the bodies of freemen and the "naturally servile" the bodies of slaves, so the appearance of bodies reflected the beauty of souls! There would then be as little difficulty determining who should rule and who should be ruled as there would, say, in judging a contest between Gulliver and the Lilliputians. Unfortunately, Aristotle remarks, nature disappoints here more often than not.

Next, Aristotle deals with the much-labored dispute (both in his own time and in the commentaries on his *Politics*)[4] whether superior strength implies superior virtue, thus the right to rule: does might make right? He avers that even the "wise" differ on this question. He demonstrates that both sides in the dispute actually hold his own position that slavery is just, *if* it is a case of a "natural ruler" and a "natural slave," and unjust if not. He later states in his own name (7.2) that successful conquerors may be in the wrong, and that superior virtue nonetheless requires equipment, the possession of which is not infrequently a matter of chance. In any case, he here claims no reasonable person would maintain that human beings of the highest nobility are slaves "by nature" because they happen to be taken captive in a war. He then extends this reasoning to the question of "nobility." Greeks regard themselves as well-born and noble everywhere, but "barbarians" as well-born only relative to other "barbarians." Aristotle says this amounts to the claim that as human being is born of human being, beast of beast, so the good are born of the good; he, himself, holds that nature may desire this result, but it frequently does not obtain. He thus distinguishes his own understanding from that of his fellow Greeks (which is again supported by reference to a poet).

Aristotle summarizes: clearly not all relationships of mastery and slavery are "natural"; the relationship between a "natural master" and a "natural slave" would be one of mutual advantage and friendship, which is not possible between a master and a slave of the other (i.e., "conventional") sort.[5] Finally, the proper employment of slaves, not their acquisition, is said to be the master's proper science. The proof of this is that whoever can employ subordinates to manage their slaves, does so, in order that they, themselves, can engage in politics and philosophy. Thus concludes Aristotle's thematic discussion of mastery and slavery.

The Conventional Slave

We expect next a discussion of relations between husband and wife, and parents and children, as constituent elements of the household, which seemed to be promised earlier (1.3), then discussions of the constituent elements of the village, and the *polis*. But, having discussed the slave as an article of property, Aristotle presents instead several chapters on the subject of property in general, and of the natural and unnatural arts of acquisition (1.8-11). We learn, among other things, that among the "natural" modes of acquisition, war must be included, for hunting is a part of war, and "should be used against wild beasts and that part of mankind that is meant by nature, but is unwilling to be ruled." These

slave-raids are said to be natural and just (cf. 4.4, 7.14).[6] Aristotle does not re-
vert to the question of the constituent elements of the household until the end of
the first book (1.12-13), and then it is again to raise the question of the nature of
the slave.[7] Indeed, oft-quoted assertions from chapter 2 to the contrary notwithstanding, Aristotle's presentation throughout book 1 of the *Politics*—his introduction to politics—clearly suggests that the slavery question is peculiarly
problematical.

Having completed his discussion of acquisition, complete with its revela-
tions concerning slave-raids, Aristotle raises the startling question, in the last
chapter of the first book (1.13), of what kinds and degrees of virtue—human
excellence—are possessed by slaves! If slaves possess virtue, and they indeed
must—more, in fact, than is required of artisans, according to Aristotle—and
they are human beings who share in reason, how are they different "by nature"
from freemen? Good question. Especially since he insists that the virtues of the
"naturally ruling" and the "naturally ruled" must differ in kind, not only degree,
just as ruling and being ruled differ in kind.

Myriad questions arise from the ensuing discussion, and those who wish
may pursue them in the voluminous literature. In a rare display of daring for an
Aristotle scholar, Hamburger remarks, "The concept of natural slave has re-
tained its basic meaning throughout the social changes of the centuries. The
abolition of slavery proper has not abolished the slave nature."[8] But critics of the
argument are legion. According to one, "Aristotle's treatment of the question
contains implicitly the refutation of his [own] theory," although he deserves
credit at least for proposing the "revolutionary" view that "Greeks should in any
case not enslave Greeks."[9] Others credit him for having been the first to appreciate the difficulties of the slavery question, although "a successful solution of it
was for him impossible"; for example, he admits a slavish soul may inhabit a
beautiful body, and vice versa, and "he cannot deny that these [examples] are
numerous; and yet he does not observe, that therefore of necessity, there must be
many cases where slavery as it actually exists is in perpetual conflict with the
law of nature, even as laid down by himself."[10] Another more cautiously observes, "Aristotle would find in the Greek society of his own day as many slave
owners who had no business to own slaves as slaves who had no business to be
enslaved. His theory of slavery implies, if followed to its results, the illegitimacy
of the relation of master and slave in a large proportion of the cases in which it
existed."[11]

I propose even greater caution. I suggest that if the logic of Aristotle's reasoning leads to the conclusion that slavery as practiced in ancient Greece was
not in accord with nature, even as understood by him, Aristotle may be aware of
this logical necessity; that if there are obvious contradictions in Aristotle's presentation, he may be as aware of them as we, so they cease to be simply contradictions—they are rather paradoxes; that if Aristotle indeed fully appreciated the
difficulties inherent in the slavery question, a successful solution of them was no
more "impossible" for him than for us.

It is time for us in the twentieth century, as we approach the twenty-first, to pass beyond the pandemic "age discrimination," which is the legacy of the "historical consciousness" of the nineteenth. At a minimum, we must acknowledge that Aristotle's teaching on "natural slavery" may properly be understood as much as an attack on as a defense of slavery as it was practiced in ancient Greece. But even a view of Aristotle's defense as a covert attack is insufficient. We must go further to appreciate his insights into the question of slavery and the human good. We must address the greatest difficulty confronting a sympathetic reading of Aristotle: not the discussion of "natural slavery" in the first book of the *Politics*, but reconciling the "revolutionary" treatment of the slavery question in book 1 with his advocacy of a slave class for his own "best regime in speech" in book 7, which is the culmination of his political philosophy.

Slavery in the Best Regime

Aristotle's "best regime" is intended to rival that of Socrates in the *Republic* of Plato. Aristotle's rule of "gentlemen" is an explicit response to the Socratic notion of rule by "philosopher-kings." The existence of this class of gentlemen seems to require the institution of a very large slave class—*larger*, in fact, than was traditional Greek practice[12]—a slave class unquestionably consisting of human beings who are slaves by convention, not "by nature."[13] That they will be conventional slaves, there can be no doubt: Aristotle says he will later discuss why it is wise that all these slaves should have freedom set before them as a reward for good service! Given the enormous difficulties this poses for his discussion of "natural slavery," we should scarcely be surprised to find that, "This promise . . . is not fulfilled."[14] We can easily surmise why not, but we must confront the problem boldly: How can the "best regime to be wished or prayed for" (1260b29) justify as its foundation so fundamental an injustice as a massive system of conventional slavery?

We begin with the obvious. Aristotle is not a democrat. The special theme of the *Politics* is the "best regime" (2.1). As Lord remarks, "The 'best regime' is in the strictest sense the way of life of the class which rules in the well-constituted city."[15] Strauss discusses Aristotle's reasonable preference for the *polis* as the political community *par excellence*, and comments on his "perfect solution" to the political problem: a city without a *demos*.[16] In Aristotle's view, the *polis* is the political association most salubrious to the practice of virtue, which practice constitutes the good life, the natural end of humanity; the institution of slavery appears to be the necessary condition for the leisure required for the life of virtue. (This life will be pursued, to be sure, only by the few; at least for Aristotle, this is preferable to its being pursued by none, in the name of "equality.") Concerning the relation of necessity and nature in Aristotle's thought, Ambler remarks, "The suggestion is not simply that necessity excuses but that necessity bestows naturalness."[17] Something akin to this is true of Aristotle's understanding of the dynamic of necessity and justice: in Aristotle's understanding of natural right, all fixed rules of justice are mutable; there are circumstances in which it is necessary to abrogate a rule of justice theretofore understood to be immutable; in such circumstances, the abrogation is not merely excusable, it may be just.[18] But the question remains: What necessity can bestow naturalness, or justice, on an institution of slavery theretofore understood to be unnatural, or unjust? Must leisure for some to pursue the good life be bought at the expense of the freedom of others? Is there no alternative preferable to slavery?

Aristotle's implicit preference for slavery over the practical alternatives is indicated in his critique of one of his few predecessors in the field of political philosophy, Hippodamus of Miletus (2.8). Aristotle presents Hippodamus as an innovator; indeed, he is presented as the first political scientist. His eccentric manner of living, grounded in his love of honor, is described in a biographical sketch that is unique in the *Ethics* and *Politics*.[19] His ambition included the desire to be learned on the whole of nature. His procedure was to organize everything in his city (apparently rationally) into "threes": three classes of citizens; three divisions of land; three kinds of laws. Among the many novel suggestions he proposed for his own "best regime" was the idea that anyone who proposes novel suggestions to improve the regime should be rewarded with honors.

Aristotle indulges in a disproportionately lengthy criticism of this proposal. The criticism revolves around Hippodamus's having confused, in Aristotle's view, what is appropriate to other arts or sciences (*technai*) with what is appropriate to political science.[20] The idea of infinite progress may be good in the *techne* of medicine or gymnastics, and Aristotle does not doubt progress in political knowledge, too, has been made. But it is the peculiar nature of laws that it is often better to leave even defective ones unaltered, for habitual custom alone, according to Aristotle, ensures obedience to law, and the consequent political stability and prosperity. On this hinges his acceptance of slavery in even the "best regime in speech." Aristotle understands that progress in the arts and sciences necessarily affects social and political life. It would perhaps be good if the "best regime" could combine "scientific progress" with the stability required for decent political life. But it is not possible. Aristotle recognizes implicitly that technology is not a "thing" human beings can pick up and put down at will. He implicitly understands the dynamism of technology. He remarks the unintended results of certain innovations (2.12), and especially remarks the adverse consequences of advances in military technology (4.13), implying, in general, the improbability of political stability, even human decency, in an era of technological progress. Aristotle's treatment of the question of slavery versus technology sheds light on the character of his political science altogether. Aristotle's *Politics* seeks to reveal the truth about political things while at the same time having a salutary effect on political life. And even his wishes and prayers for the "best regime" are limited to what is possible (1325b38-39). I believe Aristotle made the conscious political choice, in the name of the common good of humanity, against technology.

The Modern Alternative

In the modern era, different choices were made. The modern political philosophers, beginning most powerfully with Machiavelli, and in explicit opposition to
Aristotelian political philosophy, opened a new path for human endeavor. The
"clarion call of Machiavelli's *Prince*" (to paraphrase Spinoza) was to rape the
ancient Roman goddess, Fortuna, to conquer the role of chance in human affairs.
As for the new "God" of the new "Rome"—the Roman Church—He is simply,
and in chapter 25 of the *Prince*, literally, dropped from the discussion.

This Machiavellian revolution in moral-political philosophy began a generation or so before the Copernican revolution in science, and about a century
before the advent of modern experimental science, and helped prepare the
ground for them. Francis Bacon explicitly acknowledged his debt to Machiavelli, and, following him, called for the conquest of nature "for the relief of
man's estate." It was left to Descartes to discover the "new method" that would
enable the Baconian project to proceed, and to Thomas Hobbes (who, before
achieving his own fame, had been private secretary to Bacon) to elaborate the
new "natural law" teaching that would eventually lead, in John Locke's successful "natural rights" formulation of it, to the institution of the new political arrangements that were required by the "new methods" of the "new sciences" and
their projects. The most famous popular political expression of this teaching is
found in the "inalienable rights" doctrine of the U.S. Declaration of Independence.

And where has this new path for human endeavor—the revolution against
classical political philosophy and Christianity (or "Platonism for the people," as
Nietzsche calls it)—led us? We today live in the midst of the alternative Aristotle implicitly rejected. Surely we must admire Aristotle's remarkable political
prescience. All is not well in the "New Atlantis." "Alienation" is pandemic, "ni-
hilism" epidemic. Many of the most eloquent philosophic voices of our time
speak in tones of lamentation, even despair. Simone Weil sorrowfully bewails
"the need for roots."[21] Martin Heidegger tells us that our day is a dreadful night,
and warns, "an attack with technological means is being prepared upon the life
and nature of man compared with which the explosion of the hydrogen bomb
means little. For precisely if the hydrogen bombs do *not* explode and human life
on earth is preserved, an uncanny change in the world moves upon us."[22] "What
is worth doing in this barren twilight," George Grant laments, "is the incredibly
difficult question."[23]

What is worth doing? Thinking, perhaps. About Aristotle, for example. "It
is not self-forgetting and pain-loving antiquarianism nor self-forgetting and in-
toxicating romanticism which induces us to turn with passionate interest, with
unqualified willingness to learn, toward the political thought of classical antiquity. We are impelled to do so by the crisis of our time, the crisis of the West."[24]

I believe that considerate attention to the *Politics* leaves little doubt that
Aristotle was able, in principle, to envision the modern predicament. As we saw
earlier, he explicitly mentions—with reference to the legendary statues of

Daedalus and tripods of Hephaestus—the possibility of the kind of technological progress that could lead to the abolition of all human slavery, even drudgery. But Aristotle compels the open-minded at least to consider the harsh alternatives as he did: Given the choice of the liberation of a mastering science with powerful technological arms, in the name of abolishing the injustice of conventional slavery, or defending a doctrine of "natural slavery" that implies a philosophic critique of conventional slavery, but which at the same time lends political support to slavery (sans excesses), in the name of the political society he thought most salubrious to the development of human excellence, Aristotle chose the latter.

If we are willing to be thinkers, not ideologues, perhaps we might find it within our capacities to suppress our democratic *ressentiment*, to read Aristotle with our eyes open, our mouths shut, and our minds free. Confronted as we are with such boons to human excellence and the good life as social and genetic engineering, not to mention thermonuclear annihilation, surely, even in good conscience, Aristotle's "notorious" teaching on slavery should at least give us pause. There are many more kinds of slavery than one might at first think, and some things are more important than "equality." And the problem with the legendary statues of Daedalus was that once they were given life, they ran away from their master.

Notes

This chapter was originally published in *The Maine Scholar 1* (1988). Reprinted with permission. Thanks to Christopher Bruell for helpful comments on the original draft.

1. References to the *Politics* are either by book and chapter numbers as found in *The Politics of Aristotle*, trans. Sir Ernest Barker (New York: Oxford University Press, 1958), the best-known English translation, or by the standard Bekker numbers as found in the Oxford Classical Texts edition of the Greek. The best English translation is *The Politics*, trans. Carnes Lord (Chicago: University of Chicago Press, 1984). Translations in this essay are mine to the extent that I have checked them against the Greek, and altered them for accuracy and consistency.

Conventional "historical" interpretations of Aristotle's political theory may be found in Sir Ernest Barker, *The Political Thought of Plato and Aristotle* (New York: Dover Press, 1959); Sir R. J. F. Chance, *Until Philosophers Are Kings* (Washington, N.Y.: Kennikat Press, 1968); J. Ferguson, *Aristotle* (Boston: Twayne Publishers, 1972); E. A. Havelock, *The Liberal Temper of Greek Culture* (New Haven, Conn.: Yale University Press, 1964); Donald Kagan, *The Great Debate: History of Greek Political Thought from Homer to Polybius* (New York: Free Press, 1965); G. E. R. Lloyd, *Aristotle: The Growth and Structure of His Thought* (Cambridge: Cambridge University Press, 1968); R. G. Mulgan, *Aristotle's Political Theory* (Oxford: Oxford University Press, 1977); W. L. Newman, *The Politics of Aristotle* (New York: Arno Press, 1973 [1887]); W. D. Ross, *Aristotle* (London: Methuen, 1949); F. Susemihl and R. D. Hicks, *Aristotle's Politics* (New York: Arno Press, 1976 [1894]); A. E. Taylor, *Aristotle* (New York: Dover Press, 1981); and N. Wood and E. Wood, *Class Ideology and Ancient Political Theory: Socra-*

tes, Plato, and Aristotle in Social Context (Oxford: Basil Blackwell, 1978). There are, of course, differences of interpretation and emphasis among these scholars: Barker and Newman, for example, suggest that Aristotle's treatment of the slavery question makes him something of a reformer in his historical context; Havelock, Kagan, Taylor, and especially the Woods view him as especially illiberal, even for an ancient Greek.

An earlier formulation of my own views on the questions addressed in this article, "Slavery and Aristotle's Best Regime," was presented at the 1983 annual meeting of the Canadian Political Science Association. I was then, and am now, indebted above all to Leo Strauss, *The City and Man* (Chicago: Rand McNally, 1964). See also Harry V. Jaffa, "Aristotle," in Leo Strauss and Joseph Cropsey, eds., *History of Political Philosophy* (Chicago: Rand McNally, 1963). For interpretations that take a similar approach, see Laurence Berns, "Rational Animal-Political Animal: Nature and Convention in Human Speech and Politics," *The Review of Politics 38* (1976): 177-89; Mary P. Nichols, "The Good Life, Slavery, and Acquisition: Aristotle's Introduction to Politics," *Interpretation 11* (1983): 171-83; and Catherine Zuckert, "Aristotle on the Limits and Satisfactions of Political Life," *Interpretation 11* (1983): 185-206. Wayne Ambler, "Aristotle on Acquisition," *Canadian Journal of Political Science 17* (1984): 487-502; "Aristotle's Understanding of the Naturalness of the City," *The Review of Politics 47* (1985): 163-85; and "Aristotle on Nature and Politics: The Case of Slavery," *Political Theory 15* (1987): 390-410, is a remarkable series of articles that shed much light on the *Politics*, especially on book 1 and the special role of 1.2 in the plan of Aristotle's argument. A brilliant study of several important dimensions of Aristotle's thinking is Carnes Lord, *Education and Culture in the Political Thought of Aristotle* (Ithaca, N.Y.: Cornell University Press, 1982), which includes a lucid introduction discussing the general character of Aristotle's political science. As regards Strauss, *City and Man*, I find myself in the embarrassing position of having to acknowledge my enormous debt to his concise and cryptic interpretation of the *Politics*, while admitting I may not understand it. But I find confirmation of the approach I have taken in this article in the plan of Strauss's essay. The chapter on Aristotle is a mere three dozen pages, and appears to be divided into five or six parts. The first part takes up almost half the essay, and half that is devoted to Aristotle's critique of Hippodamus. In the middle of this discussion, Strauss inserts an unidentified quotation: "The very nature of public affairs often defeats reason." Strauss's commentary on this dictum begins, "One illustration taken from Aristotle's *Politics* must suffice. In the first book, Aristotle sets forth the dictate of reason regarding slavery" (22). See also Seth Benardete, "Leo Strauss's *The City and Man,*" *Political Science Reviewer 8* (1978): 1-20

2. Cf. Barker, *Political Thought of Aristotle*, 83-84.

3. Cf. Newman, *Politics of Aristotle*, 149.

4. See Susmihl and Hicks, *Aristotle's Politics*, 205-9.

5. The claim of mutual advantage is later qualified, 3.6; on friendship between masters and slaves, cf. *Nichomachean Ethics,* 1161aff.

6. Cf. Lord, *Education and Culture*, 194-95.

7. Cf. Barker, *Politics of Aristotle*, 22nD, 38nH.

8. Max Hamburger, *Morals and Laws: The Growth of Aristotle's Legal Theory* (Cheshire, Conn.: Biblio and Tanen, 1965), 139.

9. Ross, *Aristotle*, 241-42.

10. Susemihl and Hicks, *Aristotle's Politics*, 24-25; cf. 160-61.

11. Newman, *Politics of Aristotle*, 151.

12. Ibid., 152.

13. Cf. Lord, *Education and Culture*, 65, 138-39, 186; Strauss, *City and Man*, 23.

14. Barker, *Politics of Aristotle*, 305.

15. Lord, *Education and Culture*, 145; cf. Newman, *Politics of Aristotle*, 144.

16. Strauss, *City and Man*, 130-37.

17. Ambler, "Aristotle on Acquisition," 496.

18. Leo Strauss, *Natural Right and History* (Chicago: University of Chicago Press, 1953), 160-63.

19. See Jaffa, "Aristotle," 86; Strauss, *City and Man*, 18.

20. Cf. Jaffa, "Aristotle," 88; and Strauss, *City and Man*, 21-29.

21. Simone Weil, *The Need for Roots* (London: Routledge & Kegan Paul, 1952).

22. Martin Heidegger, *Discourse on Thinking* (New York: Harper & Row, 1966), 52

23. George Grant, *Technology and Empire* (Toronto: House of Anansi, 1969), 78.

24. Strauss, *City and Man*, 1.

Chapter 2

Kings, Philosophers, and Tyrants in Plato's *Republic*

At the center of the *Republic* Socrates introduces the paradox of philosopher-kings (473c-d).[1] That the notion of philosopher-kings is paradoxical is emphasized by him (472a, 473e). But the proposal is not paradoxical to Glaucon; it is shocking (473e-474a), more shocking than Socrates' proposals concerning gender equality or the abolition of the private family. It is difficult for us—cultural heirs of Plato's astonishingly successful defense of the life of philosophy—to appreciate this; indeed, it is frequently difficult for us even to notice it (cf. Bloom, 130). But this and other remarkable facts that remain unnoticed must be remarked before we can understand why the proposal of philosopher-kings is so shocking to Glaucon, why Socrates fully expects it to be, and why it is so problematical even, or especially, to Socrates himself.

Boys (Book 1)

In the opening sentence of the *Republic* we learn from Socrates that he went down to the Piraeus "yesterday" (327a) with Plato's brother, Glaucon, and that as they were making their way back up to town, the two were arrested by a party led by Polemarchus and including Plato's other brother, Adeimantus. This party had "apparently" (327c) come from the procession that Socrates and Glaucon had themselves just observed.[2] In the ensuing conversation concerning whether Socrates and Glaucon will remain in the Piraeus for the evening, Glaucon answers questions on behalf of Socrates—questions never addressed to him—three times (327b-328b). As a result, Socrates remains in the Piraeus and goes with the others to the home of Polemarchus's father, Cephalus.

At Cephalus's home are a number of invited guests, the most conspicuous of whom is Thrasymachus, the famous Chalcedonian rhetorician. By now it

13

must be clear to Socrates that Glaucon's earlier audacity is explained by the fact that Plato's two brothers have conspired with Polemarchus to arrange a confrontation at Polemarchus's father's home between the distinguished dinner guest Thrasymachus and the undistinguished and uninvited Socrates.[3] Socrates' growing awareness that he is the victim of such a conspiracy may in part explain his subsequent treatment of Cephalus, which is, at best, indelicate (especially 328e, 329e, 331c-d), and which embarrasses not so much Cephalus, who laughs it off, as Polemarchus, who earnestly comes to the rescue of his father, for whose humiliation at the hands of Socrates he must feel himself somewhat responsible (331d).[4]

The discussion of justice begins in the midst of Socrates' conversation with Cephalus, but Cephalus is never asked by Socrates how he would define justice. Socrates rather extracts a definition of justice from Cephalus's answer to a question about the greatest good he has enjoyed from possessing great wealth, and it is not clear that the definition Socrates extracts is an altogether fair inference (330d-331d; cf. Strauss, 67-68). Polemarchus, however, cites Simonides in support of his father's position, and explicitly consents to Socrates' claim that he understands Simonides to define justice as doing good to friends and harm to enemies (331e-332d). But Socrates is eventually able to persuade him that this definition of justice cannot possibly be that of Simonides or any wise man; rather, it must belong to tyrants or rich men (like Cephalus) with high opinions of what they can do with their power and wealth (335e-336a).

It is likely that at least the last section of Socrates' discussion with Polemarchus, if not the entire discussion, is really directed at Thrasymachus, whose reactions to the discussion Socrates has been observing for some time, and who bursts forth like a wild beast (336b) to defend explicitly the life of tyranny as the best possible life for a human being (344a-b; cf. Strauss, 73; Benardete, 20). Thrasymachus and Socrates are known to each other (337a, 338a, 350d); indeed, Thrasymachus's position apparently takes no one by surprise (358c).

After a series of convoluted arguments with Thrasymachus, Socrates succeeds in embarrassing him in front of his audience of potential fee-paying students (cf. 345a), succeeds in confusing if not refuting him (350d-e; Strauss, 74, says that Thrasymachus blushes only on account of the heat; cf. Benardete, 28). This embarrassment of Thrasymachus, this silencing of Thrasymachus, the *aporia* that ends book 1, is a satisfactory conclusion to the discussion of justice that took place that night in the Piraeus: satisfactory to Socrates, at least, for he tells us that with this conclusion, "yesterday's" discussion of justice, which he did not initiate, was, so far as he was concerned, at an end (357a).[5]

Kings (Books 2-4)

The aporetic conclusion of their discussion of justice was not satisfactory, however, to Glaucon. Consequently, it turned out to be only a prelude for Socrates, too, because Glaucon, who is said to be courageous in everything, would not acquiesce in the mere silencing of Thrasymachus's argument in favor of the tyrannical life: Glaucon wants—or at least Glaucon claims before this audience that he wants—a genuine refutation of Thrasymachus's argument (357a-b). It appears to Glaucon that Thrasymachus has been charmed like a snake, not refuted (358b). Glaucon will play devil's advocate (358c-d, thereby showing himself craftier than Thrasymachus, who is so unsly as to declare himself a wolf, openly, before the sheep; cf. Bloom, 339; Benardete, 29). Glaucon will restore Thrasymachus's argument (358c-362c), but on a deeper foundation than Thrasymachus had laid it, the philosophic distinction between *physis*, or nature, and *nomos*, or convention (throughout his long speech, but most explicitly at 359c).[6]

Glaucon thinks himself a real man's man (*hos alethos andra*, 359b), and with good reason, apparently: Socrates emphatically remarks his manliness (*andreiotatos*, 357a) before recounting his speech, and tells us that he marveled at the natures of both Glaucon and Adeimantus, after the latter completed the challenge to Socrates begun by the former (367e).[7] Glaucon is attracted to the life of tyranny, or at least to the life of political power and prestige, and he takes Thrasymachus's argument, that the life of the tyrant is the supreme political life, with the utmost seriousness. Indeed, Socrates is incredulous that Glaucon and Adeimantus are able to make so persuasive an argument in favor of the life of injustice, while not being persuaded by it themselves (368a). Yet, however ambivalent Glaucon's attraction to the life of tyranny may or may not be, his attraction to political life is unequivocal; this serves as the basis for Socrates' re-education of Glaucon, the "turning around" of Glaucon's soul (cf. 508c-d, 514b, 515c, 518c-519a), which Socrates effects throughout the remainder of their conversation.

Socrates claims, in response to the challenge of Glaucon and Adeimantus, that he cannot meet it, but it would be impious of him to walk away from it, so he devises a strategy for dealing with the challenge that enables him to avoid having to meet it, at least on its own terms. He suggests that, rather than looking for justice in the individual human soul, as the brothers had challenged him to do, they found a "city in speech" together, in order to view the genesis of justice and injustice in it. He suggests that the city is to the individual soul as big letters are to little letters, and that it would be a godsend for men who do not see very sharply, challenged to read the little letters, to be able to read the big letters, somewhere else in a bigger place, before attempting the little ones, "if, of course, they do happen to be the same" (368d-369a). As usual, Socrates' procedure is questionable: everything depends upon this "if." But how could we possibly know that the little letters are the same as the big letters, if our eyes are not sharp enough to read the little ones, no matter how well we had learned to read the bigger ones? Everything depends upon the identity (not mere similitude) of the big letters and the little letters, although this procedure cannot possibly establish that identity (cf. Benardete, 45-46). Regardless of how questionable the procedure is, however—and Socrates, himself, later emphasizes it (435c-d, 504b-c)—it governs Glaucon's education in the *Republic*.

Socrates founds the first city, or the first stage of the city, with Adeimantus. It arises from the fact that human beings have various needs, on the one hand,

and different capacities, based upon different natures, on the other, so that the "city of utmost necessity" would consist of four or five men, supplementing each other's different capacities in satisfying one another's common needs (369b-370b). The principle that rules the rest of the dialogue is here established: "Each thing becomes more plentiful, finer, and easier, when one man, exempt from other tasks, does one thing according to nature and at the crucial moment" (370c). "Throngs of other men" (371b) join Adeimantus's city before it has grown to completeness, at which point Socrates wonders aloud where justice and injustice would be in it, along with what things that they considered did justice and injustice come into being (371e)?

It is hardly surprising that Adeimantus is unable to answer this question, for neither can Socrates, who rather describes idyllically the manner of life the men in this city would lead, until Glaucon interrupts him (372a-b; cf. Bloom, 348). Glaucon thinks that Adeimantus and Socrates have envisioned a city of sows who must have their feasts without relishes (372c-d). Socrates prefers to call Adeimantus's city the true or truthful and healthy city, but readily agrees with Glaucon to consider the genesis of a luxurious or feverish city (372e). The feverish city's luxuries will require that it possess more land, but rather than simply posit sufficient land for the city, as was done for Adeimantus's initial territory, Socrates prefers to posit Glaucon's need to cut off a piece of his neighbor's land, which raises the question of war, which in turn calls forth an entire army for the city (373d-e). Glaucon's manliness is offended at the idea that the men of his city will not be manly enough to defend themselves; he must be reminded of their agreement that it is not possible for one man to do a fine job in many arts (374a). The importance of war for the city makes this especially true for the part of the city that has to do with war—the guardians, as they are here called for the first time (374c-e).

What nature will be best suited for these guardians? A nature conspicuous for its *thymos*, its spiritedness (375a-b). Then how will they not be savage to their fellows and their fellow citizens, gentle to their own and cruel only to their enemies (375c)? The existence, by nature, of the disposition of noble dogs supposedly establishes that the guardian nature that they are seeking is not against nature, which is amazing in itself; more amazing is Socrates' addition that these spirited men, like noble dogs, must also, like dogs (and not even noble ones!), be philosophic in their nature (375d-e). In this paradoxical, not to say baffling way, Socrates introduces philosophy in the *Republic*.[8]

Having found, then, the nature that they are looking for, what sort of nurture would be best for these guardians? Would this help us to understand the genesis of justice and injustice in the city in speech (376c)? Socrates wants neither a long nor no discussion of this matter, but Glaucon's brother certainly thinks that it warrants sustained discussion; so Socrates agrees that, like men at leisure telling myths within a myth, he and Adeimantus will educate the men in speech (376d).

After discussing at some length the content and the form of the music education of the guardians (376e-398b)—the new "theology" (379a) in which they will be instructed, and their new understanding of Hades, and what it means to be a hero, including the stricture that the guardians must not be lovers of laughter (388e)—Glaucon reenters the conversation, laughing, and resumes the place his brother had usurped as Socrates' interlocutor, for the discussion of music in the narrower sense of song and melody, which ends—fittingly—in a discussion of erotic matters concerning the fair or beautiful (398c-403c; cf. Strauss, 100; Benardete, 67). A shorter discussion of gymnastic education for the bodies follows, although it turns out that gymnastic education, no less than music education, is really education for the soul, especially the spirited part (410b-c; cf. Benardete, 59, who maintains that music education is for the philosophic nature and gymnastic for the thumoeidetic).

Next, what must be determined is who among these men will rule in this city and who will be ruled (412b), who will be the "complete guardians" and who the "auxiliary guardians" (414a-b). The paramount criterion that the rulers must care for the city (412d) leads Socrates to propound the "noble lie" (414b). While Socrates had previously asserted that they had completed their discussion of the models of education and rearing (412b), the "noble lie" is the very foundation of the education of the "auxiliary guardians" of their city, if not the "complete guardians" (414c).

No one balks at the prospect of expounding the "noble lie" in the city; but Adeimantus, who wants the good life to be not only just but easy (364a), balks at the hard living conditions that will be imposed upon the auxiliary guardians (415d-417b). He demands an apology from Socrates for failing to make these men happy (419a). Socrates would not be surprised if these were indeed the happiest of men (420b), but he is willing to leave it to nature to assign to each group in the city its share of happiness (421c; cf. 465d-466a). Socrates nevertheless tries to allay Adeimantus's concerns by assuring him that the demands being made on the guardians are not heavy; indeed, they will be easy, so long as the one great sufficient thing is adequately guarded, their education and rearing (423d-e). As for the things of so little consequence to Socrates that they may be left out of the discussion—the possession of women, marriage, and the procreation of children—these will be arranged, so far as possible, according to the proverb that friends have all things in common (423e-424a). So long as the guardians build the guardhouse from the beginning—the starting point of the education of the young—all will be well; the legislators may leave the founding of temples, sacrifices, and whatever else belongs to gods, demons, and heroes, to Apollo at Delphi; thus the city in speech is founded (427b-c), Glaucon's luxurious and feverish city, purged of its fever (399e).

Now justice must be found. But just as he did after founding Adeimantus's initial city with him, Socrates tries to avoid having to seek it himself. As he did then, so now Glaucon interrupts and will not permit Socrates to back away (427d-e; cf. 371e-372c).

Pressed by Glaucon, Socrates uses yet another questionable procedure—the questionableness of which is widely remarked (Strauss, 105-8; Bloom, 373-74; Nichols, 88-91)—to establish that the city possesses the four virtues (they just "happen" to be the four cardinal virtues) of wisdom, courage, moderation, and justice. He suggests that they first find and factor out the three other virtues, and the fourth—the justice for which they have been searching from the beginning—will be the "remainder" of the city's supposed perfect goodness (427e-428a). But why only four virtues in the city? And why these four? What about, for example, piety? After all, Socrates has just mentioned Apollo at Delphi and the arrangements concerning the things of Apollo in their city (cf. Benardete, 82). Glaucon has just reminded Socrates that he said it would be impious of him not to assist justice with all his power (427e; cf. 368b-c). And in the music education of the auxiliary guardians, "The first place is occupied by education to piety" (Strauss, 98). Nevertheless, Socrates proceeds, without objection.

Wisdom, or good counsel, is found in the city, because the smallest part of the city, the ruling part, possesses "that knowledge which alone among the various kinds of knowledge ought to be called wisdom": the skill appropriate to true guardians (428a-429a). Courage, or "political courage," as opposed to a "still finer" kind, is found in the city, because the soldiers have been trained to preserve the opinion produced by law, through their education, about what sorts of things are and are not terrible (429a-430c; there are also "vulgar" and "fine" versions of moderation and justice—indeed, virtue entire; cf. 442e, 500d; Strauss, 108; Bloom, 378-79, 395-97).

Socrates would evidently prefer to avoid the question of what constitutes moderation (430d)—already backing away from his already questionable procedure—in part, we suspect, because he disappoints our expectation that moderation will be found to be the virtue possessed by the part of the city that is constituted by the farmers and artisans. He finds it instead in a kind of harmony and accord among the three classes in the city; an accord in which the smaller and better part, with the aid of the middle part, controls the inferior multitude (430e-432a).⁹ It is also not clear, after Socrates has described the role of moderation in the city, that there *is* any "remainder" left of the city's goodness that we could ascribe to its justice (cf. Strauss, 105-6; Bloom, 374; Nichols, 91; Benardete, 88). Little wonder Socrates cautions that we are operating in the realm of opinion (432b).

So where is justice? Glaucon cannot discern it. Yet it has been ridiculously rolling around at their feet from the very beginning in that rule they originally established, "that each one must practice one of the functions in the city, that one for which his nature made him naturally most fit." This, the practice of "minding one's own business and not being a busybody . . . when it comes into being in a certain way, is probably justice" (432d-433b): Justice in the city is nothing other than a certain form of this rule. Consequently, "the money-making, auxiliary, and guardian classes doing what's appropriate, each of them minding its own business in a city—would be justice and would make the city just" (434c). We are halfway through the fourth of ten books of the *Republic*, and the regime—the *politeia* of the title of the dialogue—is complete, and justice has been found. Why, then, six and a half more books? "This is perhaps," as Strauss (105) remarks, "the strangest happening in the whole *Republic*."

First and foremost, because Glaucon has forgotten about the little letters. Does this form (*eidos*) apply also to individual human beings, and is it also justice there (434d)? If so, fine, but if not, if something different should turn up in the individual, they must go back to the city and test it; then, "by considering them side by side," Socrates says, "and rubbing them together like sticks, we would make justice burst into flame" (434e-435a).

Now, it's no slight question they have stumbled upon, whether the human soul has three forms in it, like their city (435c). Before they proceed, Socrates warns Glaucon that in order to get a precise grasp on this profound question, they would have to travel a longer and further road; they will never get anywhere on the basis of the procedures they have been using so far in the argument, but they could do it an a way worthy of what they have done so far— which is to say, in an unworthy way (cf. 504b-c)—which contents Glaucon, so it will content Socrates, too (435d).

The shortcut Glaucon has chosen to take with Socrates soon leads to the conclusion that the human soul does, indeed, have three parts corresponding to the three parts of their city (435e-441c). The soul is wise in the same way and because of the same thing; it is courageous in the same way and because of the same thing; and it is just, too, in the same manner that the city was said to be just, when each of its parts minds its own business (441c-e).

We are not to suppose it an utter lie that we have now found the just man and the just city, and what justice is in each (444a). Glaucon agrees with Socrates that justice in the individual human being is a certain health, beauty, and good condition of the soul; he volunteers, in light of this, that the challenge that he and Adeimantus had posed to Socrates, the challenge that occasioned their whole discussion of the city in speech, now looks ridiculous to him (444d-445a). Socrates has fulfilled, it seems, the obligations of piety—if not of philosophy— having not walked away from, although he has not genuinely met, the challenge of two of the three sons of Ariston (cf. 368a-c).

Glaucon readily accepts all this, although Socrates has repeatedly cautioned him not to be in such a hurry; all of it is, of course, problematical, but for the present this is not our concern. Our concern, rather, is to notice that while Glaucon and Adeimantus are fully aware that this city is best, in part because it possesses wisdom, and it possesses wisdom because the wise rule in it, they are utterly unaware that Socrates means *philosophers* will be ruling in their city. Apparently, that philosophers are wise, at least in any respect that has to do with ruling, is a notion that has never occurred to Glaucon or Adeimantus.

In any event, Glaucon is satisfied that their discussion has come to an end. But Socrates insists that they push on, that they now consider how many forms vice has, or rather, the forms that are worth noting from among an unlimited number, the four that characterize types of soul, and that correspond to types of regimes (445b-c). Socrates is not permitted, however, to push on. He is once again arrested by Polemarchus and Adeimantus, in fact, by the entire group, including even Thrasymachus, who is well on his way to becoming "friends" with Socrates (449a-450a; cf. 498c-d). Adeimantus accuses Socrates of robbing them of a whole section of the argument: He had asserted that as for women and children, the things of friends would be in common (423e), and now he presumes to go on without explaining what he meant by this extraordinary assertion (449c). Socrates' interlocutors think that how children will be begotten and reared makes all the difference in the world concerning the rightness or wrongness of a regime (449d). Socrates admits that he had intentionally attempted to slip this by them without going into it, on account of the swarm of arguments it would stir up, from the beginning again (450a-b); however, he acknowledges the propriety of completing the "female drama," now that the male drama is complete (451c).

Philosophers (Books 5-7)

The most remarkable and least remarked fact about the three "waves" (457b) of book 5 of the *Republic* is that these young men do not find the first and second waves insurmountable—complete gender equality, and the abolition of the private family—but they do find the "third wave"—philosopher-kings—impossible to accept without a fight. Furthermore, this is precisely what Socrates expects. Were one to ask a contemporary audience unfamiliar with the *Republic*—or for that matter, one familiar with it—to predict the degree of difficulty that these young men would have in accepting the three waves as requirements of a just society, the vast majority would almost certainly get it backwards. Contemporary readers would expect a group of aristocratic young men in ancient Athens to find the notion of philosopher-kings relatively palatable; that of the communal possession of women and raising of children, somewhat palatable; and the notion of complete gender equality, utterly unpalatable. That the reactions of these young men are, in fact, exactly the opposite of our contemporary expectations speaks volumes about the prejudices of current readers of the *Republic* (cf. Bloom, 390).

Socrates warns concerning the two waves upon which he is being impelled to elaborate—and his interlocutors are expecting discussion of only two; the third comes as a complete surprise (cf. Benardete, 122)—that they may admit of many doubts, as regards both their possibility and their goodness (450c-d; cf. 456c). They nevertheless come to an agreement that complete gender equality is possible (451d-456c) and would be best for their city (456c-457c). The second "wave"—that all the women and children will belong to all the men in common, the abolition of the private family—is susceptible of greater doubts concerning both its possibility and its goodness (457d), so much so that Socrates requests permission, which Glaucon grants, to put off until later the question of its possibility (457e-458b). Certainly a "throng of lies" (459c), in addition to the "noble lie," would be needed, not to mention divine sanction for incest (461e). To make matters worse, when Socrates eventually reminds Glaucon that they have taken a holiday from considering the question of the possibility of the second wave, he does so only to change the subject abruptly (or, at least, apparently change it) to how they will conduct themselves in war (466d-e; cf. Bloom, 388; Benardete,

120).

Glaucon finally loses patience. He has by now become such an enthusiastic adherent of their city in speech that he will hear nothing further, other than how they can bring their new regime into existence (471c-e). But Socrates will not satisfy Glaucon, at least not before reminding him, at some length, of the real purpose of their discussion (472b-473b). It was not to prove the possibility of founding such a city, in deed, that they founded it, in speech; it was rather for the sake of a pattern to be used to understand the perfectly just human being. Strictly speaking, the question of the possibility, in deed, of the city in speech is irrelevant to the real issue under discussion—the question of who is the perfectly just human being, and who the perfectly unjust, and what relationship exists between perfect justice or perfect injustice and human happiness. For these reasons, among others, Socrates would have postponed indefinitely the question of "realizing" their city. (As Benardete, 123, remarks: "Glaucon's demand that the good city in speech be realized measures exactly the degree to which he has not understood the *Republic.*")

Socrates calls the "third wave" the "biggest and most difficult"—he has already told us that this means the most questionable as regards both its possibility and its goodness (457d)—and "paradoxical" (472a), nay, "very paradoxical" (473e):

> Unless the philosophers rule as kings or those now called kings and chiefs genuinely and adequately philosophize, and political power and philosophy coincide in the same place, while the many natures now making their way to either apart from the other are by necessity excluded, there will be no rest from ills for the cities . . . nor for humankind, nor will the regime we have now described in speech ever come forth from nature, insofar as possible, and see the light of the sun. (473d-e)

But these words are not merely paradoxical to Glaucon: they're fighting words. Does Socrates expect to be able to say such things and not provoke violence? The notion that philosophers should rule is, in Glaucon's opinion, preposterous or worse (473e-474a).

According to Socrates, however, this reaction—which he fully expected—is grounded in ignorance of who the real philosophers are (on the part of the many, if not the universality of men) (474b-c). First of all, true philosophers are, like Glaucon, erotic men (474d). (Glaucon balks at Socrates' characterization of him as erotic, perhaps because Socrates is here linking *eros*, heretofore so condemned in the dialogue, and philosophy, with which Glaucon, a "real man," does not want to be associated [475a].[10]) Socrates proceeds not only to explain to Glaucon, "through a somewhat lengthy argument" (484a), who the real philosophers are and who the counterfeits (474b-484a), but to prove to him that since true philosophers possess the four cardinal virtues of wisdom, moderation, courage, and justice—since true philosophers are individual embodiments of their city in speech—it makes perfect sense that they should rule in their city

(484b-487a).

Adeimantus interrupts with perhaps the most intelligent objection made to Socrates in the *Republic*. One can never beat Socrates at his game of clever questioning and answering, but the truth is unaffected by his ability to win these contests, and the truth is plain to see for whomever has eyes to see. The vast majority of those who linger with philosophy beyond their youth turn out very strange, even vicious, and the few who don't have at least the defect of being useless for political life (487b-d).

Socrates admits that Adeimantus's perception of philosophers is accurate, at least so far as their political uselessness is concerned, if not their viciousness; however, this needs to be explained through an "image" (487d-488a), the first of the great series of images in the *Republic*, the image of "the ship."

According to this image (488a-489a), a big and strong, but rather deaf, shortsighted, and ignorant shipowner (the demos) is forever pestered by sailors who endlessly fight among themselves over who should pilot the ship. None has been educated in the art of piloting (political science) and they all deny, and are prepared to kill anyone who says otherwise, that an art of piloting even exists or is teachable. They are constantly begging the shipowner for control of the ship. Sometimes, they succeed. Sometimes, if they fail at begging and persuading the shipowner, they resort to violence, kill or expel their rivals, mesmerize the shipowner with soporifics, and steer the ship exclusively to their own advantage. These "sailors" think that the art of piloting is the art of getting control of the helm, by persuasion or force; all else they consider useless. Is it any surprise that on ships run like this, the true pilot, the one who pays attention to the true art of piloting, rather than to the art of gaining control of the ship, is called useless?

It doesn't take much, according to Socrates, to see that the predicament of the true pilot on the ship is that of the true philosopher in the city, and that the sailors on the ship correspond to the current rulers in cities (489a-c). So much for the perceived political uselessness of the true philosophers. But what about the many "philosophers" who are downright vicious (489d-e)?

First, Socrates reminds Adeimantus of the *nature* of the true philosopher—a very erotic nature, described in terms redolent of love, procreation, and child-birth (489e-490b; Bloom, 462n9)—then addresses the problem of the *nurture* that the city provides for this extraordinary nature. For, according to Socrates, the vast majority of the very small minority of human beings who possess a perfectly philosophic nature are corrupted in their education by the things that the city calls good; these being the best natures, they turn out the worst when provided with inappropriate rearing, barring divine intervention (491a-e).

Thus it is the many in the city who blame "sophists" for corrupting the young who are in fact the "greatest sophists," and who fashion all the human beings in the city just as they want them to be—in their own image (492a-c). Furthermore, when these "educators" fail, they punish with dishonor, fines, and death (492d). The very attempt to counter this political education of the young is foolish (492e). Indeed, even those usually called "sophists" by the multitude are only its flatterers, with the result that both the multitude, which is incapable of philosophizing, and its sophistical educators slander genuine philosophy (493a-494a). In such circumstances, what are the chances that a talented and fortunate young man could escape damage? Moreover, would there not be dire political consequences for whomever attempted to rescue the extraordinary young from the multitude and its flatterers (494c-e)? Thus, those very few who are best suited for philosophy are almost always drawn away and corrupted, and it is these, having been corrupted, who do the greatest harm, both to cities and to individuals (495a-b). As for philosophy, she is left abandoned to herself, the prey of inferior, unsuitable natures, a few of whom are useless, but many of whom are vicious (495c). We note, then, that two kinds of human beings earn philosophy its bad reputation: philosophic natures without a philosophic nurture, and nonphilosophic natures who consort with philosophy. The crucial implication is that while philosophy is harmed by the wrong men coming to her (i.e., *political* natures), the city, too, is harmed by the wrong men (i.e., *philosophic* natures) to whom "human life [does not] seem anything great" (486a), coming to political life (cf. Brann, 94-95; Nichols, 113).

In any event, it is a very small group that remains to keep company with philosophy in a suitable way, a group that includes Socrates. This group knows well how to mind its own business: abjure participation in political life (from which Socrates' famous *daimonion* saved him), where no one can really come to the aid of justice and live to tell the tale (496a-e; cf. Benardete, 148-49, on Socrates' saving grace, in at least two senses). No extant city is an exception to this rule (497b).

Difficult as it may be for any city to take philosophy in hand (497d), Socrates wishes to insist (for reasons having more to do with his love of Glaucon than his love of truth) that it *is* possible that something should constrain true philosophers to take over a city and the city to obey them, or that something divine should inspire the sons of kings, even the kings themselves, with true erotic passion for true philosophy (499b-c). Is it impossible that one child of one king could be born with a philosophic nature and chance to receive a genuine philosophic nurture (502a-b)?

What remains, then, is to speak of what study and what practices would constitute genuine philosophic nurture (502c-d). It would have to be, of course, the greatest study: we are now walking on that longer road that earlier was said to be the only one that would enable us to get a precise grasp on the questions of justice, moderation, courage, and wisdom in the human soul. Heretofore, the arguments were so lacking in precision that they may have been without any value whatsoever (504a-c).

Socrates has many times in the past spoken of the great study he has in mind: the *idea* of the good (505a). According to Strauss (119), no one has ever succeeded in giving a satisfactory or clear account of the "utterly incredible" doctrine of ideas introduced here and discussed elsewhere in the Platonic dialogues, so no one should expect one now. Nevertheless, we must say something about Socrates' dazzling presentation of the images of the "sun," the "divided line," and the "cave."

Adeimantus wants to know whether Socrates thinks the good is knowledge, or pleasure, or something else (506b). Socrates demurs with his customary claim of what has come to be called Socratic ignorance (506c; what Thrasymachus preferred to call his habitual irony, 337a): Should one presume to express one's ugly opinions when one lacks knowledge? Glaucon, perhaps provoked by the fact that Socrates has just called his brother a "real man" (506b), interrupts, refusing to allow Socrates to withdraw from the discussion when he has come so close to completing it; so Socrates must complete it, even if the discussion of the good should be only on the inadequate level of the previous discussion of justice, moderation, and the rest (506d). But Socrates still balks. Even at Glaucon's urging, he will not express even his *opinion* about the good; he will utter only his opinion of what looks like a child of the good and most similar to it (506e). He will speak in similes.

First, Socrates distinguishes between the realm of things seen and the realm of the *ideas*, which are apprehended by intellect, not sight (507b). He then says that the role that light plays in the realm of things seen is similar to the role that the good plays in the realm of intellection (507d-e; Strauss, 119, points out that Socrates speaks synonymously of "the idea of the good" and "the good"). And what being—which of the gods in heaven—is the source of light in the visible realm, if not the sun (508a)? So the existence of the sun in the visible realm is analogous to the existence of the good in the intelligible realm (507b-c).

Glaucon requires further explanation, so Socrates points out that just as one sees clearly or dimly, depending on whether one's eyes are turned toward the light of day or toward the dark of night, one's soul has access to knowledge when it is turned toward being, which is illumined by truth, but merely opines when it is turned toward becoming, which is mixed with darkness (508d). The good provides both the truth to all things known and the soul's ability to know them. Just as light and sight are somehow of the sun without being the sun, truth and knowledge are of the good without being the good; just as the sun also provides what is seen with generation, growth, and nourishment, so the good also provides what is known with existence and being. Yet "the good isn't being but is still beyond being, exceeding it in dignity and power" (508e-509b). Dazzling as all this is to Glaucon, Socrates reminds him that he is only expressing opinions, and assures him that he is leaving many things out (509c).

Socrates declares the sun to be king in the visible region and the good to be king in the intelligible region, and proceeds to construct the famous "divided line" (509d-511e). The divided line purports to sketch an outline of all being. Socrates posits different levels of being and describes the different "experiences of the human soul" (*pathemata en te psyche*, 511d)—not just the "mind"—that correspond to the different levels of being. The divided line (which is itself an "image" in speech) purports to help us understand how the human soul can experience reality, from the lowest level of things that really exist, images or icons (e.g., shadows or reflections in water, as opposed to unicorns or satyrs, which do not exist), to the highest level of things that really exist, the *ideas* (*eide*). (Note that the only "god" mentioned—the sun—exists in the visible region.)

Jacob Klein[11] has succeeded in giving us a satisfactory and clear account of the divided line. The key to that account is the meaning of *eikasia*, the experience of the soul in apprehending *eikons*, or "images," the name assigned to those things in the lowest subdivision of the divided line. *Eikasia* is the soul's capacity "to see an image *as an image*" (Klein, 114), a capacity that distinguishes human beings from all other beings. Klein (119) explains how a kind of *eikasia* operates all the way up the line, how "in our thinking we exercise a kind of *eikasia* which is different from the one we exercise in the realm of visible things," and he calls this "*dianoetic eikasia*." This capacity enables our intellect to understand things in the visible realm as somehow dependent upon things in the intelligible realm in a way analogous to the dependence of an "image" on an "original."

With the divided line, Socrates purports to illustrate how the soul can ascend from the apprehension of shadows and reflections, the lowest level of being, to the apprehension of the *eide*, the highest level of being, over which the *idea* of the good is sovereign, a being that is somehow "beyond being, exceeding it in dignity and power" (509b; according to Brann, 56, the good, itself, which is "beyond being," cannot be placed anywhere on the line, itself). Klein (125) notes that immediately after constructing the line, Socrates presents the "image" of the cave:

> This "image" gives us an opportunity to exercise our fundamental power of *eikasia* . . . so as to enable us to refer the "imagined" cave back to a "real" one. But at the same time our faculty of *dianoetic eikasia* makes us understand that this "real" cave images our natural and civic life within the familiar world around us.

Klein then concludes his discussion by noting that Socrates takes us on an ascending path in both images, cave and line (125).[12]

But we should rather like to *begin* our discussion of the line here, for it cannot be emphasized too much that Socrates insists that what he would have us understand can be grasped only by connecting the image of the cave as a whole with the image of the divided line, making the two images into one. We are to liken the visible realm on the line to the cave in the image of the cave, and the ascent from the cave up to the place above in the image of the cave to the soul's ascent from the visible realm to the intelligible realm in the image of the divided line (507b).

This does not mean, as is frequently supposed, that the image of the divided line and the image of the cave say the same thing twice, in two different ways; it means rather that the two images, taken together, say one thing once. And what is that one thing? The key will again be *eikasia*.

The image of the cave is said to be an image of our nature in its education and its lack of education (514a). The cave in the image represents, of course, political life: The rulers and ruled together comprise the prisoners in the cave (516c-d). These prisoners are chained throughout their lives by their legs and necks so that they cannot turn around, but can only look straight ahead toward the back wall of the cave, onto which are projected shadows of all sorts of artifacts and statues of human beings and animals. These artifacts are carried by other human beings who walk along a road, behind the prisoners, separated from the prisoners by a wall, over which they display their artifacts, which serve as the "originals" of the "images" on the wall facing the prisoners; the light in the cave is a fire far above and behind all these human beings. Some of the carriers of the artifacts utter sounds; others do not (514a-515a). Would such prisoners ever have seen anything of themselves and one another, or anything of the things carried by behind them, other than shadows cast on the cave wall? When the carriers uttered sounds, would the prisoners suppose anything other than that the passing shadow had uttered the sound (515a-b)? When discussing these shadows among themselves, then, these prisoners would certainly believe that they were discussing the beings themselves, thus mistaking shadows of artificial things for real things (515b-c).

Socrates next describes what the "release and healing from bonds and folly" (515c) would be like for such prisoners. It occurs in two main stages: first, the turning around and looking about within the cave (515c-e); second, the ascent from the cave and looking about in the place above (515e-516c). In the first stage, at every point, the released prisoner must be compelled: he is forced to stand up and turn around toward the light in the cave; he experiences physical pain, emotional distress, and mental confusion; he persists in believing that the shadows on the cave wall are more real than their "originals," of the existence of which he had been heretofore utterly ignorant. In the second stage, there is no talk of compulsion, once the prisoner is freed from the cave: he slowly grows accustomed to his new surroundings in the place above, gradually able to discern with increasing clarity the beings in his brave new world. Once he finally discerns the sun itself, by itself, in its own region, he will understand that it is somehow ultimately the source of all those things that he and his companions chained in the cave had been seeing; when he recalls the cave and what passed for wisdom there, he will be grateful for his freedom and will pity the prisoners. He will in no way desire the honors and rewards available to those in the cave who are sharpest at discerning the shadows and predicting their order; nor will he envy those who hold power among the prisoners. He will very much prefer, as Homer says, "to be on the soil, a serf to another man, to a portionless man," and suffer anything rather than share the life and opinions of the prisoners (516d).

The quotation, of course, is the lament of Achilles to Odysseus when the latter visits him in the underworld (*Odyssey* XI, 489-91). Socrates had earlier quoted it more directly and fully: "I would rather be on the soil, a serf to another/ To a man without lot whose means of life are not great/ Than rule over all the dead who have perished" (386c). The message could not be clearer. The liberated prisoner would value life in the cave as Achilles valued being in Hades; the difference between being liberated from the cave or being a prisoner within it is as radical as that between life and death; the liberated man would rather undergo anything than rule in the cave, even though it would mean the granting of honors, praises, prizes, and power from the prisoners; i.e., the philosopher would rather undergo anything than rule in the cave as its philosopher-king. (Soon, Socrates will contrast life in and out of the cave in even more extreme terms: it is an ascent from Hades up to the gods, and that ascent is called "philosophy" [521c].)

The fire in the cave represents the city's version of the good. And just as fire really is something like the sun, and firelight something like sunlight—otherwise it could shed no light whatsoever—so every city's version of the good is something like the good, otherwise it could not function as a city (or even as a gang of robbers; cf. 351c-352c). As Nietzsche's Zarathustra saw in his travels to many lands, a tablet of the good hangs over every people (*Thus Spoke Zarathustra*, book 1, chapter 15: "On the Thousand Goals and One").

Socrates completes his presentation of the image of the cave with a description of what the plight of the liberated prisoner would be, were he to return to the cave. Having come suddenly from the sunlight, he would find his eyes infected with darkness; if, while his eyes were still infected—which they would be for a considerable time—he had to compete in forming judgments about the shadows with the perpetual prisoners, he would be laughed at. It would be said of him that he had returned from the place above with eyes corrupted, and that attempting to go up to that place was vain and foolish. As for the liberator who had first unchained him and forced him on the long, difficult ascent, wouldn't the cavemen kill the liberator (516e-517a)? Our *dianoetic eikasia* assures us that the "original" of this part of the "image" is obviously the fate of Socrates in Athens.

Glaucon's soul has been completely "turned." After all this elaboration of the paradoxical proposal of philosopher-kings, he is still shocked and opposed to the idea. Before he was outraged from the perspective of the city (473e-474a); now he is outraged from the perspective of the philosophers. Compelling the philosophers to rule in the city—to make them live a worse life when a better one is possible for them—would be a terrible injustice (519d). And, indeed, Glaucon is right: it is contrary to the city's own definition of justice (cf. Brann, 20-21; Bloom, 407; Benardete, 180-81). As Benardete (195) remarks: "The hyphen in 'philosopher-king' cannot conceal the divergence of these two elements even in the best regime." The perfect city is perfectly impossible (Bloom, 409; cf. Strauss, 127), even before Socrates puts the last nail in the coffin of its possibility, that the philosopher-kings (and queens, 540c) must expel from the city everyone over the age of ten (cf. Strauss, 124-27; Benardete, 124, 128-29). The *Republic* is truly "the greatest critique of political idealism ever written" (Bloom, 410; cf. Strauss, 65).

From the image of the ship, it appeared that "philosopher-kings" were problematical because it would be most difficult to persuade the city to accept philosophers as rulers. From the image of the cave, however, we learn that that problem pales into insignificance compared with the problem of how to persuade the true philosophers to accept kingship. Indeed, since it is against their own true interests, it would be impossible to persuade them; certainly rhetoric would not suffice (cf. Brann, 20; Bloom, 407).

The image of the divided line and the image of the cave, taken as a whole, teach us why (to paraphrase Cicero) Socrates was the first to call philosophy down from the heavens, to settle her in the cities, even introduce her into private homes, and to ask her questions about things good and bad; in other words, why Socrates was the founder of political philosophy (cf. Benardete, 152-53).

On the divided line, *eikasia* is the human soul's capacity to see an image *as an image* of an "original." The soul's ascent imagined on the divided line begins with "images," ascends by means of *eikasia* to the "original" objects of trust (*pistis*) in the visible realm, and proceeds by *dianoetic eikasia* to ascend from the visible to the intelligible realm, ultimately to intellection of the *eide*. But the cavemen do not perform *eikasia*; indeed, they cannot, as they are utterly unaware of the existence of the "originals" of the shadows on the cave wall. Furthermore, were they to perform *eikasia*, the "originals" to which their souls would ascend are themselves "images," not real "originals." The "originals" in the cave are artifacts (there is no mention of anything artificial outside the cave). These "artifacts" are fabricated by poets, represented in the cave by those who carry the artifacts and statues along the road behind the wall, the shadows of which are cast before the eyes of the prisoners.[13]

These "poets" are not chained in the cave: they are free to leave, if they so desire. The poets are in the cave because poetry qua poetry is at home in the cave, and only in the cave. To the extent that a poet were genuinely liberated from the cave, he would be a philosopher; to the extent that a philosopher went down into the cave, and wished to communicate with the prisoners there, he would be a poet: hence the form of the Platonic dialogue. Indeed, the philosopher-king needs must be the poet-king: "The poets are the *unacknowledged* legislators of mankind" (Benardete, 223).

The image of the divided line and the image of the cave, taken together as one, teach us that a metaphysics that is too eager to address itself to the question of being runs the risk of forever closing itself off from being, because it fails to liberate itself from the cave. Taken together as one, the images show us that our link to being is our nature—self-knowledge—and that the beginning of self-knowledge is the awareness that we are bound. (As Benardete, 185, remarks: "There is no ascent from the cave without self-knowledge.") The cave is an image of our nature and our nurture (514a). Human nature, including one's own nature ("Know thyself"), can be studied properly only in its natural habitat, the cave of political life.

The importance of self-knowledge for liberation is revealed within the image of the cave by the fact that in the case of *themselves* alone, the prisoners can observe on the shadow-wall the "image" of a real being, an authentic "original," and not just the shadow of an artifact. *Eikasia* could work for the prisoners in the sole instance of their own individual shadows. It may be possible for the prisoners to observe discrepancies between the shadows of the statues of human beings, which are carried by behind their backs, and their own shadows. Furthermore, it may be possible for the prisoners to perform the finger exercises that Socrates describes in his discussion of number and calculation (523c-e), "the lowly business of distinguishing the one, the two, and the three" (522c), the first of the studies that draw the soul from becoming up to being (521d); after all, their legs and necks are chained, not their arms and hands.[14] These observations may go some way toward relieving us of a pessimistic reading of the cave image according to which only the force of an outsider can begin to liberate the individual from the cave.[15] How else could the cave image account for the liberation of Socrates himself?

The image of the divided line and the image of the cave, taken together as one, teach us that political philosophy is first philosophy. Philosophy without Socratic or Platonic political philosophy would have remained forever in the cave. This is why Socrates, the exemplar of the political philosopher, should be on the one hand so interested in studying political life, and on the other hand, so uninterested in participating in it.

Tyrants (Books 8-10)

At the beginning of book 8, Socrates asks Glaucon to recall where they were when they took their long detour, so that they may return whence they came (543a-c). Remarkably, Glaucon responds that Socrates had described the good city and good man (i.e., books 2-4), and was about to compare four inferior cities and human beings, in descending order from the best to the worst (book 4, end), but it turned out that Socrates had a "still finer city and man to tell of" (543c-544a; i.e., books 5-7). More remarkably, Socrates affirms that Glaucon's recollection is correct (544b). This means that the city and man of books 2-4, and the city and man of books 5-7 are agreed explicitly by Socrates to be two different pairs (cf. Benardete, 190). It means that, however much the long digression launched near the beginning of book 5 may appear to be a continuation of the discussion of the city and corresponding human being of books 2-4—the kingly soul—at some point it ceased to be (if it ever was) and became a discussion of something else. In having his Socrates explicitly confirm Glaucon's recollection, Plato calls our attention to this fact. In having his Socrates thereafter make every effort to hide from Glaucon the significant implications of this fact, to obfuscate the distinction between the two versions of the "best" city and the "best" human being in the *Republic*, Plato reveals to us what Socrates has learned about Glaucon from "yesterday's" events and conversation.

There are various combinations of the inferior regimes, which Socrates is about to elaborate for Glaucon, but there are basically four, to which correspond four types of human beings (544c-d). Which means, says Socrates, that there are five arrangements of cities and five human souls; he thus abandons the distinction between the two different versions of the best regime and "the man who is like aristocracy" immediately after affirming it (544e). What they must next go through is the declension of worse men, so that they can conclude their discussion with a comparison of the most unjust man and the most just man (545a). The obvious question—never posed by Glaucon—is: Which of the two versions of the "best" human being is the "most just"? Or, put another way: Is the "best" human being identical to the "most just"?

Socrates proceeds with the well-known declension of regimes and corresponding human beings, likening them to Hesiod's races of men: gold, silver, bronze, and iron (546e). Many peculiarities characterize this declension: Socrates now speaks as if the "best" regime actually existed—in the distant *past*—but has become impossible for the *future*. It is unclear how gold, silver, bronze, and iron—four metals—are to correspond with aristocracy, timocracy, oligarchy, democracy, and tyranny—five regimes (not to mention the sixth).[16] Throughout the declension, the man who is like the regime differs from the man who dominates in the regime, and so on. But these are not our present concern. Our concern, rather, is to notice how the tripartite soul of books 2-4 has become so much more complex after books 5-7, and that this has everything to do with the elevation of *desire* over *thymos* after the central books. As Brann (43) notes, in the central and later books, the calculating part of the soul has an alternative name, "the wisdom-loving" (*philosophon*, 586e); love of wisdom is often called an *epithymia*, or desire (e.g., 475b, 517b6; an allusive connection between *thymos* and *epithymia* cannot be missed); and "when tyranny is discussed the three parts of the first soul are even explicitly connected to three 'pleasures' or 'desires'" (see my note 10).

After the central books, it is the various *desires* of human beings that characterize what *kinds* of human beings they are, and how they compare with the best (e.g., 554d-e). The dominance of desire in the human soul has become obvious by the time we reach the discussion of the oligarchic man in the declension (553-554), but is even more prevalent in the discussion of the democratic man (558c-561d). Before discussing the tyrannic man, Socrates first wishes to distinguish more adequately the kinds and numbers of desires (571a). He contrasts a human being in whose soul the wild and bestial part, gorged on food and drink, completely overwhelms the calculating, tame, and ruling part when he sleeps—one who neither shrinks from attempting intercourse, in his dreams, with a mother, gods, or beasts, nor from committing the foulest murder (571b-d)—with a man who has a healthy and moderate relationship with himself, and what he does to prepare himself for sleep. First, he feeds his calculating part on its proper food; second, he takes care of the desiring part; and third, he soothes the spirited part in the same way (571d-572b; note that for the first time, the usual order of discussion of the three parts of the soul has changed). *Eros* has long been called a tyrant (573b); perhaps it even is a tyrant (573d). Once *eros* has established itself as tyrant in the soul, what one has dared to be in one's dreams, one will become while awake (574e-575a). "The tyrant is *Eros* incarnate" (Strauss, 133).

"With respect to virtue," Socrates asks Glaucon, "what is the relation between a city under a tyranny and the one under a kingship such as we *first* described?" (576d, my emphasis). This can only mean the regime of books 2-4, not the "still finer" one of books 5-7. Glaucon responds, "Everything is the opposite. The one the best, the other the worst . . . it's plain to everyone that there is no city more wretched than one under a tyranny and none happier than one under a kingship" (576d-e). Glaucon agrees that it follows from this that the life of the tyrant is most wretched (578b-c); that the tyrant lives an even more wretched life than the one he, himself, had described (in his challenge to Socrates at the beginning of book 2; 579d; cf. Benardete, 209). Calling our attention to that challenge, Socrates cannot but remind us, whether or not it reminds Glaucon, that he speaks of a tyrant who is known to be a tyrant (580a), whereas Glaucon had spoken of the perfectly unjust man with the perfectly just reputation (361a).

Socrates persists in speaking of five, not six, human beings, and asks Glaucon to rank them in order of happiness: kingly, timocratic, oligarchic, democratic, and tyrannic. Glaucon, of course, ranks them as prompted (580b). Playing on Glaucon's father's name, Socrates proclaims that the son of Ariston has decided that the best (*ariston*) and most just human being is happiest, the kingly one; the worst and most unjust is most wretched, the tyrannic one; and this is true, whether or not their respective justice and injustice escape the notice of all human beings and gods (580b-c). (Glaucon has now twice failed to notice the significance of the fact that the injustice of the tyrant that they just discussed escaped the notice of *no* human beings.)

Glaucon also fails to notice that in the new discussion of the tripartite soul, the immediate sequel to his proclamation that the most just life is best, each of the three parts of the soul has its specific desire, so that human beings may be categorized according to whether they are lovers of wisdom, lovers of victory or honor (which two are conflated into one), or lovers of gain (580d-581c). And that in the contest among them for who has the sweetest life, pleasure is the standard for choosing the life of the lover of wisdom over the other two (581c-583a; cf. Bloom, 424; Nichols, 134-35). And that the kingly soul of the first proof of the superiority of the most just life over the most unjust (580b-c) becomes the philosophic soul, the lover of wisdom, in this second proof. (Socrates compares the "worst" with whichever of the two "best" furthers his pedagogical goal with Glaucon.)

The kingly and the philosophic souls both figure in Socrates' third proof. When the whole soul follows the philosophic part, pleasures are the best and truest (586e); when what is most distant from philosophy and argument (*logos*), and from law and order (*nomos* and *taxis*), is followed, pleasures are worst and least true (587a); since the kingly is least distant from law and order, and the tyrannic most distant, the tyrant lives most unpleasantly and the king most pleasantly (587b). Socrates finally adds the pertinent qualification to all this— "if we count the aristocratic and the kingly man as the same" (587d)—but Glaucon again fails to grasp its significance, and the miraculous conclusion is reached that the kingly man lives 729 times more pleasantly than the tyrant (587e).

Socrates now constructs his final image of the soul to clarify what it means to say that injustice is profitable for the perfectly unjust man with the reputation for justice (588a-e). Somehow fused are the separate *ideas* of a many-colored (cf. 557c), many-headed monster of tame and savage beasts, with regenerative powers; of a lion; and of a human being. Molded about them on the outside is a single image of a human being. One who says it is profitable to practice injustice is in effect saying that it is profitable for this human being to feast and strengthen the manifold beast and lion, and to starve the human being within (588e-589a). One who says that it is profitable to practice justice is saying that it is best for the human being within, making the lion its ally, to control the many-headed beast, nourishing the tame heads and stunting the growth of the savage ones (589a-b). (This is, of course, reminiscent of the *first* good city in speech and the corresponding human being, where the rational part of the soul, with the spirited part as its ally, masters the desiring part. But in accord with the interim elevation of desire, there are desires, or heads, that are to be nourished and culti-vated.)

At the conclusion of this discussion in book 9, Glaucon blurts out that the well-ordered human being they have described won't be willing to mind the political things; Socrates swears by the dog—the philosopher-dog?—(for the third and last time; cf. 399e, 567d) that he will, at least the things of his own proper city (592a). Glaucon thinks this means he will mind the things of the city in speech, which they earlier elaborated, but Socrates corrects him: he will mind the things of the city within himself, he will care for his own soul.

It is no surprise, then, that Socrates wins from Glaucon, in the end, permis-sion to restore to justice and the rest of virtue its rewards and prizes, in their quantity and quality, from both human beings and gods, both while the human being is alive, and in the afterlife, for the immortal soul (608-621).

And no one could fail to notice later, in Socrates' recounting of the Myth of Er (614b-621b), that after the thousand-year journey of punishments, it is the tyrant alone who is not permitted to choose a new life and be reborn; that for the tyrant alone, punishment is unremitting and eternal (615c-616a). Nor can we fail to notice that the philosopher alone escapes the eternal exchange of evils and goods that most human beings suffer; that for the philosopher alone, rewards are unremitting and eternal (619d-e). For the first man to choose a new life, after a thousand-year journey of rewards, having lived his previous life in an orderly regime participating in virtue, chooses tyranny, for he practiced virtue by habit, without philosophy (619b-c; cf. Bloom, 435-36).

Kings, Philosophers, Tyrants

Near the end of book 9, Socrates wished his interlocutors to recall "those words because of which we are here" (588b), meaning the argument of Thrasymachus in book 1, restored by Glaucon in book 2, according to which the best life for a human being is the life of tyranny. In opposition to the tyrant, Socrates pre-sented, in books 2-4, the king. In book 5, Socrates appeared to continue his dis-cussion of the kingly city and man of books 2-4, in his discussion of the first two waves, but once he introduced the third wave, philosopher-kings, as the indis-pensable means of actualizing the first two, the discussion moved to a new plane, so that eventually we realized that in books 5-7, a still finer city and hu-man being—a better version of the best, acknowledged explicitly by Socrates at the beginning of book 8—had been presented: the philosophic city and the philosopher.

What the entire dialogue has been building toward is a confrontation between *the* "best" and *the* "worst" human life, and the purpose of that confrontation is to cure Glaucon of his deadly attraction to tyranny. The problem, however, is that the truly best soul, the philosophic soul, is not, in fact, the polar opposite of the worst, the tyrannic soul. The philosophic soul and the tyrannic soul are twins, fraternal, not identical; the philosopher is a very erotic man, like the tyrant. Thus, Benardete (148) can remark both that *eros* is the "essence" of the *philosophic* nature, and that "The tyrant is *Eros*" (Benardete, 205, 208; cf. Bloom, 422-26).

The several discussions of the tripartite soul lead us to conclude that there are three fundamental ways of combining the rational, the spirited, and the erotic parts of the soul, each representing one of the three most important human alternatives presented in the *Republic* (see chart).

King (Books 2-4)	Philosopher (Books 5-7)	Tyrant (Books 8-9)
Reason Spirit	Reason Desire	Desire Spirit
Desire	Spirit	Reason

The kingly soul, corresponding to the city of books 2-4, is the harmony of reason and spiritedness, with its desire suppressed (cf. Strauss, 110-112). The philosophic soul, corresponding to the city of books 5-7, is the harmony of reason and desire, with its spiritedness suppressed.[17] These are the two versions of the best soul, corresponding to the two versions of the best regime, in the *Republic*. The tyrannic soul, the worst soul for a human being, is the harmony of desire and spiritedness, with reason suppressed (cf. Benardete, 208). The philosopher and the tyrant are both, in a sense, the opposites of the king: in both the philosophic and tyrannic souls, desire is liberated; in the kingly soul, it is suppressed. The difference between the philosopher and the tyrant is that philosophic *eros* is in harmony with reason, while tyrannic *eros*, with *thymos* as its ally, is at war with reason.

Glaucon is very spirited and very erotic, and he is attracted to the life of tyranny: the most dangerous combination. He is not a potential philosopher, he is a potential tyrant. The best that can be hoped for from him is that he will master his unlawful desires, allying his spiritedness with reason, whether that reason should be under his own or another's command. This is why Socrates wishes to obfuscate the distinction between the two versions of the best city and the best soul, after it appears in the central books, and is affirmed at the beginning of book 8.[18] This is why, "The repugnance with which the tyrant must be held politically nowhere lets up in the *Republic*" (Benardete 94), even if the repugnance with which *eros* is held, does. Socrates cannot turn Glaucon into a philosopher, like his brother, Plato; however, he can save him from being a tyrant, like his uncle, Charmides.

Xenophon, *Memorabilia* (III.vi.1) reports that Socrates took an interest in Glaucon for the sake of his uncle, Charmides, and his brother, Plato, and saved him from entering political life. It cannot surprise that our reading of the *Republic* should be consistent with the report of so reliable an authority as Xenophon.

Notes

This chapter was originally published in Michael Palmer and Thomas L. Pangle, eds., *Political Philosophy and the Human Soul: Essays in Memory of Allan Bloom* (Lanham, Md: Rowman & Littlefield, 1995). Reprinted with permission.

1. Eva Brann, "The Music of the Republic," *The St. John's Review 39* (1989-90): 1-103 (hereafter cited as Brann, followed by page references), has explored at length the construction of the *Republic* as a ring composition. All my references to the *Republic* are to the standard Stephanus numbers as they appear in *The Republic of Plato*, 2nd ed., trans. with notes and an interpretive essay by Allan Bloom (New York: Basic Books, 1991). My reading is indebted from the ground up to Bloom's "Interpretive Essay" (hereafter cited as Bloom, followed by page references); which is, in turn, explicitly indebted to Strauss, "On Plato's Republic," in Leo Strauss, *The City and Man* (Chicago: Rand McNally, 1964): 50-138 (hereafter cited as Strauss, followed by page references); which prepared me (if anything could) for Seth Benardete, *Socrates' Second Sailing: On Plato's Republic* (Chicago: University of Chicago Press, 1989) (hereafter cited as Benardete, followed by page references).

2. This is how it "appeared" to Socrates. All the speeches and deeds of the *Republic* are narrated by Socrates, as he perceived them "yesterday." To whom is Socrates "repeating" them "today"? Plato? It would certainly be odd for Socrates to introduce Plato's own brothers to him the way he does (327a, 327c). Plato and a group of people? It would certainly be wonderful that he could find, on two successive days, two groups of people who would be willing to listen to such a long conversation, which, unlike "yesterday's," is never interrupted (cf. Strauss, 50-62; Benardete, 58-59). Not the *Apology of Socrates*, but the *Republic*, is the longest speech of Socrates ever vouchsafed us by Plato. Brann (78) suggests that the *Republic* is not addressed to anyone, that it presents Socrates practicing the Pythagorean discipline of "recollecting" to himself his conversation of the previous day.

3. Both Brann, 21, and Benardete, 110, refer to the "arrest" of Socrates at the beginning of book 5 in terms of a "conspiracy," but neither characterizes the arrest that opens the dialogue as one (cf. Benardete, 11).

4. Since Cephalus declares at the outset that he has no intention of remaining with Socrates and the others for the discussion that ensues (328d), Socrates' discourteous treatment of Cephalus cannot be explained by any need to expel him from that discussion, as Bloom, 312, suggests. Had Socrates not badgered him, Cephalus might have departed sooner. Strauss, 66, says of Socrates' opening question to Cephalus, at least, that it is "a model of propriety."

5. Not so "today's" conversation, for which Socrates almost never evidences any lack of enthusiasm for every detail. "Almost": for rare exceptions, see 342d, 350c-d; cf.

Benardete, 9, 43.

6. As Benardete, 39, remarks: "Glaucon is not only the first to introduce into the *Republic* the word for nature (*phusis*), but he is also the first to introduce a word for kind (*eidos*)."

7. In this essay, I attend almost exclusively to Socrates' pedagogical project with Glaucon, who is presented as Socrates' sole chosen companion, "yesterday." It is not that Socrates has no pedagogical goal with Adeimantus; he does, but it is a different one, dictated by the differences between the two brothers' natures, as reflected in their speeches; see Strauss, 90-91.

8. Bloom, 350-51, thinks the claim that dogs are philosophic by nature is not serious. Mary P. Nichols, *Socrates and the Political Community: An Ancient Debate* (Albany: SUNY, 1987), 206n14 (hereafter cited as Nichols, followed by page references), disagrees, suggesting that the comparison is more "serious" than it at first appears. Serious or not, we need only remark that the first mention of philosophy in the *Republic* alerts us to the questionableness of spiritedness in the philosophic soul.

9. What about the virtue of moderation in the human soul? Is it the appetitive part of the soul, possessing modest appetites, working in harmony with the calculative and spirited parts, or is it the angry will's ability to suppress strong, immoderate appetites? And there are other possibilities, too; cf. Strauss, 107-8; Benardete, 86-88. An interpretation of Socrates' presentation of the story of Leontius is essential to addressing these questions. For the most thorough discussions, see Strauss, 109-12, and Benardete, 91-102; cf. Brann, 40-41; Bloom, 375-77; Nichols, 92-93.

10. It is of paramount importance that after the central utterance of the *Republic*—the paradox of philosopher-kings—the teaching on *eros*, or desire, changes: virtually unqualified condemnation of *eros* gives way to an elevation of its status vis-à-vis *thymos*; cf. Strauss, 110-12; Brann, 42-43; Bloom, 392; Nichols, 134.

11. Jacob Klein, *A Commentary on Plato's Meno* (Chapel Hill: University of North Carolina Press, 1965): 112-25 (hereafter cited as Klein, followed by page references).

12. Although we speak of the soul "ascending" the divided line, as Eva Brann, *The World of the Imagination: Sum and Substance* (Lanham, Md: Rowman & Littlefield, 1991), 37, points out, "The divided line is meant to be read from the top down."

13. Bloom, 428, remarks, "The poets are the authentic, the only, teachers about the gods." All the more remarkable, then, that the image of the cave is silent about the gods. Putting the line and cave images together implies that "gods" exist only in the cave.

14. Yet Benardete, 172, insists that "Socrates goes out of his way to have the prisoners cast *stationary* shadows of themselves on the wall while watching moving shadows of images of themselves" (my emphasis); cf. Benardete, 165-67, 171-72. Both Nichols, 117-19, and Julia Annas, *An Introduction to Plato's Republic* (Oxford: Oxford University Press, 1981), 252-69, whom she cites approvingly (Nichols, 214n22-216n26), appear to have missed these details.

15. Cf. Strauss, 128, who says that the image of the cave "presents the ascent from the cave to the light of the sun as entirely compulsory."

16. Strauss, 129-33, elaborates the significance of Socrates' comparing the five cities of the declension to Hesiod's races of men, of which he mentions only four. Socrates omits the age of heroes, which, when supplied, corresponds to democracy, pointing to his implicit praise of democracy, the actual regime that is least hostile to philosophy; cf. Bloom, 421-22. We might add that this is anticipated in the myth of the metals in the noble lie (415a-c): The god mixes one of four metals into people's souls—gold, silver, iron, and bronze—to determine to which of three classes they will be assigned. The rulers must be careful guardians of nothing more than this; indeed, the declension of regimes

eventually begins because the psychic metals get mixed up (546d-e). If we unmix them, we find that three are pure and one an alloy—bronze, of copper and tin. Hence, there are five or six metals in the myth, depending on how we count, just as there are five or six regimes, and five or six human types in the *Republic*, depending on how we count.

17. "Let us also never forget," writes Strauss, 110-11, "that while there is a philosophic *eros*, there is no philosophic indignation, desire for victory, or anger (consider 536b8-c7)." In his reading of the "Myth of Er," Bloom, 436, observes: "Achilles no longer exists, alive or dead, in the new poetry or the new Socratic world. Correspondingly, the wise voyager Odysseus gains higher status. All he needed was to be cured of love of honor (a form of spiritedness), and he could live the obscure but happy life of Socrates" (cf. Bloom, 355, 376, 420-21).

18. Brann, 13, remarks on the two versions of the best city, but sees a closer kinship between them than I do: "The guardian city therefore differs from the philosopher city as the best pattern differs from its realization, and, as it has now turned out, as the impossible differs from the possible" (23).

Chapter 3

Alcibiades and the Question of Tyranny in Thucydides

"Thucydides," writes Thomas Hobbes, "is one who, though he never digress to read a lecture, moral or political, upon his own text, nor enter into men's hearts further than the acts themselves evidently guide him: is yet accounted the most politic historiographer that ever writ."[1] But Thucydides studies have traditionally been the domain of historians and classicists who generally preoccupy themselves with the question of how well or ill Thucydides measures up to the modern standard of the "scientific historian."[2] Despite Thucydides' never calling his book a "history" and never calling himself a "historian," we persist in treating his book almost exclusively as a "historical" narrative. Usually implied in our labelling him a "historian" is the view that his writing does not present a comprehensive teaching about politics. I believe, with Hobbes, that it does. To say the least, the "most politic" character of Thucydides' writing has not received the attention it deserves.[3]

What is it that makes Thucydides' writing "most politic"? Hobbes continues:

> He filleth his narrations with that *choice* of matter, and *ordereth* them with that judgement, and with such perspicuity and efficacy expresseth himself, that, as Plutarch saith, he maketh his auditor a spectator. . . . So that look how much a man of understanding might have added to his experience, if he had then lived a beholder of their proceedings, and familiar with the men and business of the time: so much almost may he profit now, by attentive reading of the same here written. He may from the narrations draw out lessons to himself, and of himself be able to trace the drifts and counsels of the actors in their seat.[4]

In another place, Hobbes writes: "Digressions for instruction's cause, and other such open conveyances of precepts (which is the philosopher's part), he never useth, [rather] the narration itself doth secretly instruct the reader, and more effectually than can possibly be done by precept."[5] Thucydides presents his political thought *as* a narrative and teaches *through* the narrative.

The reticence of Thucydides to comment on his own text and in general to make judgements in his own name is so widely acknowledged as to require no references to scholarly opinion (although, for a writer with this reputation, Thucydides does make a remarkable number of very clear and significant statements of his own judgement; for example, 4.28.5, 7.30.3, 7.86.5, 8.73.3, 8.97.2).[6] There is, however, as Hobbes suggests, one way in which Thucydides speaks to his readers directly on every page of his writing; that is, by which events he chooses to present to the reader and in what order he chooses to present them.[7] Together with explicit statements made in his own name, especially revealing of Thucydides' own thought would be those passages where he inserts so-called "digressions" into his text, particularly when he dramatically interrupts his narrative to do so. Taking Hobbes's view of how Thucydides wrote his book as the starting point for determining how to read it, in this essay I examine Thucydides' presentation of the fateful events surrounding Alcibiades' recall to Athens from the Sicilian expedition, his defection to Sparta with its disastrous consequences, and Thucydides' dramatic interruption of this account with his so-called "digression" on the end of the Pisistratid tyranny at Athens.[8] In what follows, I shall try to emulate Thucydides by entering into his heart no further than the text itself evidently guides me. While I use Hobbes to suggest how we should read Thucydides, I hope my method will be justified more by the outcome of my analysis than by resort to even so eminent an authority.

The Recall of Alcibiades and the "Digression" on the Athenian Tyrants

In the first book of his work, Thucydides tells us that the Athenians have a false understanding of their own tyrants (1.20). Thucydides himself possesses the true understanding; he briefly indicates wherein the common Athenian understanding is deficient. However, it is not primarily in the first but rather in the sixth book, when he retells the story of Harmodius and Aristogiton's attempt to overthrow the Pisistratids, that Thucydides chooses to correct adequately the common understanding. Just as the Athenians are about to act decisively in Sicily, the stateship *Salaminia* arrives for Alcibiades and certain others who are accused of defiling the Hermae in Athens and profaning the Mysteries. They are to be returned to Athens for trial and execution on the ground of impiety. Book 6 had begun with the Athenians at the peak of their power about to embark on the conquest of all of Sicily. At the end of book 6, we have a very different picture. On the one hand, Athenian domestic life is in a state of disintegration while the timid Nicias is now alone in command of the Athenians' greatest and most daring foreign adventure. On the other hand, a domestically secure Sparta, with the audacious and brilliant Alcibiades now directing her war effort, is coming to the aid of Sicily, prepared to pursue the war with enthusiasm. This situation must spell disaster for Athens, as the sequel reveals in Thucydides' most powerful prose.[9] The immediate cause of this reversal is the affair of the defiling of the Hermae, the suspicions that arose about Alcibiades, implicated in some mock performances of the Mysteries in some private homes, his subsequent recall from Sicily, and his consequent defection to Sparta. These events have a profound effect on the outcome of the war. Why should Thucydides be so anxious to correct the common understanding of the Athenian tyranny, which had come to an end almost a century earlier, as to interrupt his narrative right in the middle of recounting these crucial and dramatic events? There is obviously a connection in Thucydides' mind between the Athenians' misunderstanding of the old tyranny at Athens and the recall of Alcibiades with its disastrous consequences for Athenian democracy. What is the connection and, to borrow Hobbes's formulation, what lessons does Thucydides intend for the reader to draw out to himself from these narrations? Clearly, these passages on the Athenian tyrants provide the perfect Thucydidean gloss on the hysterical witch-hunt that ensued at Athens after the affair of the Hermae, hysteria that was motivated by the *demos*' extreme fear of tyranny.[10] Thucydides says the Athenian *demos* was always afraid of tyranny and regarded everything suspiciously (6.53.3); Athens is the tyrant city of Greece and the city whose citizens most fear tyranny (cf. 1.122.3, 124.3, 2.63.2, 3.37.2). Where Thucydides stands on the question of tyranny is essential for determining his judgement of Alcibiades' notorious career.

In reading the "digression," it must be borne in mind what the prevailing view of Harmodius and Aristogiton, the so-called "tyrannicides," was. They were held in the highest esteem by the city, which created the impression in the public mind that the murdered Hipparchus, not his brother Hippias, had been the ruling tyrant, and that with his murder, they,[11] not the Spartans and the exiled Alcmaeonids, had overthrown the tyranny.[11] But what, according to Thucydides, is the truth?

Harmodius was a beautiful youth and Aristogiton, an older man, was enamoured of him, as was, unfortunately for all concerned, Hipparchus, son of Pisistratus and brother of Hippias, the ruling tyrant (6.54.1-2, 55). Hipparchus's vain attempts to solicit Harmodius caused Aristogiton "lover-like" resentment and he, fearing Hipparchus's power, lest he take Harmodius by force, resolved to overthrow the tyranny (54.3). Thucydides states explicitly that Hipparchus had no intention of resorting to violence, that rather he contrived to insult Harmodius covertly by publicly humiliating his young sister (54.4, 56.1). To insure that the import of Hipparchus's intending no violence be fully appreciated, Thucydides takes time to pronounce on the character of the Pisistratid tyranny. He tells us that in general the government did not give offence and was not oppressive to the many; indeed, these tyrants practised virtue (*arete*) and intelligence (*xynesis*) to a very high degree; they exacted from the Athenians no more than 5 percent of their incomes, and with this money they splendidly adorned the city, carried on the wars, and provided sacrifices for the temples (54.5). And the city was left to enjoy its established laws, too, except that the precaution was taken that one of the Pisistratids should always be in office (54.6). This is very high praise from Thucydides. He praises the tyrants in the same tone he uses to praise the rule of Pericles and with the very words he uses to describe the virtue and intelligence of Brasidas (4.81.2) and the intelligence of Themistocles (1.138.3), Theseus (2.15.2), and Hermocrates (6.72.2), among the most admirable characters we find in his book. Only three individuals in Thucydides are credited with *arete*: Brasidas (4.81.2), Nicias (7.86.5), and Antiphon (8.68.1), and that of Nicias is qualified as conventional.[12] The tyrants are the only rulers credited with *arete* by Thucydides.

Thucydides next shows us that the tyrants were also pious (6.54.6-7). The theme of piety is important for understanding Thucydides' presentation of Alcibiades, but for the moment let us return to his account of the daring deed.

Harmodius and Aristogiton are to begin the action and to be aided immediately by their accomplices, who are not many. It is "hoped" that others will rise up spontaneously to support the conspirators (56.3), a hope that does not appear to have been very well founded. In any case, the attempt is aborted. What happens instead is that the would-be tyrannicides panic when they see one of their accomplices talking familiarly to Hippias—who was, Thucydides says, easy of access to all—and wrongly conclude they have been betrayed (57.2). These would-be tyrannicides are suspicious and fearful while the tyrant is trusting and calm. (Ironically, at this moment, both the conspirators' fears and the tyrant's confidence are not justified.) In their panic, Harmodius and Aristogiton resolve at least to revenge themselves upon Hipparchus, by whom they feel wronged and on whose account they risked so much. They rush to where he is in the city and cut him down, both in anger; the one, Thucydides tells us, affected by *eros*, the other by *hubris* (57.3). It should be remarked that the lovers are no longer, even as a pretext, acting to overthrow the tyranny; they believe their conspiracy has been betrayed already. They simply murder in a vengeful passion.[13] The immediate result of this murder is that all three members of the lovers' triangle perish. The enduring result is rather more unfortunate. Thucydides summarizes:

> It was in such wise, for an affront of love, that the plot of Harmodius and Aristogiton was first conceived and their reckless attempt made under the influence of their momentary alarm. After this the tyranny became harsher for the Athenians, and Hippias, being now in greater fear, not only put to death many of the citizens, but also began to look abroad, to see if in any quarter he might find a door of safety open to him in case of a revolution. (59.1-2)

In the end, Hippias is expelled from Athens by the Spartans and the exiled Alcmaeonids, eventually finding refuge with King Darius of Persia, with whom he returned to Marathon twenty years later to try to recover Athens (59.4). The refuge of Persia was one that Hippias had had the foresight to cultivate after the murder by marrying his daughter, Archedice, to the son of the tyrant of Lampascus, whose family had great influence with Darius. Thucydides quotes in full, in elegiac verse, the epitaph of this Archedice (attributed to Simonides),[14] whose father, husband, brothers, and children were all tyrants. The epitaph is unique in his writing and praises Archedice for being free of the very vice most likely to be associated with tyranny in the common understanding—vainglory. Simonides evidently found this remarkable; given Thucydides' consistently sympathetic presentation of the Pisistratids, we should not.

Thucydides' "digression" utterly overturns the common understanding of Harmodius and Aristogiton and the Pisistratids: Hipparchus was not the ruling tyrant; the motive for this murder, far from being public-spirited, arose from the most private of concerns, a love affair (54.1); the murder did not end the tyranny; the tyranny that was later overthrown by the Spartans and the Alcmaeonids was not the usual Pisistratid tyranny, but the tyranny after it had gone bad as a direct result of the murder; the Pisistratids were praiseworthy men and their hereditary tyranny was grievous to the Athenians only during the relatively brief period between the murder of Hipparchus and their final expulsion. We may summarize thus: from considerations of interest and honor, the Pisistratids established and maintained a mild hereditary tyranny that was generally neither oppressive nor offensively administered; indeed, these tyrants were benefactors of the city; after the murder of his brother, however, Hippias, under the compulsion of fear of violent death, became harsher and the Athenians suffered. Far from being an account of how noble and public-spirited self-sacrifice brought down a very bad regime, the true story of Harmodius and Aristogiton is an account of how a very good regime came to ruin, undone by the most private of concerns—*eros*.

The "Digression" on the Story of Cylon

That the tyrants were pious and that the themes of tyranny and piety are linked in the thought of Thucydides should come as no surprise to any careful reader of his work. He links them persistently. For example, in the so-called "archaeology," the account of olden times, in the first book, the first tyrant named, Polycrates, performs the first act of piety mentioned in Thucydides: he consecrates an island to the Delian Apollo (1.13.6; cf. also 3.104.2). But the most remarkable passage linking the themes of tyranny and piety is Thucydides' account of the story of Cylon (1.126.3-12).[15] This passage recalls in many ways the "digression" on the Pisistratids. Both passages relate events contemporaneous with the archaeology but are recounted, in apparent digressions, in contexts outside it. Both stories concern events in the past in which the Alcmaeonids, the family of Pericles and Alcibiades, are involved. Thucydides' account of the story of Harmodius and Aristogiton relates the end of the Pisistratid tyranny at Athens; the story of Cylon is his account of the first attempt to establish a tyranny in the city.

The context in which Thucydides recounts the story of Cylon is intimately connected with the question of piety: the Spartans want the "greatest pretext" (*prophasis*) possible for waging their war against the Athenians; they demand that the Athenians expiate a curse by expelling Pericles and others (who would include Alcibiades) from the city because of a pollution the Athenians had incurred some two hundred years before (126.1-2, 127). The story of Cylon is the story of how the Athenians incurred this pollution.

Cylon was (like Alcibiades) a well-born and powerful Athenian and an Olympic victor (126.3; cf. 5.43.2, 6.16.2) and, like the Pisistratids, pious. He has inquired at the Delphic oracle and has been told to seize the acropolis of Athens on the great festival day of Zeus (126.4); Cylon's attempt to establish a tyranny at Athens is in obedience to an oracle. When it came time for the Olympic festival in the Peloponnese, he seized the acropolis; this was not only the greatest festival day of Zeus but was connected with him on account of his Olympic victory (126.5). "But," Thucydides writes, "whether the oracle meant the greatest festival in Attica or somewhere else, he did not consider, and the oracle did not make it clear" (126.6). Now we might suggest that this oracle business is all nonsense, or that the oracle was obscure on purpose (as Hobbes does),[16] or even that this is one of those semimythical stories of *hubris* being punished by the gods, but we must note that Thucydides does none of these things. He does call into question whether Cylon chose the right festival day to seize the acropolis, that is, his interpretation of the oracle on this point, but he does not call into question the oracle itself or Cylon's intention of establishing himself as tyrant in accordance with it. Thucydides vindicates this oracle, which, not so incidentally, concerns a festival day of Zeus—and who, after all, is Zeus but the divine protector of the rule of kings who established himself by overthrowing his own father? We must note, too, that Cylon and his brother escape unscathed after his unsuccessful attempt (126.10). Some of his party are not so fortunate. They seat themselves on an altar on the acropolis as suppliants, are raised up by the Athenians on the understanding that they will not be harmed, and are treacherously murdered. It was with this deed that the Athenians brought upon themselves the pollution that the Spartans are now demanding they expiate (126.11, 127.1).

As was noted above, this story is contemporaneous with the archaeology. One of the striking things about Thucydides' treatment of olden times is his almost total silence about the gods, the only mention of a god being the one noted above in connection with Polycrates the tyrant.[17] The story of Cylon is the only indication we are given in Thucydides of divine intervention in human affairs in olden times, and that glimpse into the past calls into question the traditional linking of piety and justice, the view that there is divine support for traditional justice: the Delphic oracle encourages a tyranny and the Athenians are cursed as a result of an action taken to punish those who supported Cylon's unsuccessful attempt. Perhaps the gods of olden times, like the men (see the archaeology), were not so scrupulous about justice as they later became. In any case, the question of piety is clearly linked to the question of tyranny in Thucydides' account of politics, and both, too, are linked to the question of the justice of the Athenian empire.[18] The "pentecontaetia," or account of the fifty years (1.89-118), shows us how the Athenians proceeded from hegemony to empire after the Persian war, making Athens the tyrant city of Greece. Central to the principles according to which the Athenians rule their empire is the view that piety consists in doing as the gods do, or at least that the gods will not punish men for imitating them (cf. 4.98.1-6, 5.105.2), especially when men are acting under compulsion.[19] The most striking thing that emerges from the story of Cylon is this: piety may indeed consist in doing as the gods do, not as men say the gods say.

What is the connection between Thucydides' persistent linking of the themes of tyranny and piety, and the recall of Alcibiades from Sicily with its disastrous consequences? What lessons does Thucydides intend for the reader to draw out to himself from these narrations?

The Affair of the Defiling of the Hermae

The Hermae were boundary-marker statues that oversaw the fertility of the property they marked. The facts of the affair of the defiling of the Hermae, as Thucydides presents them (6.27-29, 53, 60-61), are as follows. One night, as the Athenians are preparing for the sailing of the Sicilian expedition, the Hermae are mutilated. This disturbs the Athenians inordinately. They take it as an ill omen for the expedition and as an affront to their democratic regime. The deed was, of course, a gross flouting of traditional piety. It was not surprising, perhaps, that the Athenians should link overt impiety and political conspiracy.[20] Nevertheless, in this instance, widespread concern about piety in Athens results not in the suppression of conspiracy but in the city being thrown into an hysteria, in which atmosphere conspiracies and counterconspiracies thrive. A savage witch-hunt ensues and all the old suspicions about Alcibiades and his *paranomia*, his lawlessness, come to the surface (cf. 6.15.4). This culminates in his recall from Sicily to Athens for execution on the ground of impiety and plotting to subvert the democracy.

Thucydides says in his own name that no one knew who were the perpetrators of the sacrilege (27.2, 60.2). Rewards were offered and citizens, strangers, or even slaves could testify; in fact it was certain metics and slaves who did (28.1). From this testimony arose stories of some mock celebrations of the Mysteries in private homes. Alcibiades was implicated and his enemies took up the charges and magnified them, because they were jealous of his being an obstacle to their being first in the city and holding sway over the *demos*. That is, for reasons that are in no way public-spirited, certain politically ambitious men in the city who are overshadowed by Alcibiades appeal to fears of the *demos* about his *paranomia* in order to condemn Alcibiades for not being public-spirited (28.2).[21] We may at least wonder whether, with the possible exception of Nicias, Alcibiades' political enemies are any more public-spirited and any less impious than he. (Certainly, if they are more pious, they are not above making use of piety as a political weapon. Nicias is not mentioned in this context.) Alcibiades is prepared to stand trial and pay the penalty (29.1), but his enemies insist that the expedition sail with him as planned; they are intent on condemning him in his absence, and they are afraid of his influence with the army on account of his responsibility for the participation of the Argives and the

Mantineans in the expedition (29.3). It would also, as Alcibiades warns, be easier to get a trumped-up charge against him in his absence; Alcibiades says it
would be wiser (*sophronesteron*, literally "more moderate") to try him immediately rather than send him out at the head of an expedition with suspicions
hanging over him, but his exhortation to moderation is ignored (29.2).

After the departure of the expedition, the Athenians continued to investigate
the affairs of the Hermae and the Mysteries. Thucydides describes their method
of investigation:

> And the Athenians, instead of testing the witnesses, in their suspi-
> cious temper accepted everything, arresting and imprisoning the best
> citizens on the credit of base ones, thinking it more expedient to sift
> the matter to the bottom, than that anybody, even one reputed to be
> good and accused only through the villainy of an informer, should es-
> cape without close investigation. (53.2)

The man who made the accusations that finally purged the city of its delirium
did so after being persuaded that it made no difference whether there was any
substance to his charges, but that some charges and trials were necessary to
purge the city of its violent fever (60.3). Thucydides concurs. He says that many
noteworthy men were already imprisoned, there seemed to be no end to the
matter (60.2), and that, regardless of the question of injustice, the city as a whole
clearly benefited from this action (60.5). This constitutes a strong condemnation
of the Athenian *demos*: every so often, it seems, they feel the need for the judicial murder of a number of their outstanding citizens in order to calm their ap-
prehensions about the insecurity of their regime. (The Spartan counterpart is
their vicious murder of the best of the helots [4.80.3-4].)

As a result of all this, the *demos*, wrongly believing that it now has the truth
about the impieties, is even more convinced that Alcibiades is guilty of conspiring to overthrow the democracy (60.1), evidence of which Thucydides provides none. A Spartan force has appeared nearby (61.2) and friends of Alcibiades at Argos are being accused of revolution (61.3). Alcibiades' political
enemies have succeeded, and the *Salaminia* is sent to Sicily to bring him home
for trial and execution (61.4). Here Thucydides reaches the point in the narrative
where he had dropped it, with the arrival of the *Salaminia* in Sicily (Cf. 53), in
order to recount the story of Harmodius and Aristogiton discussed above.

We have noted that when Thucydides interrupts the dramatic events of book
6 to recount this story, he is in fact retelling a story from book 1. Is it not strange
that Thucydides, renowned for his economy of expression, should tell this story
twice? If his purpose was merely to correct the Athenians about an incident in
their city's past, which is Gomme's explanation for the "digression" in book 6,
why not simply correct them adequately on the occasion of first telling it? The
answer, of course, is that Gomme's explanation of Thucydides' motive for telling the story in the first place is inadequate.[22] If we compare the respective contexts of the two occasions for telling the story, something interesting comes to
light that clearly indicates Thucydides' intention and the significance of the

story for his presentation of Alcibiades and the question of tyranny. In book 6, he says he will tell the story of the would-be tyrannicides "in order to show that neither the Greeks in general nor the Athenians themselves give an accurate account of their own tyrants or about this incident" (54.1); Thucydides is relating contemporary events when he pauses to tell the story of Harmodius and Aristogiton in order to correct men's understanding of an event in the distant past. The context of the story in book 1 is a mirror image: Thucydides has just finished relating events of the distant past (the archaeology) when he pauses to tell the story, immediately after which he says, "there are many other matters, too, belonging to the present and not forgotten through lapse of time" about which men are mistaken, and he cites two minor examples. "So averse," he concludes, "to taking pains are most men in the search for the truth, and so prone are they to turn to what is ready at hand" (1.20.3). I hope I shall not be accused of frolicking in some esoteric garden if I contend that in instructing us to call to mind certain ancient events when he is recounting contemporary events involving Alcibiades' defection from Athens, and certain events belonging to the present when he again recounts those same ancient events, Thucydides clearly implies that the most important contemporary events about which the men of his time have a false understanding is the series of events involving Alcibiades.[23]

Harmodius and Aristogiton attempted to overthrow the tyranny of the Pisistratids from private motives; Alcibiades' enemies at Athens attack him from private motives; in both cases the Athenian *demos* mistakenly believes that the motives were public-spirited and that the acts conduced to the public benefit. In fact, in both cases, the Athenians suffer as a result of these deeds: in the first because the tyranny becomes oppressive, Hippias fearing for his life; in the second because Alcibiades, the one Athenian leader who could have won this war for them, if any living man could, defects from their side, fearing for his life.[24] Both Hippias and Alcibiades, while in the ranks of Athens' enemies, are in fact conspiring to return to the city that expelled them (6.59.4, 8.47.1). Just as the tyranny of the Pisistratids does not deserve the calumny of the many, Alcibiades does not deserve their blame. Thucydides' primary intention in correcting the common opinion about the Athenian tyrants and the would-be tyrannicides is to correct the common opinion regarding Alcibiades and his relations with the Athenian democracy.

The "Digression" on the Career of Themistocles

The intention of Thucydides to correct the common opinion regarding Alcibiades reveals itself in at least one other important passage in his work, where he corrects the common understanding of another extraordinary Athenian's relations with the Athenian democracy. Curiously enough, the passage in question is, like the one on the tyrants, one of the outstanding passages in Thucydides' writing that appears to be a digression, the purpose of which Thucydides scholars have had some difficulty determining. I refer to the passage where Thucydides, in Gomme's words, "betrays a strong biographical interest, that interest which he so sternly represses . . . in his main narrative," a passage that is "irrelevant to the narrative," that is, Thucydides' "digression" on the fate of Themistocles.[25]

The context of the "digression" on Themistocles (1.135.2-138) is the same as the context of the story of Cylon, but there is something remarkable to observe. The Athenians are charged with one pollution and the story of Cylon explains it; the Spartans are charged with two, and the stories of the curse of Taenarus (128.1) and of Pausanias (128.2-35.1) explain these. These stories arise directly out of the Spartan and Athenian charges and countercharges of impiety. The story of Themistocles does not arise in this manner; it has nothing to do with any pollution incurred by anybody. Rather, the occasion for Thucydides' recounting this episode from his city's past is that the Spartans, having punished Pausanias (and in the process incurring a pollution) for trying to betray the Greeks to the Persian king, demanded at the time that Themistocles, implicated in the same treason, be similarly punished by the Athenians. And so Thucydides recounts the story of Themistocles, the most distinguished Athenian of his time.[26]

Thucydides presents no evidence that Themistocles was guilty of the charges made against him by the Spartans (compare this with Alcibiades and the Hermae affair), which is appropriate, for the Athenians do not even bother to investigate the charges, which is all we need know to judge the Athenians in this affair. Whereas the Spartans, faced with abundant evidence of his guilt, treated Pausanias with almost ludicrous indulgence, the Athenians no sooner hear the charges against Themistocles than they proceed against him. Themistocles' flight eventually takes him to the court of the king of Persia, from whence he never returns. Thucydides reproduces the letter Themistocles wrote to the Persian king to gain access to his court (137.4). That such a letter was necessary sufficiently exonerates him of having been, like Pausanias, working in collusion with the Persians to betray the Greeks. But what of his earlier favors to the Persian king, his warning him to retreat at Salamis and the failure of the Greeks to destroy the bridges? How are we to understand them? He is not even as guilty as his own letter claims he is: of the latter favor, Thucydides tells us outright that Themistocles lied, and the former he did only after the Persians already had been beaten. We must note that Themistocles is praised in unparalleled terms by Thucydides for having the greatest measure of practical wisdom (and Thucydides says in his own name that his greatness arose from his "nature" [138.3]). Themistocles was best at seeing far into the future.[27] It is in the light of this great virtue, I contend, that Themistocles' "treason" must be understood. Themistocles has insight into the Athenians' nature. He fully understands his tenuous position at Athens. He knows that the Athenians, as Thucydides amply reveals, are capable of moving, from envy and suspicion, against their greatest benefactors on not particularly solid evidence. He must make contingency plans. He must have a refuge to which he may someday flee, so, like Hippias, he cultivates his interests at the Persian court. In his letter, his claim to have done the Persians a favor he did not do is easily understood, given his circumstances, as is his reminding the king of a favor he did do. But is Themistocles not lying, too, when he claims to have done even this favour for the king?[28] The least that can be said is that while the favor conduced to his own benefit as well as the king's, it did not effectually harm the Athenians. But can we not say more, for, in the long run, did not his action conduce, not to his own as well as the king's benefit, but to his own and the Athenians' benefit, at least as he saw it? Themistocles' career was devoted to laying the foundation of the Athenian empire. Would he not, with his amazing farsightedness, be understandably reluctant to see the Persians' power utterly crushed so as no longer to represent a potential threat to the Greeks, thus obviating the need for the Delian alliance?[29]

If the story of Themistocles is not needed to explain any of the impieties that are purportedly the subject of the long "digression" in which we find it, why does Thucydides tell it? Is it not meant precisely to provide narrations from which the reader is to draw out lessons to himself? I concur wholeheartedly with J. B. Bury's contention that the point of Thucydides' including in his book this story of the most distinguished Athenian of former times is to provide a point of comparison for the career of the most distinguished Athenian of Thucydides' own time.[30] The lessons drawn from that comparison confirm that the event of Thucydides' own time that was most misunderstood was the career of Alcibiades.

The Problem of Tyranny and the Question of Piety

Alcibiades as presented by Thucydides is the outstanding representative of the post-Periclean generation of prominent Athenians, the core of whose political education consisted in pondering the speeches and deeds of Pericles, especially the funeral oration, with its exaltation of the glory that derives from empire. Alcibiades, the ward of Pericles, was nurtured by the city of Athens at a time when the principles informing the Athenian empire were being clearly revealed in the speeches of Pericles—the first in Thucydides' pages to speak of the empire as a tyranny, and to the *demos*, too—the speeches of the Athenian envoys at Sparta and Melos, for those who were privy to their words (or could have espoused them, themselves),[31] and in the deeds of Athens, for all those who had eyes to see. Thus was Alcibiades' generation nurtured, all the while holding that impressive Athenian empire before their eyes. It is with the career of Alcibiades that the principles informing Athenian foreign policy, the principles of the tyrant city of Greece, are introduced into domestic politics in the most uncompromising way. Alcibiades is as frank about his desire for predominance in Athens as the Athenians are about their desire to dominate Greece. The problem of Alcibiades' relations with the Athenian democracy, the question of tyranny, brings into question most forcefully the Periclean solution to the political problem as presented in the funeral oration: that wholehearted devotion to glory as the greatest good will resolve the conflict between the private and the public good.[32] What is Thucydides' judgement on Alcibiades and the question of tyranny?

In Thucydides' presentation of the debate on the Sicilian expedition (6.8-

26), it is revealed, among other things, that his possession of law-bred virtue does not prevent Nicias from being precisely one of those Athenians who, as much as Alcibiades, cares about his personal interest and reputation (9.2), and that he must be included among those post-Periclean Athenian leaders who contributed to the factional strife that brought ruin upon Athens (12.2-13.1; cf. 15.4). With the account of the defiling of the Hermae (27-29, 53, 60-61) and the parallels between the lives of Themistocles and Alcibiades, we have seen that it can be questioned whether Alcibiades' political enemies were really his moral superiors. From Thucydides' presentation of the assembly at Syracuse (32-41), the question arises whether we are to understand him as the moral inferior of his enemies in Sicily. Hermocrates sees a great opportunity in the Athenians' coming to Sicily: From the ashes of Athenian ambitions in Sicily will arise a Syracusan empire, just as the Persian invasion provided the opportunity for the Athenians. Like Themistocles, he exhorts his fellow citizens to take to their ships (33-4; cf. 7.56.3).[33] Athenagoras' speech contains the highest praise found in Thucydides, and the only theoretical defense, of democracy qua democracy (Pericles' praise being a paean to Athens, not democracy). Thucydides puts these sentiments into the mouth of the worst sort of democratic politician: Athenagoras calumniates his opponents; he warns against faction, then calls for a city in which the kind of atmosphere that leads to Alcibiades' break with Athens is that of everyday political practice. And why? In order to save the city from tyranny (38.3-4; it is appropriate that "Athenagoras" should personify the destructive forces at work at Athens). The reaction of the Syracusan general is undoubtedly approved by Thucydides: he rebukes Athenagoras and calls an immediate halt to any further democratic debate (41). From the plans of the three Athenian generals at Syracuse (47-49), we learn that Alcibiades is as capable as others of espousing "measured" policies (his plan being central, both in order of presentation and as a mean between the extremely diffident and extremely daring plans of Nicias and Lamachus, respectively).[34] In his speech at Sparta after his defection (89-92), Alcibiades' message is essentially the same as the one he earlier (6.6-17.1) gave the Athenians: not to permit prejudices against him to lead to a less favorable hearing being given to matters of public concern (cf. Diodotus's advice to the Athenians about judging the substance of, not the motives behind, advice given in the assembly; 3.41.2-6).

    In Thucydides' account of events in book 7, what is especially important to see is the extent to which the tension that seems so clearly to be at the heart of Alcibiades' problematic relations with Athens, the tension between the private and the public good, is also at the heart of Nicias's, that the Athenians meet utter destruction in Sicily not only because of his numerous egregious errors,[35] but because at crucial junctures Nicias places his private interest before the public interest with disastrous consequences for the latter.[36]

    As for book 8, there may be much confusion (though, without going into the question of its being unfinished, not as much as is usually supposed), but this much is clear: we see the eventual return of a kind of moderation to Athenian politics, followed by the return of Alcibiades to Athens, and that followed by a remarkable Athenian revival. Thucydides associates these events. The only direct discourse in the eighth book is a portion of a speech by Pisander that exhorts the Athenians to do two things: change their *politeia* to a more moderate (*sophronesteron*) form, and recall Alcibiades (53.3). While still at Samos, Alcibiades receives very high praise from Thucydides. The democrats are intent upon sailing against the Piraeus and warring on the oligarchy, but Alcibiades dissuades them; Thucydides ranks this among the greatest services ever done the city and remarks that Alcibiades was the only man alive who could have done it (86.4-5). And why were the democrats so angry? Because the Four Hundred had, almost a century after the expulsion of the tyrants, deprived the Athenian *demos* of its freedom (68.4). The democratic regime that has flourished at Athens ever since the Spartans and Alcibiades' ancestors expelled the Athenian tyrants is finally overthrown not by Alcibiades but by his enemies.[37] After the deposition of the Four Hundred, Athenian affairs are put into the hands of the Five Thousand. Thucydides writes: "And during the first period the Athenians appear to have enjoyed the best government they ever had, at least in my time, for there was a measured blending of the few and the many, and this it was that first caused the city to recover from the wretched plight into which it had fallen. And they voted to recall Alcibiades" (97.2-3). This was, in Thucydides' view, the best Athenian regime of his lifetime; that is, superior to Periclean Athens. (Need it be remarked that the highly praised rule of the Pisistratids was not of Thucydides' lifetime?) The last significant event of Thucydides' book is the Athenian naval victory at Cynossema; the city has reconciled itself to Alcibiades and is on the rebound.

Book 8 is the book in which the tyrannical principles of Athenian foreign policy become, pervasively, the principles of Athenian domestic life. The specter of civil war hangs over Athens. For Thucydides, no less than for his greatest student, Hobbes, the *summum malum* of politics is civil war (cf. the account of the civil wars at Corcyra [3.70-84]), and this is what Alcibiades alone among the men of his time could, and did, prevent. Thucydides knows well that Alcibiades' presence poses a threat to any regime except one in which he rules (note what Phrynichus "rightly thought" of Alcibiades, that "he cared no more for oligarchy than for democracy" [8.48.4, 63.4]).[38] The last book of Thucydides appears to point to a regime in Athens that can accommodate the ambitions of both Alcibiades and the Athenians, that is, a regime in which Alcibiades holds sway in the city in the position of predominance once held by Pericles. In practical terms, this means the measured tyranny of Alcibiades.[39] Thucydides' "digression" on the Athenian tyrants teaches us that he does not share the Athenians' extreme fear of tyranny. His blame of the Athenian *demos'* treatment of its greatest potential benefactor consists in his demonstration that there is such a thing as a moderate and beneficent tyrant.

It cannot be denied, however, that if this was Thucydides' prescription for Athens, it cuts both ways. It is surely a mistake to think that Alcibiades is the primary target of Thucydides' blame of Pericles' successors (2.65.10-11): Thucydides believed the Sicilian expedition could have succeeded with the right leadership, that is, Alcibiades, and his presentation makes it clear that Alcibiades' presence in the city was not the cause of the Athenians' ambitions in Sicily.[40] Nor is his explicit judgement of Alcibiades (6.15.3-4) to be read so much as a blame of Alcibiades as a blame of his fellow Athenians. He makes the statement that the way Alcibiades lived his private life was precisely the sort of thing that later ruined the city, but then explains what he means:

> For the many, fearing the greatness of his lawless and sensual self-indulgence in his manner of living, and also of his designs in every action in which he was involved, became hostile to him on the ground that he was aiming at tyranny, and, though publicly he managed the affairs of the war most excellently, at his private life, every man took offense, and so entrusting the city to others, after no long time they brought it to ruin.

The Athenians, not Alcibiades, brought the city to ruin by rejecting (as Nicias had urged them to [12.2-13.1]) Alcibiades' leadership in the war.

However, in the final analysis, Alcibiades cannot escape unscathed. For if, on the one hand, Thucydides' teaching about the question of tyranny culminates in the prescription for the measured tyranny of Alcibiades at Athens, on the other, his writing includes a teaching about why that measured tyranny did not, and perhaps could not, come about, and Alcibiades must share responsibility. In the private realm, Alcibiades' flaw is the same as that which brought down the Pisistratids. For, when we say that the story of the end of the tyranny is the story of how a good regime came to ruin, undone by *eros*, it is primarily the *eros* of Hipparchus, not Aristogiton, that we must have in mind. In the public realm, the theme of tyranny and piety is paramount. What, more than anything, distinguishes Alcibiades from the Pisistratids but the latter's piety?

Alcibiades' essential flaw is that he cannot, or would not, appreciate the link between successful tyranny and piety. In fact, Thucydides teaches that piety is an essential ingredient of all political life.[41] This is the truth that Nicias divines, which is why, despite his damnable share of responsibility for the Athenians' destruction in Sicily, he is singled out in such an extraordinary way by Thucydides. Nicias believes there are just gods who rule the affairs of men and reward justice (see especially his last speech [7.77]). These pious hopes of Nicias are not fulfilled. Like the Melians, he clings to hopes in powers invisible, and like them, he is utterly destroyed. However, it is not only in spite of this, but precisely because of it, and in the very context of his having shown the folly of Nicias's hopes, that Thucydides calls Nicias "the man who, of all the Greeks of my time, least deserved to be brought to so great a degree of misery, because of his practice of law-bred virtue" (86.5).[42] For if Thucydides does not share the view of Nicias, neither does he share the view of the Athenians at Melos, who believe that because there are no gods who reward justice there will be no penalties for injustice. Nicias divines this truth of piety: the Athenians cannot carry on in their "Athenian" ways without limit; they are courting disaster. The Athenians live in the light of an understanding that rejects what is true in piety. But no city can long survive in that light. (Whether an individual can—for example, a Diodotus or a Thucydides—is another question, but no individual can who wants to flourish, as Alcibiades does, in the public realm.)

The fundamental defect of Alcibiades' understanding, paralleling the fundamental defect of the "Athenian" understanding, that of the "new" imperial Athens of which he is the individual incarnation, is the inability or refusal to recognize what is true in piety. But the city qua city can never abjure entirely what is at the core of the "old" political understanding, namely, concern for the question of piety. Thus the piety of the Athenians, which persisted in Athens in the face of the "new," became a problem for both Alcibiades and the city. "Old" Athens did not feel it could trust Alcibiades, so placed its trust in pious Nicias; "new" Athens could not flourish, could not achieve its objectives in Sicily and beyond, without a man like Alcibiades at the helm.[43] Because of a fortuitous combination of circumstances and his own great political prudence, the problem of tyranny and the question of piety did not arise so irremediably for Pericles. And perhaps it need not have for Alcibiades, for had Alcibiades understood the problem of tyranny, as Athens' ancient tyrants apparently did, he *may* have been able to combine successfully the interest of Athens in ruling the Greek world and beyond, and his own interest in ruling the Athenians.[44] But had he been able to understand sufficiently the importance of the question of piety for the problem of tyranny, could he have any longer been an Alcibiades, and would he have aspired to tyranny?

Notes

This chapter was originally published in *The Canadian Journal of Political Science 15* (1982). Reprinted with permission. Thanks to Christopher Bruell, Clifford Orwin, and anonymous referees for helpful comments on earlier drafts.

1. Thomas Hobbes, *English Works*, Sir William Molesworth, ed., vol. 8 (London: J. Bohn, 1843), viii.

2. For brief discussions of the gamut run by the literature, see Virginia Hunter, *Thucydides The Artful Reporter* (Toronto: Hakkert, 1973), 3-8, and W. P. Wallace, "Thucydides," *Phoenix 18* (1964): 251-61. The literature on Thucydides is enormous and I would tend to follow the dictum of G. F. Abbott that students should "take as their principal instructor in Thucydides Thucydides himself" (*Thucydides: A Study in Historical Reality* [New York: A. Routledge, 1925], vi.)

3. The outstanding exception is Leo Strauss, *The City and Man* (Chicago: Rand McNally, 1964). Strauss's discussion reveals that Thucydides' writing is "most politic" as regards its subject, its object, and its method. Werner Jaeger (*Paidaia: The Ideals of Greek Culture*, trans. Gilbert Highet, vol. 1 [Oxford: Oxford University Press, 1939]) began down this road in his essay on Thucydides, but did not travel it as far.

4. Hobbes, *Works*, viii; my italics.

5. Ibid., xxii.

6. References to Thucydides will be included in parentheses in the text, citing book, chapter, and, where relevant, sentence. Successive citations from the same book will

usually omit the book number. Translations are my own to this extent; while they tend to follow the Loeb, they are in fact an amalgam of several translations, corrected by me for accuracy and consistency, and I take responsibility for them.

7. Wallace ("Thucydides," 258) speaks of the effect of Thucydides' writing being almost that of "subliminal persuasion" and describes it well (252); cf. Hunter, *Artful Reporter*, 8, 40, 115, 180. Although they would seem to be unaware of the fact, the efforts of scholars like Hunter, Jacqueline de Romilly (*Histoire et Raison chez Thucydide* [Paris: Les Belles Lettres, 1956]), and Wallace were substantially anticipated by Hobbes's view. Would that in following his methods they also shared his concerns! R. G. Collingwood (*The Idea of History* [Oxford: Oxford University Press, 1961], 29) thinks that Thucydides has a "bad conscience" about writing history and is not really writing history at all. I doubt that Thucydides has a "bad conscience." Cf. Thomas S. Engeman, "Homeric Honor and Thucydidean Necessity," *Interpretation 4* (1974): 66n5.

8. I say "so-called" because Thucydides is himself capable of calling a passage a digression when he wants to; for example, 1.97.2.

9. If a regime could be established, and endure, that practiced Spartan domestic policy and Athenian foreign policy, it would undoubtedly be the most impressive regime Thucydides could imagine. One of the things we learn from reading Thucydides, however, is that such a regime could not endure. Athens and Sparta represent the peaks of fundamental alternatives, according to Thucydides. The Athenian principle is "motion," the Spartan "rest," and there can be no more be a synthesis of "Athenianism" and "Spartanism" than there can be a synthesis of motion and rest. Cf. Lowell Edmunds, *Chance and Intelligence in Thucydides* (Cambridge, Mass.: Harvard University Press, 1975), 120-30, and Strauss, *City and Man*, 145-63.

10. For other views on the role of the "digression" on the end of the tyranny at Athens, see Abbott, *Historical Reality*, 101-02; F. E. Adcock, *Thucydides and His History* (Cambridge: Cambridge University Press, 1963), 25-26; F. M. Cornford, *Thucydides Mythistoricus* (London: E. Arnold, 1907), 132-33; and H. D. Westlake, *Individuals in Thucydides* (Cambridge: Cambridge University Press, 1968), 221-22. J. B. Bury, *History of Greece* (New York: Macmillan, 1959), 470-71, appears to view Alcibiades and the question of tyranny in much the same light as I, but in his *The Ancient Greek Historians* (New York: Macmillan, 1958), 89, he sees no significance in this "digression." I suspect that the narrations themselves have secretly instructed Bury, and more effectually than could possibly have been done by precept. See Strauss, *City and Man*, 196-97.

11. See the article "Aristogiton" in the *Oxford Classical Dictionary*.

12. On the question of Nicias's "virtue," see A. W. Gomme, *A Historical Commentary on Thucydides*, 4 vols. (vol. 4 rev. and ed. A. Andrewes and K. J. Dover: [Oxford: Clarendon Press, 1945-1970]), 462-63; Westlake, *Individuals*, 209; Strauss, *City and Man*, 208-09; and my note 42, below.

13. I suspect that Gomme, *Commentary*, vol. 4, 318, in objecting to Thucydides' tone at 54.1 and 59.1, has not attended sufficiently to this fact. See Strauss, *City and Man*, 196.

14. Aristotle, *Rhetoric*, 1367b19. Thucydides lifts Archedice out of the obscurity that Pericles recommends for women (2.45.2). Women are seen to participate in political life on occasion, as at Thebes (2.4.2 and 4) and in the Corcyrean civil war (3.74.1), but Thucydides calls their participation "beyond nature" (*para physin*). Cf. Engeman, "Homeric Necessity," 76n24.

15. Cf. Cornford, *Mythistoricus*, 244-49.

16. Hobbes, *Works*, 127n3. It is on this passage that an ancient commentator made the oft-quoted remark, "Here the lion laughed."

17. This is particularly striking in his revisionist interpretation of the Trojan war, the essence of which is to ascribe a mundane cause to those things that Homer's version links with the divine; for example, fear of Atreides' power, not an oath, bound the suitors to his cause (1.9.1 and 3), and the *aitia* of the siege of Troy lasting so long was not the power of the gods but the weakness of the Greeks: they lacked money (11). Cf. Seth Benardete, *Herodotean Inquiries* (The Hague: Martinus Nijhoff, 1969), 20, 33; and Strauss, *City and Man*, 154-62, and 235-36 (on Thucydides, 3.104).

18. The most renowned book dealing with Athenian imperialism is Jacqueline de Romilly's *Thucydides and Athenian Imperialism*, trans. P. Thody (Oxford: Blackwell, 1963). But see the excellent discussion of Christopher Bruell ("Thucydides' View of Athenian Imperialism," *American Political Science Review 68* [1974]: 11-17), who argues that the differences between his own and Romilly's conclusions, "on the meaning of the opposition of right and force or compulsion . . . are not unrelated to the greater seriousness with which I take, and argue that Thucydides takes, the issue of justice, the issue of the justice of Athenian imperialism, in the first place."

19. At Delium (4.98.1-6), the Athenians attempt to avoid the charge of impiety while admitting committing acts traditionally viewed as impious. Their excuse is that they acted from compulsion. But if piety is the highest compulsion—this is the traditional view: cf. Nicias at 4.44.5-6 and Hobbes, *Works*, 429n1—they are still impious. Their solution is to interpret piety itself as sanctioning acts committed under the constraints of compulsion.

20. Gomme, *Commentary*, vol. 4, 284-85; cf. Westlake, *Individuals*, 221n1. Of course, why Alcibiades should be suspected in an affair that could do nothing but raise doubts about an expedition he so strongly supported is another question. Nevertheless, although the informers implicated Alcibiades not in this but in a related affair (28.1), his enemies insisted that he was involved in both and more (28.2).

21. Gomme, *Commentary*, vol. 4, 289, contrasts this with 2.65.11 and makes an important point: "Here there is an important difference, in that Thucydides treats Alkibiades' enemies as a group ('preventing *them* from leading the people *themselves*'); Alkibiades was a giant, and men who were potential rivals of one another combined to overthrow him" (Gomme's italics).

22. Ibid., 329: "The most plausible explanation is that he succumbed here to the temptation before which all historians and commentators are by their very nature weak, the temptation to correct historical error wherever they find it, regardless of its relevance to their immediate purpose." Gomme should not be so generous in ascribing his own weaknesses to all other historians and commentators, especially to Thucydides; it is "unhistorical." As for the story's being told twice, Gomme (ibid., vol. 1, 137) suggests that not only the first, but the second account also would have been eliminated if Thucydides had had time for a final revision. I see no reason to doubt that the text as we have it, with the possible exception of the eighth book, is substantially as Thucydides wanted us to have it.

23. L. E. Lord, *Thucydides and the World War* (Cambridge, Mass.: Harvard University Press, 1945), 189-90, has a different view of the purpose of this as well as other "digressions": they serve to heighten dramatic suspense; cf. Hobbes, *Works*, 29. See also K. J. Dover, *Thucydides* (Oxford: Clarendon Press, 1973), 30; Edmunds, *Chance and Intelligence*, 194-95; J. H. Finley Jr., *Thucydides* (Cambridge, Mass.: Harvard University Press, 1942), 222-25; Hunter, *Artful Reporter*, 173-74; Liesbeschuetz, "Thucydides and the Sicilian Expedition," *Historia 17* (1968): 304-06; Romilly, *Athenian Imperialism*, 4n1, 207-09; A. W. Saxonhouse, "Nature and Convention in Thucydides' *History*," *Polity 10* (1978), 483-84; Hans-Peter Stahl, "The Speeches and Course of Events in Books Six

and Seven of Thucydides," in Philip A. Stadter, ed., *The Speeches in Thucydides* (Chapel Hill: University of North Carolina Press, 1973), 70; and Mabel Lang, "The Murder of Hipparchus," *Historia 3* (1955): 395-407. Lang is clearly convinced of the importance and relevance of the "digression," but her primary concern is to determine, by comparing Thucydides' account of the murder with other ancient accounts, what happened historically; this is not my concern.

24. Thucydides gives his account of how the Pisistratid tyranny "went bad" in the context of his account of how Alcibiades "went bad." On the question of Alcibiades' abilities and the Sicilian expedition, see David Grene, *Greek Political Theory* (Chicago: University of Chicago Press, 1965), 68-69; Liebeschuetz, "Sicilian Expedition," 289-306; and M. F. McGregor, "The Genius of Alcibiades," *Phoenix 19* (1965): 33. P. A. Brunt, "Thucydides and Alcibiades," *Revue Des Etudes Grecques 65* (1952): 59-96, agrees that this is Thucydides' judgement of Alcibiades and that Thucydides blames the Athenian *demos* for not trusting him, but feels compelled to account for this judgement (rather than by simply saying that Thucydides thought it was true) by maintaining that Thucydides had a personal bias in favour of Alcibiades, having fallen under the spell of, and been blinded by, his *virtù* (Brunt's usage). The supposed similarity between Thucydides' *arete* and Machiavelli's *virtù* is remarked also by Bury (*Greek Historians*, 145; cf. Lord, *World War*, 204).

25. Gomme, *Commentary*, vol. 1, 26-27, 447.

26. That Thucydides' purpose in recounting the stories of Pausanias and Themistocles is at least two-fold is indicated by the difference between what he says when introducing these "digressions" and when concluding them. In his introduction, he states his purpose to be to explain how each of the pollutions was incurred (1.126.3, 128.1-2). At the end of his discussion of the episodes involving the two famous men, he writes, "Such was the end of Pausanias the Spartan and Themistocles the Athenian, the most distinguished Greeks of their time" (138.6). See Strauss, *City and Man*, 211-12.

27. This is a virtue that he shares with Thucydides, although they see well into the future in very different ways: Thucydides' book can be a "possession for all time" only if he can see the future in the very relevant sense that he can know the limits of human things and that these limits will not change (1.22.4); cf. my note 9, above.

28. When Alcibiades finds himself at Sparta in similar circumstances to those of Themistocles in Persia, he, too, is willing to tell a fib or two (for example, 6.90.3, 91.1). Alcibiades has also courted favor with the enemies of his city and he emphasizes this for the same reason Themistocles does in similar straits (89.2; cf. 5.43.2). Alcibiades and Themistocles were the two most successful Athenians at Sparta (Gomme, *Commentary*, vol. 1, 258).

29. The story of Pausanias (cf. 1.94-5) is linked to Spartan decline and loss of allies; of Themistocles, to Athenian ascendancy and acquisition of allies (cf. 1.89-93). That Thucydides is aware that complete destruction of one's enemies is sometimes not in one's own best interest is evidenced in his account of Demosthenes' exploits in Acarnania (3.113.6). Cf. Bury, *History*, 283.

30. Bury, *Greek Historians*, 127-28; cf. N. M. Pusey, "Alcibiades and *to philopoli*," *Harvard Studies in Classical Philology 51* (1940): 227. For other opinions about the purpose, if any, of Thucydides' including the story of Themistocles in his writing, see Adcock, *Thucydides*, 23; Cornford, *Mythistoricus*, 135-37; Finley, *Thucydides*, 139; Romilly, *Athenian Imperialism*, 230-35; and A. G. Woodhead, *Thucydides on the Nature of Power* (Cambridge, Mass.: Harvard University Press, 1970), 91. Woodhead (81) quite rightly points out that while the Athenians doubtless wondered, "How far can we trust Alcibiades?" it is remarkable how little consideration has been given to the reverse ques-

tion, that is, "How far can Alcibiades trust the Athenians?"

31. Cf. Romilly, *Athenian Imperialism*, 242-44, 273.

32. For an elaboration of these themes, see my "Love of Glory and the Common Good," *American Political Science Review 76* (1982): 825-36.

33. Hermocrates accepts the "Athenian" understanding of human nature and politics. Cf. Bury, *Greek Historians*, 136; Edmunds, *Chance and Intelligence*, 29; Grene, *Greek Political Theory*, 43-44; and Romilly, *Athenian Imperialism*, 304-05.

34. Whenever Thucydides speaks of Athenians and their policies, including Pericles, he uses the word *metrios* as opposed to *sophrosyne*, which he does use of Spartans and others. I am translating, respectively, "measured" as opposed to "moderate." There is one exception that proves the rule. After Cleon's famous taunt to Nicias that he, himself, could capture the Spartans trapped on the island of Sphacteria in twenty days, Thucydides says that the "moderates" in Athens, the "*sophrones*," preferred to rid the city of Cleon than to capture the Spartans; that is, they, like the Spartans, habitually cared more for domestic stability than for victories in foreign affairs (4.28.5; cf. 108.7). A "measured" as opposed to a "moderate" policy is merely a means to an end, which end, in itself, may be immoderate. It would be possible for a policy *not* to be "measured" because it *was* "moderate."

35. Nicias's bungling is responsible for the large size of the original expedition (6.8.4., 19.2), and the Athenians' great confidence that it will succeed (24.2-3), therefore, the greatness both of the Athenians' expectations from it and of the final disaster. He contemns the coming of Gylippus to Sicily (104), a big mistake (cf. 6.103, and 7.2). He is also responsible for the doubling of the size of the expedition and, therefore, of the disaster (7.15.1). Cf. also 7.4.4 and 6, 24.3, 42.3, and 50.4: the Athenians still had time to escape Sicily with their power and empire intact. Cf. Finley, *Thucydides*, 216-17.

36. Especially 7.48.3-4: His view before the final debacle is that he would rather die in Sicily, taking the Athenian army with him, than unjustly suffer at the hands of the Athenian *demos* for having abandoned Sicily. Nicias commits a kind of treason rather than return to Athens to an unjust trial on the charge of treason. The congruence of Nicias's interest and the Athenians' interest has broken down, just as it did with Alcibiades. By contrast, Demosthenes appears to be thinking only of the public good at this crucial juncture (7.47.3-4: And whose arguments is he echoing? Cf. 6.9.3., 10.1, 11.1, and 12.1). Cf. Edmunds, *Chance and Intelligence*, 86-88, and Westlake, *Individuals*, 198.

37. This simplifies the situation in a way that may be misleading, for it must be acknowledged that it was Alcibiades who initiated the movement against the democracy, even though those who completed it were his political enemies. His enemies knew that Alcibiades really cared no more for oligarchy than for democracy (8.48.4, 63.4).

38. In the Loeb edition, the words "*hoper kai en*" at 8.48.4 are left untranslated, although they appear in the Greek.

39. Cf. Woodhead, *Nature of Power*, 87.

40. Cf. 1.36.2, 44.3, 3.86.4, 115.4, 4.2.2, 59 and 6.76; Thucydides introduces Alcibiades at 5.43.2; the question for Thucydides is not *whether* the Athenians will go to Sicily, but *who* will lead them there. What must be remarked about the Sicilian expedition is not that it failed, but how close it came to succeeding, even without Alcibiades. That the presence of a man like Alcibiades in Athens facilitated the launching of the expedition is not to be denied. Cf. Finley, *Thucydides*, 220, and Grene, *Greek Political Theory*, 47.

41. The civil wars at Corcyra are characterized precisely by the abandonment of all the traditional constraints of piety (3.70-84). It is in this context that Thucydides tells us that war is a "violent teacher" (82.2). The harshest teaching of that harsh teacher is the

revelation of how precarious are the supports that permit civilization, in Thucydidean terms, "Greekness," occasionally to emerge from barbarism. Cf. his account of the moral effects of the plague at Athens, which follows immediately upon his presentation of Pericles' funeral oration, which is strikingly silent about the gods. See my "Love of Glory and the Common Good"; Strauss, *City and Man*, 146-48; and Saxonhouse, "Nature and Convention," 470-73.

42. Bury, *Greek Historians*, 119-20, maintains that Thucydides is being ironic here. This is better than taking the statement at face value, but to leave it at that is to fail to go far enough. For other interpretations of the econium, see C. N. Cochrane, *Thucydides and the Science of History* (Oxford: Oxford University Press, 1929), 136; Edmunds, *Chance and Intelligence*, 140-42; and Westlake, *Individuals*, 209-11. Cf. also Hobbes, *Works*, xv and n1, where it is asserted by Hobbes's nineteenth-century editor that 7.86 was corrected by Bekker by deleting "*es to theion.*" If Bekker was correct in deleting these words, whoever added them to Thucydides' text was certainly on the right track.

43. Strauss, *City and Man*, 195-209. Pondered in the context of Thucydides' presentation as a whole, does the fact that we can understand eclipses of the moon as "natural" phenomena render the eclipse in Sicily (7.50.4) at that particular time and place—a seemingly "chance" event with such monumental consequences—any less "miraculous"? Could an avenger god have meted out any more appropriate punishment to the hubristic Athenians?

44. There is an indication (not in Thucydides, but in Plutarch, *Alcibiades*, 34, and Xenophon, *Hellenica*, 1.4.20) that Alcibiades may have learned a lesson from his experience at Athens: ever since the occupation of Decelea, for which he was so responsible, the annual sacred procession by land from Athens to the Eleusian shrine had had to be suspended and the trip made by sea. After his return to Athens, the procession marched out under his auspices, in the customary fashion, Alcibiades protecting it with an escort of troops. It was over the Eleusian Mysteries that he had gotten into trouble originally. Cf. Bury, *History*, 500. Does Thucydides teach that piety is essential for successful politics merely in some Machiavellian sense, or in a more genuine sense? I find no clear answer, that is, no definitive text, in Thucydides. But see also my preceding note, and Leo Strauss, "Preliminary Observations on the Gods in Thucydides' Work," *Interpretation 4* (1974); 1-16.

Chapter 4

Thucydides on Ambition to Rule

Steven Forde's *The Ambition to Rule: Alcibiades and the Politics of Imperialism in Thucydides*[1] is an outstanding contribution not only to our understanding of the deepest concerns of Thucydides' narrative of the Peloponnesian War but also to our understanding of the highest and purest forms of political ambition, regardless of time and place, of the perennial tensions between the private good and the public good as they manifest themselves in the relations between individuals of superlative virtue and their political communities. The book is a study "not of the historical Alcibiades but of Thucydides' understanding of Alcibiades, of Alcibiades' place in Thucydides' writing and of his relation to the deepest of Thucydides' themes" (Forde, 1). We must approach Forde's *Ambition to Rule*, therefore, as indeed we must approach Thucydides, with interests that transcend the "historical." Forde's is the first book-length interpretation of Thucydides to be published the ground for which was prepared by the excavations of Leo Strauss in *The City and Man*.[2] It follows a remarkable series of papers by a number of like-minded scholars working on Thucydides, most notably a half-dozen prominently placed articles by Clifford Orwin, and a few books which at least parallel Strauss's approach (whether or not they were based upon it), either consciously, as in the case of Lowell Edmunds's *Chance and Intelligence in Thucydides*,[3] or unconsciously (apparently), as in the case of W. R. Connor's *Thucydides*.[4] This is not to detract from Forde's accomplishment: *Ambition to Rule* is now the premier comprehensive interpretation of Thucydides' portrait of Alcibiades and the politics of Athenian imperialism in English or any other language.

Forde's book contains a brief introductory chapter and four long substantive ones. In the introduction, he outlines what he calls "The Problem of Thucydides and the Problem of Alcibiades" and adumbrates the argument of his book. Thucydides spent his adult life writing about the Peloponnesian War not because of a compelling allegiance to some "historical" task like the "ideal of factual accuracy" but because "the Peloponnesian War is a historical event that has proved especially revealing of permanent truth" (Forde, 4): "more sharply than any other war, it exposed the grave ambiguities that attend the character, and the force, of justice in relations between states" (Forde, 5); furthermore, it "unsettled the conventional understanding of domestic politics and morality more thoroughly than it did the corresponding understanding of international politics" (Forde, 6). Forde himself has focused on Thucydides' presentation of Alcibiades both because these questions of justice and power in international relations are thrown into highest relief by Athens' most daring attempt at imperial expansion—the attempt to conquer Sicily, an expedition for which Alcibiades was Athens' most vociferous advocate—and because Alcibiades' career in general compels us "seriously to reconsider traditional views of the place of statesmen in political society and of their legitimate obligations to the community" (Forde, 7). Thucydides' presentation of Alcibiades "brings us closer to the heart of Thucydides' understanding of the human and political world than does almost any other part of his work" (Forde, 1).

Chapter 1, "The Alcibidean Moment," that is, the climactic "moment" of the Sicilian expedition, when "the most daring of cities and the boldest of its bold commanders set in motion an imperial scheme of the greatest audacity" (Forde, 12), treats generally Thucydides' view of Athenian imperialism. In a lengthy analysis of the Athenian character, Forde explores more carefully than has ever been done Thucydides' account of the "national character" of Athens. He particularly investigates Thucydides' attribution of the quality of daring (*tolma*) to the Athenians, painstakingly demonstrating that Thucydides reserves the word *tolma* almost exclusively for the Athenians, rendering it practically a technical term, and in particular distinguishing it from courage (*andreia*), which is rarely attributed to Athenians. Forde subtly analyzes this and related distinctions and their import for understanding the emergence of Athenian self-assurance after the Persian War, how Athenian daring represented an innovative transformation of traditional courage along lines that called into question any inhibitions about the enormous potential of purely human power, inhibitions ultimately grounded in traditional piety. Connected with this is the question of the political sublimation of *eros*, "a significant if somewhat concealed theme in Thucydides' work" (Forde, 31), which Forde deftly develops in a direction quite different from the "mythic" sense in which F. M. Cornford presented it almost a century ago in his classic *Thucydides Mythistoricus*.[5]

Chapter 2 investigates more particularly the ambitions and political understanding of Alcibiades as revealed especially in his speeches at Athens favoring the Sicilian expedition and at Sparta, after his defection, attempting to justify his behavior to the sceptical Spartans. Forde shows how extreme, and thus revealing, Alcibiades' ambitions really are: Alcibiades inverts Pericles' Funeral Oration exhortation to the Athenians to bask in the glory of imperial Athens, exhorting them to bask instead in the reflected light of his own splendor; he inverts Nicias's view that the individual's prosperity depends on the prosperity of the city, urging the Athenians to understand instead that the prosperity of Athens depends on his own political success. Alcibiades' ambition is

> so free from every external restraint, free even from attachment to
> any goal outside itself, that it practically leaves politics behind. . . . At
> the moment of the speech at Sparta, Alcibiades' unsated thirst for
> glory and accomplishment continues to drive him. We learn from
> non-Thucydidean sources that at a later juncture, after his return to
> Athens and some brilliant military successes in the East, Alcibiades
> did content himself with a kind of political retirement upon falling
> again into disfavor at Athens. Thucydides' presentation makes this as
> comprehensible as Alcibiades' earlier frenetic activity. (Forde, 114)

What distinguishes Forde's discussion of Alcibiades' ambition is his insistence
on combining this kind of analysis with the full force of the implications of Thucydides' own insistence that by the time of the Sicilian expedition Athens was
indeed dependent on Alcibiades for its success, perhaps even its survival, that
"Alcibiades' argument concerning his usefulness to the city is nevertheless
valid, for all its implausibility from the point of view of ordinary civic consciousness" (Forde, 169).

Chapter 3, "Book Eight of Thucydides' History," is my personal favorite. I
found particularly helpful Forde's discussion of Alcibiades and Phrynichus
(Forde, 130-39), especially combined with his lucid argument denying that Alcibiades aspired to tyrannical power in Athens (Forde, 92-95, 184-87). In general, recent scholarship has begun to develop a more sympathetic assessment of
the quality of book 8 than had been prevalent (e.g., Connor, 210-30), but Forde
does the best job yet of demonstrating its coherence and its place in the context
of the narrative as a whole. Indeed, one of the greatest strengths of Forde's book
is his repeated persuasive demonstrations that what earlier critics viewed as
contradictions in the work, contradictions "explained" by attending to the "composition question" and discerning allegedly "earlier" and "later" layers in the
narrative, are not contradictions at all, but in fact developments in a coherent
Thucydidean argument. Other scholars, of course, have made this argument, but
Forde really demonstrates it to an unprecedented degree (with the exception,
perhaps, of Strauss).

Forde's last chapter draws all the questions and themes of his book together,
offering a final account of Alcibiades' politics and a final judgment of him
(guided, of course, by Thucydides): "We should not be surprised," he cautions,
"if the final estimation of this man, whose career and whose very existence
breathe ambiguity, contains some irreducible measure of that ambiguity itself"
(Forde, 11). Peter Pouncey, discusses very well some of the ambivalencies of
Thucydides' presentation of Alcibiades,[6] especially as a man so adept at, yet in
important ways superior to, factional party politics, but Forde elaborates this
much further (in a somewhat different direction) and at the highest level of sophistication.

I could, of course, offer some criticisms of *Ambition to Rule*; rather, I could
express some differences between Forde's views and my own on certain ques-

Chapter 4

tions. Forde (91) implicitly endorses the widely held view, for example, that the Sicilian expedition was a departure from Pericles' strategy for the war. I believe, however, that we need not think that Pericles would have adopted the Thucydidean view of the "Peloponnesian War" as one continuous war rather than two ten-year wars separated by a seven-year peace; this was, after all, the prevailing opinion among Thucydides' contemporaries against which he was compelled to argue. I suspect, in fact, that Pericles, had he survived, would have sanctioned the Sicilian expedition. Not, I think, an expedition of the magnitude that the Athenians sent, but it was Nicias, not Alcibiades, who was responsible for the enormous size of the expedition, and Forde himself shows very well (Forde, 90-91) that Alcibiades' strategy for the expedition did not depend on the large military force that Nicias advised sending to Sicily. In any case, where I would question Forde, even disagree with him, I have learned from him. I would prefer the book were written with greater economy—some arguments are first adumbrated, then presented and reiterated, finally summarized—but more general readers probably would not mind, indeed, might even appreciate it.

In sum, Forde's *Ambition to Rule* is an enormously useful book, one of the best ever written on Thucydides. All the major themes and passages in the narrative are discussed in insightful and refreshing ways. All the important scholarship is not only cited but engaged in critical discourse. The writing is perspicuous: general readers will be instructed. The arguments are perspicacious: seasoned scholars will be both instructed and delighted.

Notes

This chapter was originally published in *The Review of Politics 52* (1990). Reprinted with permission.
    1. Steven Forde, *The Ambition to Rule: Alcibiades and the Politics of Imperialism in Thucydides* (Ithaca, N.Y.: Cornell University Press, 1989) (hereafter cited as Forde, followed by page references).
    2. Leo Strauss, *The City and Man* (Chicago: Rand McNally, 1964).
    3. Lowell Edmunds, *Chance and Intelligence in Thucydides* (Cambridge, Mass.: Harvard University Press, 1975).
    4. W. R. Connor, *Thucydides* (Princeton, N.J.: Princeton University Press, 1984).
    5. F. M. Cornford, *Thucydides Mythistoricus* (London: Arnold, 1907).
    6. Peter Pouncey, *The Necessities of War* (New York: Columbia University Press, 1980).

Chapter 5

Machiavellian *virtù* and Thucydidean *arete*: Moderation and the Common Good

Introduction

This chapter illumines an important aspect of the political thought of Thucydides by examining an apparent kinship between the political thought of Machiavelli and Thucydides, which was remarked on at least as long ago as the nineteenth century.[1] About eighty years ago, for example, J. B. Bury, famed classical historian, asserted of Thucydides, *"his object is to examine and reveal political action from an exclusively political point of view. He does not consider moral standards. . . .* If, instead of a history, Thucydides had written an analytical treatise on politics, with particular reference to the Athenian empire, it is probable he would occupy a different place from that which he holds actually in the world's esteem; he would have forestalled the fame of Machiavelli."[2]

Bury goes on to compare Machiavellian *virtù* and Thucydidean *arete*: it is especially in his understanding of "virtue" that Thucydides is asserted to have anticipated Machiavelli.[3] But no comparative study of Machiavellian *virtù* and Thucydidean *arete* is even initiated by Bury, nor has anyone else undertaken one. While many readers are likely to have noticed apparent kinships between Machiavelli and Thucydides, on the question of Machiavellian *virtù* and Thucydidean *arete*, assumptions and assertions loom large, textual examination and interpretation, small. Yet the question, specific and relatively limited in scope, is relevant to one of the biggest controversies currently animating scholarly studies in what we call the "history of political philosophy." Is it proper to conceive our studies in terms of "the great tradition" of political philosophy, comprised of a canon of "classic" texts? And in what sense does "the tradition" constitute a "history"? Or, is the idea of a "history of political philosophy," divided into "periods"—each with its characteristic assumptions, "ancients" versus "moderns," for example, with "three waves of modernity"[4]—a tendentious intellectual construct, "a piece of academic folklore"?[5] The scholarly debate that has raged over these questions is too pervasive to require (or even attempt) exhaustive citation, but major contenders include Leo Strauss (virtually his entire *corpus*), his critics, and his allies.[6]

The political thought of Thucydides is an excellent touchstone for investigating the question of the alleged radical disjunction between "ancient" and "modern" thought. It has recently been remarked of Thucydides that he is one of the few writers who still commands the attention of both political scientists and political theorists.[7] This is undoubtedly a consequence of his much heralded "realism." Thucydides is perhaps the outstanding ancient "realist," and it is on their "realism" (among other things) that thinkers like Machiavelli, Hobbes, and Locke so prided themselves, and urged the superiority of "modern" political philosophy to "ancient." The clarion call of chapter 15 of Machiavelli's *Prince* exhorts political thinkers to abandon inquiries into "imaginary republics and principates that have never been seen or known to be in truth":[8] Plato's "best regime in speech"; Augustine's "City of God"; the "Prince of Peace" of the gospels. Yet Thucydides presented his political thought not as a treatise on some "ideal utopia," but as a narrative of the very real war between the Peloponnesians and the Athenians, which was tearing the known world asunder, and which he spent his mature life observing. Indeed, one of the greatest "moderns," Thomas Hobbes, commended to the public as his first publication, his own translation of Thucydides, with an important introduction and notes.

In addition to shedding some light on our understanding of Thucydides, this chapter aspires to make a modest contribution to our understanding of the "ancients" versus "moderns" distinction by initiating a (long overdue) comparative study of Machiavellian *virtù* and Thucydidean *arete*.[9] It presumes not to settle the question but, for the first time, to raise it properly, to stimulate reflection, and to suggest the lines along which it might profitably proceed. In my concluding section, I offer an interpretation of Thucydides' complex presentation of the career of Nicias in support of my suggestion that, when read in their proper contexts within the narrative as a whole, Thucydidean utterances of *arete* do not support the apparent kinship between Machiavelli and Thucydides on the question of "virtue."

Machiavellian *virtù*: A Reprise

"Modern" political thought is today widely understood to have emerged around the turn of the sixteenth century as a reaction against "ancient" political thought, all earlier political thought in both its classical and Christian forms. The thinker who is held chiefly responsible for this intellectual revolution is Machiavelli. The turning point of the Machiavellian revolution is his allegedly wholly new teaching concerning "virtue." What constitutes *virtù*, according to Machiavelli, must be henceforth understood solely instrumentally. This Machiavellian teaching is commonly identified with the phrase, "the end justifies the means." It enables Machiavelli to ask such questions as whether it is "virtuous" to be cruel, and to reason that cruelty is "virtuous" when it is in fact politically expedient and expeditiously executed, vicious when not.

In *The Prince*, chapter 8, Machiavelli discusses Agathocles the Sicilian, who "always led a wicked life" but "nevertheless accompanied his wickednesses with such virtue [*virtù*] of mind and body" that he was able to raise himself to the rank of praetor of Syracuse. Machiavelli is sensitive to the view that "one cannot call it virtue [*virtù*] to kill his fellow citizens, to betray his friends, to be without faith, without pity, without religion"; nevertheless, he calls it *virtù* in the very next sentence. While there remains some ambiguity as to whether Agathocles' "brutal cruelty and inhumanity and his infinite wickednesses" permit him to be named among the "most excellent *celebrated* men" (my emphasis), before the end of the chapter, Agathocles is named among those who may "have some remedy for their state with God and with men" on account of their cruelty having been "well used."[10]

Any residual ambiguity is dispelled in Machiavelli's later discussion of the "inhuman cruelty" of Hannibal when leading his armies against Rome. Among the "wonderful actions of Hannibal," Machiavelli notes how remarkable it was that he could lead such great armies, "combined of infinite races of men, which he had conducted to war in alien lands," without dissension arising: "That lack of dissension could not have proceeded from anything other than his inhuman cruelty which, together with his infinite virtues, always made him, in the eyes of his soldiers, venerated and terrible. Without that cruelty his *other* virtues would not have been sufficient."[11] Hannibal's "inhuman cruelty" is one of his virtues, is, indeed, his paramount virtue! Machiavellian *virtù* consists in being "virtuous" (in the traditional sense) when it is politically expedient, and "vicious" (in the traditional sense) when it is politically expedient.[12]

I do not dispute the understanding of Machiavellian *virtù* that I have reprised. That Machiavelli's teaching represents a radical break with the political philosophy of Plato and Aristotle, and with Christian moral-political doctrines, is not here in question. But does it so clearly represent a radical break with the teaching of Thucydides concerning political life and its exigencies? Bury and others who assert the kinship of Machiavellian *virtù* and Thucydidean *arete* imply that it does not.

Thucydidean *arete*: Catalog and Comments

The catalog of occurrences of *arete* in Thucydides' narrative of the war between the Peloponnesians and the Athenians is intriguing. According to my own count and the index of Bétant, *arete* appears forty-three times.[13] All but seven instances are found in the speeches of Thucydidean characters. A full third of the remaining thirty-six occur in Pericles' Funeral Oration alone. It should go without saying that we must carefully distinguish the speeches of Thucydidean characters and Thucydides' own speech.[14] I take the seven instances of *arete* uttered in Thucydides' own name to be of primary interest for initiating inquiry into

Thucydidean *arete*.[15]

The first Thucydidean utterance of *arete* is in the so-called "archaeology" ("account of olden times") at the beginning of the narrative. Thucydides is there concerned to show that the war he treats was the "greatest motion" that had ever affected the Hellenic world. The ancient times are characterized as ones of constant motion, but of no great motions. The Athenians were the first people in Greece to attain a settled existence, because the sterile soil of Attica made it an unattractive island of rest in a sea of migratory motion. It was because of the *arete* of their land, Thucydides says, that other communities in Greece were plagued by factional strife and external threats for so long (1.2.4).[16]

In the second instance, before presenting his Funeral Oration of Pericles, Thucydides reminds us of the customary ceremony at Athens for the burial of warriors fallen in battle, and notes that the custom was broken when those who fell at the critical battle of Marathon (during the Persian War) were interred on the battlefield, because their *arete* was judged preeminent by the Athenians (2.34.5). Thucydides does not explicitly say that he shares the Athenians' view of the Marathon fighters, but his remarking it serves ironically to depreciate the *arete* of those who are presently to be eulogized by Pericles in the very speech in Thucydides' narrative containing the greatest density of utterances of the word *arete*.

In his account of the terrible plague that ravaged Athens, which is the immediate sequel in the narrative to Pericles' Funeral Oration, Thucydides notes that foremost among the victims were those who made any pretensions to *arete*, holding it a point of honor to visit their afflicted friends (2.51.5). These would be the kind of Athenians most prized by Pericles, those whose concern for their reputation for honor dominated their concern for personal safety and gain. Unfortunately for these virtuous "Pericleans," their wish to profess the good in everything led to their ruin rather than their preservation.

Thucydides' central attribution of *arete* is to the remarkable Spartan, Brasidas. Speaking of his startling successes in cajoling the Athenians' allies into revolt from the empire (for which some of these cities would later pay atrociously), Thucydides remarks, "after the events in Sicily, it was the *arete* and intelligence of Brasidas at this time, experienced by some, and heard about by others, that did most to inspire in the allies of the Athenians a sentiment favorable to the Lacedaemonians" (4.81.2). Those who had first-hand experience of the *arete* and intelligence of Brasidas included Thucydides, whose failure to rescue Amphipolis from Brasidas's machinations occasioned his own exile from Athens. (Thucydides' impartiality in this and other instances is astonishing.)[17]

In the so-called "digression" (Thucydides, never so calls it) on the Pisistratid tyrants who had ruled in Athens a century before this war, with which Thucydides interrupts his dramatic account of the fateful recall of Alcibiades from the Sicilian expedition on the capital charge of impiety, Thucydides notes that these tyrants, in addition to piety, possessed an extraordinary degree of *arete* and intelligence (6.54.5), the very words he had used in speaking of the almost universally admired Brasidas.

Sixth is the ambiguous case of Nicias. At the conclusion of his horrific and deeply pathetic account of the final destruction of the Athenians in Sicily, Thucydides eulogizes Nicias: "The man who, of all the Greeks of my time, least deserved to be brought to so great a degree of misery, because of his life-long devotion to the practice of law-bred *arete*" (7.86.5). Unfortunately, the manuscripts disagree on the wording, and the philologists dispute the meaning of this passage, but interpretation of it is critical for any understanding of Thucydidean *arete*.[18]

Thucydides' final attribution of *arete* in his own name occurs in the context of a discussion of the oligarchical conspirators who succeeded in depriving the Athenian *demos* of its freedom almost a century after the expulsion of the Pisistratid tyrants (8.68.4). Pisander was their chief spokesman, but it was Antiphon, Thucydides tells us, who put the whole thing together, and devoted himself to it longest. Thucydides says Antiphon was second to none of the Athenians of his time in *arete* (8.68.1). He was also ablest (*krakistos*) both at thinking and speaking his mind, but was unable to contend before the democratic assembly, because the many greatly suspected him on account of his extreme cleverness. Thucydides adds that later, on the occasion of his capital trial, Antiphon gave the best *apologia* ("defense speech") that had ever been given in Athens.

At first blush, this catalog of Thucydidean attributions of *arete* may appear to support the assertion that Thucydides was a "Machiavellian" (if we are permitted the anachronism) in his understanding of "virtue." He first employs the word in a morally neutral sense, referring to the quality of land. Then it occurs twice in the role of somewhat ironic gloss on Pericles' Funeral Oration, with its great density of Periclean references to *arete*. The central Thucydidean utterance attributes *arete* to a named individual for the first time, Thucydides' own military adversary, Brasidas, who "presented himself before the cities as just and measured," but whose "justice" Thucydides apparently doubts. The final three utterances attribute *arete* to tyrants, Nicias, and an oligarchical conspirator who was, in the words of a modern historian, "responsible for a reign of terror."[19] To make matters worse, only concerning the *arete* of Nicias does there appear to be any doubt in Thucydides' own mind. Thucydides appears, that is, to suggest a distinction between "virtue" and "law-bred virtue" that could remind us of Machiavelli's distinction between what one is permitted to *call* "virtue" and what *is* "virtue" in the case of Agathocles.

In the broader context, this all might appear to support the view that an epic rendition of the history of political philosophy that alleges a radical break with classical thought, a break initiated by Machiavelli, and grounded in his radically novel understanding of "virtue," is a tendentious myth. I believe, however, that closer examination supports the advocates of the so-called "Straussian" interpretation on this point. What is required is scrupulous attention to the question of the narrative contexts of Thucydidean attributions of *arete*.

Machiavellian *virtù* and Thucydidean *arete*: Preliminary Observations

"We are much beholden to Machiavelli," says Francis Bacon in a famous remark, because he "wrote what men do, not what they ought to do." But this cannot mean that Machiavelli simply taught us to do what we already do, or that he taught us to abandon the notion that there are things we ought to do. We ought to do what Machiavelli tells us to do, and we need telling, because we are not currently doing it. That we *can* do what Machiavelli tells us to do, that he is not asking the impossible of us (as he believed classical political philosophy and Christianity did), is proved by the fact that some of us have done it, as he demonstrates in his historical studies. Whatever else it is, Machiavelli's revolutionary teaching concerning *virtù* is as "normative" as Aristotelian ethics.

Thucydides, too, has a normative teaching, but it differs significantly from Machiavelli's. I submit that the purpose of Thucydides' selective attributions of *arete* in his own name differs significantly from the purpose of Machiavelli's attributions of *virtù*, in accord with his different normative teaching. Where Machiavelli is prescribing a new moral perspective in ascribing *virtù* to particular individuals, Thucydides is rather reflecting the moral perspectives of particular individuals to whom he ascribes *arete*.

Concerning the status of the speeches in Thucydides, it is generally appreciated that they are written from the points of view of the speakers, that Thucydides' own views can be gathered only by reflecting on the contexts of the speeches in the narrative, that there is a reciprocal relation between the speeches and the narrative: the speeches inform our understanding of the narrative, and the narrative informs our understanding of the speeches.[20] The suggestion I wish to pursue is that even explicit judgments presented in Thucydides' own name, in this instance, his attributions of *arete*, can be understood properly only with reference to their narrative contexts, and are, in turn, meant reciprocally to guide us in our understanding of those narrative contexts. These, in turn, cannot be extracted from their context within the dramatic structure of the narrative as a whole. Thucydides' very selective employment of *arete* in his own name is thus in accord with his complex and reticent manner of writing altogether.[21]

I will illustrate these contentions with further observations on Thucydides' most apparently "Machiavellian" attributions of *arete*, the cases of the Athenian tyrants and Antiphon; then I shall examine the case of Nicias. The "digression" on the Athenian tyrants is presented in the context of Thucydides' exciting narration of the fateful Sicilian expedition. The "digression," which interrupts this narrative at the critical moment of the recall of Alcibiades to Athens to be tried on the capital charges of impiety and conspiring to overthrow the democracy, has been taken as proof of the cogency of the arguments of the "separatist" critics by some of the highest authorities of Thucydidean scholarship.[22]

In fact, the "digression" is indispensable for Thucydides' presentation of his political teaching. His praise of the tyrants (6.54.5-7) rivals his eulogy of Pericles (2.65): they possessed the intelligence (*xynesis*) attributed to Themistocles (1.138.3), Theseus (2.15.2), Brasidas (4.81.2), and Hermocrates (6.72.2); they practiced piety and liberality to an admirable degree; and, of course, they are credited with *arete*. The purpose of the "digression" as a gloss on Alcibiades' troubles in Athens is clear: the Pisistratid tyrants no more deserve the calumny that they have suffered throughout a century of Athenian democracy than Alcibiades deserves judicial execution at the hands of the Athenian *demos*. In the context of the question of Athenian tyranny, Pisistratid or Alcibidean, it serves Thucydides' purpose to emphasize the "virtues" of "tyrants," including their paramount *arete*.[23]

After the account of the disastrous Sicilian expedition comes book 8, the end of Thucydides' narrative. This ending represents almost a new beginning, with almost an entirely new cast of characters. But Alcibiades, above all, is not new, and his machinations are at the center of every significant development in book 8: he pits two Spartan factions against each other, and two Persian satraps, the Athenians at Samos against the Athenians at Athens, the democrats against the oligarchs, and so on, all to further his own schemes. Book 8 presents a picture of Athenian domestic politics in which the "Alcibidean" understanding of patriotism, "Ask not what you can do for your country, but what your country can do for you," rules supreme. It is thus within its "Alcibidean" context that Thucydides' remarks concerning the *arete* of Antiphon, too, must be understood.[24]

Apparently "Machiavellian" attributions of *arete* reflect not Thucydides' "Machiavellian" understanding of politics, but his attempt to depict accurately, by reflecting, the variety and complexity of political life, and the moral permutations that the exigencies of political life foster when war, that "violent teacher" (3.82.2), is given full scope to impose its lessons. It is a separate question whether and to what extent Thucydides' own perspective would or would not correspond to the particular individual's perspective in each instance, a question that can be answered only by reflecting upon its place within the dramatic structure of the narrative as a whole.[25]

But that Thucydides' normative teaching does not prescribe the rejection of traditional virtue, as Machiavelli's does, is above all indicated in his complex presentation and assessment of the career of Nicias.

Moderation and the Common Good:
Nician *arete* in Thucydidean Context

Thucydides is not what we would call a "progressive." He is aware, of course, that important changes occur in the world, but "history is progress" is not a Thucydidean dictum. Thucydides is not at all sanguine about the future: he is not inclined to believe that change is necessarily change for the better, even over the long term.

In the first score or so chapters of the narrative, the so-called "archaeology," Thucydides is concerned to justify taking up contemporary matters as the subject of his narrative rather than the "old things."[26] The oldest things were traditionally held to be the greatest and most important things (cf. 1.21.2). But Thucydides is concerned to demonstrate that the contemporary war of the Peloponnesians and the Athenians is the peculiarly revealing war, perhaps, indeed, the singularly revealing human phenomenon. And it is so because the earlier times where somehow decisively inferior to Thucydides' own time (1.3).

According to Thucydides, the Greek world was at its *akme* when this war broke out. This war was the "greatest motion" that had ever affected the Greek world (cf. 1.2 and 21.2). The olden days are characterized as times of constant motion, but no great motions. Thucydides' description sounds like the "state of nature" of Thomas Hobbes or John Locke: there was no commodious living, because there was no peace, no rest. "Progress" in settlement, commerce, and such has occurred since the olden days, but this "progress" is a decidedly mixed blessing. It culminates in this "greatest" of all "motions," this war, but this war effects nothing so much as a great decline from the *akme* of Greek civilization; this is a war of unparalleled human suffering and destruction.

In the beginning, there were no Greeks, no "Hellenes," neither in name nor in fact; there was only "barbarism." "Greekness" arose out of "barbarism"; it is not clear when, or how. (But "Greekness" and "barbarism" are not racial distinctions for Thucydides: he speaks of people whose native tongue is Greek as non-Greeks, in the decisive respect [1.5].)[27] In earlier times, men lived like pirates and went armed (1.5). The emergence of a kind of justice, the establishment of some kind of "law and order," was the result of Minos' suppression of pandemic piracy, which Minos alone was able to do, he being the biggest pirate; "justice" arose from injustice, and was imposed by force (1.4).

The first people to cease to go armed in their city were the Athenians, who were able to attain peace, or come to rest, in Attica, because its sterile soil made it an unattractive island in the antique sea of migratory motions. The Athenians were consequently the first people to acquire considerable wealth. The Spartans, on the other hand, were the first to adopt "moderate" (*metria*) dress in their city, from which we might infer the overcoming of "barbaric" ostentation; they were also the first to go undressed, to exercise naked, from which we might infer an overcoming of "barbarism" concerning sexual matters (1.6).

Desire for gain eventually led the many to accommodate themselves to the few in the early Greek cities (a kind of "common good" was recognized), which led in turn to the more powerful walled towns subjugating the weaker ones, and this facilitated the Trojan War (1.8).

Thucydides debunks Homer's account of the Trojan War (1.9-12). The war was not, in fact, fought for the alleged noble reasons; the suitors accompanied Agamemnon and Menelaus to Troy from fear of their power, which derived from their wealth. Thucydides discounts the role attributed by Homer to the gods: not the power of the gods, but the weakness of the Greeks accounts for the ten years it took to conquer Troy.

With increased wealth and settlement, tyrannies and navies arose. The tyrants proved a temporary setback to "progress": they were concerned chiefly with security, so they achieved little; that is, they fought no great wars (1.17).

But eventually all the tyrannies in mainland Greece, including the tyrants at Athens, were suppressed by the Spartans. Thucydides here praises the Spartans for both the quality and the stability of their regime: they have enjoyed domestic peace and freedom from tyranny for four centuries (1.18).[28] Sparta is, indeed, the most highly praised city in the "archaeology."

Before the war of the Peloponnesians and the Athenians, the Persian War was the greatest, but it was not nearly so great as the contemporary war (1.23). Why not? What is Thucydides' standard for "greatness" in a war? Is it the unparalleled displays of heroism? The nobility of the principles over which the war was fought? The durability of the peace that followed? No. The "greatness" of the Peloponnesian War consists, it seems, in its terrible destructiveness; the Persian War was insufficiently destructive. In particular, the Persian War was not destructive of "Greekness." On the contrary, it was a noble war of liberation of "Greeks" from "barbarians." This is why it was not "the great war" in the Thucydidean sense, a sense not foreign to an earlier generation in the contemporary West, which persists in attaching this epithet to what later generations call the First World War.[29]

The destruction of "Greekness" and resurgence of "barbarism" is a central theme of Thucydides' narrative. One sees it most poignantly in the story told late in the narrative of an incident that would loom very small in the perspective of a "scientific historian," but which figures importantly in Thucydides' presentation. When Nicias is bogged down in Sicily with an enormous Athenian expeditionary force, a second large force is brought together and sails out from Athens. Unfortunately, a group of some 1,300 light-armed Thracian troops arrived at Athens too late for the departure for Sicily, and the Athenians could not afford to retain these barbarians for their war effort in Attica (7.27). In this context, Thucydides pauses to sing virtually a paean to the greatness of Athens (7.28). Athens was suffering great hardships; greatest of all was carrying on two wars at once, but what an amazing miscalculation of the power and daring of Athens was made by the Greek world, which thought at the beginning of this war that Athens could hold out for one, two, or at most three years![30]

In any event, the Athenians were currently unable to keep the Thracian peltasts in pay, so they were sent home. On their way home (after having camped at the temple of Hermes, no less), the Thracians descend upon the city of Mycalessus, a veritable model of "Greekness" (7.29): a small city with a large school full of young boys, a city utterly at rest and peace, utterly undefended and unsuspecting. Thucydides compels us to observe the complete destruction of this "Greek" haven of leisure by unmitigated "barbarism." What is most striking is the Thracians' utter disregard for any standards of "civilized" behavior—this is wanton and gratuitous slaughter: children, animals, every living thing is butchered indiscriminately.

Thucydides says of the events at Mycalessus that the loss it received was no less to be lamented than any that occurred in this entire war. That Thucydides should pause to call our attention to this matter in the context of his paean to Athenian power and daring, which is itself sung within the context of his general account of the terrible destruction of the Athenians in Sicily, is the most awful and beautiful way that this "artful reporter"[31] could impress upon us how "barbarism" was again making inroads into the heart of the "Greek" world as a consequence of the Peloponnesian War (or, as most of the Greek world would have called it, the Athenian War).

And what is Thucydides' posture before this spectacle? Resignation. But before what? To what does Thucydides' resign himself before the spectacle of such barbarism?[32] I believe we can derive the answer to our question most clearly from his unforgettable account of the paradigmatic *stasis*, revolution or civil war, that erupted at Corcyra in the midst of this great war (3.70-85). This description is of paramount importance for understanding Thucydides' teaching concerning the relation between moderation and the common good, traditional virtue and political wisdom. Thucydides' description of the plague that ravaged Athens in the first years of the war is grim—the lawlessness that pervaded the city, the abandonment of any concern for what was considered noble—but his account of human nature as it reveals itself in the man-made plague of civil war is even grimmer. And this account contains the longest statement presented in Thucydides' own name in the entire narrative.[33]

What occurred at Corcyra is the epitome, according to Thucydides, of what occurred throughout virtually the entire Greek world during this war (3.82). There was what we might call a "Machiavellian transvaluation of values" (Thucydides emphasizes the permutations that occurred in the meanings of words), the result of which was political, social, and moral chaos. There was a complete triumph of daring (the "Athenian" characteristic) over moderation (the "Spartan"). Thucydides says that the cause of all these troubles was "desire to rule," from avarice and ambition. Concern for justice was overcome by desire for revenge, and oaths were no longer able to impose any limits on human deeds. Dishonest men were more readily praised for their cleverness, than simple and moderate men were for their honesty. Contracts became nothing but pretexts for betrayal. Thucydides describes the dissolution even of family bonds that accompanied the abandonment of concern for the divine law.

Here Thucydides offers his only personification of war: war is a "harsh schoolmaster," a "violent teacher." A violent teacher, nevertheless, a teacher; most importantly, Thucydides' own teacher, especially concerning human nature. War is a violent teacher because war brings necessity to bear on human affairs.[34] Civil war, the most violent of political phenomena, is a danger coeval with political life, and the experience of it teaches Thucydides that whatever restraints forestall civil war are sacred (if only metaphorically).

But it is important to recognize Thucydides' resignation before the limits of political life imposed by the limits of human nature. He explicitly says that his account of the civil wars is intended to show us how things were during these revolutions, and always will be. Thucydides does not think that his having written this account will significantly affect the future; these horrors cannot be eliminated or prevented by the writings of historians and political theorists! Thucydides leaves to others the futile attempt to change the world; the point is to understand it.[35]

It is equally important to recognize that men of traditional virtue, moderate, pious men, such as Nicias, and those much rarer individuals who possess political wisdom, such as Thucydides and his character, Diodotus,[36] are natural allies against all "sophisticates," such as Cleon, whose views succeed in liberating us from conventional restraints, but fail to elevate us.[37] Indicative of this is what Thucydides tells us about the fates of certain types of individuals during *stasis*: citizens who belong to neither extreme party, those in the middle, the "moderates," we could say, are continually destroyed by the partisans on both sides (3.82.8); citizens of meaner intellectual capacity, fearing the intelligence of their opponents, simply resort to the preemptive strike; those of superior intelligence (*gnome*) thus perish in greater numbers (3.83.3-4).

This common good that is shared by the "Niciases" and "Diodotuses" of the world is the key to many aspects of Thucydides' narrative that have puzzled various critics, especially his "unscientific" attention to many and various acts of piety, pollutions, and omens, but above all his paradoxical presentation of the career of Nicias, culminating in his remarkable "eulogy" (7.86.5).

We have seen how Sparta is the most highly praised city in the "archaeology": she is praised for the quality, stability, and longevity of her regime; she has always been free of tyrants, and she liberated the other Greek cities from tyranny. At the outset of this war, many Greek cities looked to Sparta with the hope that she would liberate them from the "tyrant city," too (see the two Corinthian speeches at Sparta [1.68-71; 120-24]). And the Delphic oracle proclaimed that Apollo would aid the Spartans in this war, called or uncalled, and that the Spartans would win the war, if they waged it with vigor (1.118.5); sure enough, despite the remarkable Athenian superiority in resources and resourcefulness, Sparta wins the war.

The Spartans are the city of tradition and moderation. The first Spartan we hear in Thucydides is King Archidamus, speaking before the official outbreak of hostilities (1.80-85). He was reputed, Thucydides tells us, to be "wise" and "moderate" (1.79.2). In the Corinthians' comparison of the Athenian manner with the Spartan manner, Spartan "lethargy" is attacked, but Archidamus contends that this apparent "slowness" is in fact "moderation," a virtue that is the product of traditional Spartan education. In what does Archidamus's "wisdom" and "moderation" consist? He is an advocate of traditional virtue: he is moderate enough not to esteem himself wiser than the laws of the city, wiser, that is, than the ancestors who made the laws.

Compare this Spartan king with the de facto king of Athens, Pericles. Pericles' renowned Funeral Oration constitutes an attack on old, traditional Athens. His famous speech opens with criticism of the ancestral law requiring the speech (2.35). He esteems himself wiser than the laws and the ancestors who established them; he conspicuously lacks moderation in this respect. In fact, Pericles and his Athenians are conspicuously lacking in moderation (*sophrosyne*) altogether: Pericles never utters the word, and Thucydides never utters it in reference to Pericles, or to any other Athenian. There is one exception that proves the rule: after Cleon's famous tirade against Nicias and his generalship at Pylos, in which he boasts that he, himself, could conquer or capture all the Spartans trapped on the island of Sphacteria in twenty days, if only he were in command, Thucydides says that the supporters of Nicias in Athens, the "moderates" (*sophrones*), saw this as an opportunity to rid the city of Cleon; it seems that they actually preferred this outcome to the capture of the Spartans, i.e., they, like the Spartans, habitually cared more about domestic peace and stability than military victories on foreign soil (4.28.5; cf. 108.7).[38]

It is worth remarking that the moderate Spartans, virtually alone among the Greeks, never succumbed to the "civil plague" of civil war, nor, indeed, did the plague proper infect Sparta. And Thucydides dramatically supplies his graphic account of how the plague ravaged Athens as the fitting response to the apparent *hubris* of Pericles' Funeral Oration. It is really quite beautiful: Pericles, whose speech is silent about the gods, who boasts that Athens is so beautiful that she needs no Homer to beautify her, answered by Apollo, the Homeric god of plagues, in the tradition of epic poetry![39] Pericles perishes. But after all, had not Apollo oracularly declared that he would come to the aid of Sparta in this war?

Far overshadowing the dramatic sequence of the Funeral Oration answered by the plague is the Melian Dialogue answered by the Athenian disaster in Sicily. In that infamous dialogue (5.84-113), the Melians ultimately stake everything on their hopes for divine (and Spartan) assistance, while the Athenians hold that there are no gods from whom to expect rewards for justice or punishments for injustice. And exactly what the Athenians predict will happen, happens: utter destruction for the Melians (5.114-16). But is not the immediate sequel in the narrative, the vivid account of the equally utter destruction of the Athenians' Sicilian expedition, Thucydides' and the gods' response to what the Athenians say at Melos: divine retribution for Athenian *hubris*?

Probably not. But Nicias, at least, believes it so. Now, on one level, of course, the *cause* of the Athenians' final destruction in Sicily is the incompetence of Nicias.[40] Thucydides makes this perfectly clear in his account of the expedition, from the debate at Athens to the final destruction. Nicias's rhetorical ineptitude, for example, is responsible for both the inflated size of the original expeditionary force (6.8.4; 19.2) and the Athenians' inflated hopes for its success (24.2-3); later, the doubling of the size of the expedition and, thus, the disaster (7.15.1). He commits the egregious error of contemning the arrival of Gylippus in Sicily (6.103-4; 7.2). Having failed to complete the wall of circumvallation around Syracuse before the arrival of Gylippus, Nicias fortifies Plemmyrium as a place to deposit the armament's equipment and to moor the fleet; Thucydides says that this was above all the cause of the deterioration of the naval force (7.4.4-6). Later, when the forts at Plemmyrium are captured by the Syracusans, along with food, equipment, and ships, Thucydides says that this was the greatest blow suffered by the land force (7.24). Finally, there is Nicias's famous response to the eclipse of the moon (7.50.3-4), which seals the fate of the Athenians in Sicily, preventing them from escaping Sicily with their power intact. This turns what would have been merely a military defeat in far-off Sicily into a mortal blow to both the Athenian empire and the democracy at home.

But Nicias believes his own disastrous fate in Sicily to be the result of his having always subordinated his private interest to the public good; thus, he now finds himself sharing in the public suffering that he does not deserve to suffer (7.77). Thucydides makes it clear, however, that the disaster in Sicily results not only from Nicias's incompetence, but from the fact that at crucial junctures (especially 7.48.3-4) he prefers his private interest to the public interest. Thucydides is nevertheless sufficiently concerned to preserve, indeed, perhaps to augment Nicias's good reputation that he echoes Nicias's self-understanding in his eulogy of him: "The man who, of all the Greeks of my time, least deserved to be brought to so great a degree of misery, because of his life-long devotion to the practice of law-bred *arete*" (7.86.5). This eulogy of Nicias is indicative of the affinity between the political vision of Thucydides and the man of traditional virtue and piety. It is in part because of this affinity, and in part because of the common good that they share, that Nicias is treated in so singular a manner in Thucydides' narrative.

Nicias is presented as a "Spartan" Athenian: he possesses, like the "moderate" Athenians whom he represents, a "Spartan" understanding of political life. Nicias believes there are just gods who rule the affairs of men and reward justice. Like the Melians, he clings to hopes in powers invisible, and like theirs, his hopes are utterly dashed. It is not only in spite of this, however, but precisely because of it, and in the very context that reveals the folly of Nicias's "Melian" hopes, that Thucydides eulogizes him in accord with his self-understanding. For Thucydides would have us know that, however misguided may be his "Melian" hopes, Nicias divines something true that escapes the Athenians at Melos (whose views reflect those of Nicias's political nemesis, Alcibiades): the Athenians cannot persist in their "Athenian" manner without courting disaster. Nothing, indeed, would be more hopeful than to think otherwise. Nicias, the "Spartan," is ultimately diffident about the power of human beings to control the world. But however hopeful Nicias may be about cosmic support for justice, the hopefulness of "Athenians" ultimately surpasses even that of "Melians." Thucydides thus adopts Nicias's own perspective in his eulogy of him, because he wishes to lend support to Nicias's less sophisticated anticipation of his own perspective on Athenian imperialism.[41] And he must do so especially at the moment when more discerning readers are likely to be feeling little or no sympathy for Nicias.[42] (This explains, too, I believe, why the death of Demosthenes, perhaps the most loveable individual in the narrative [7.57.10], on whom the sympathy of Thucydides' more discerning readers is likely to be lavished, must go unremarked in this context.)[43]

In conclusion, taking together the various contexts that Thucydides artfully constructs for his readers, and placing them in the context of his narrative as a whole, we can see *why* Thucydides echoes Nicias's self-understanding at the end of the seventh book, and why, in the end, he is not a "Machiavellian," even though he employs the word, *arete*, in specific contexts, in an apparently "Machiavellian" way. The "Alcibidean" context, in which Thucydides utters his apparently "Machiavellian" pronouncements, especially following the catastrophe in Sicily and the death of Nicias, is one in which *all* the prominent Athenians conceive themselves in light of a political understanding that rejects what is true in the "Nician" understanding, and dedicate themselves to limitless self-aggrandizement. But the normative intention of Thucydides includes an appreciation of what is true in the "Nician" understanding: Thucydides wishes his most discerning readers to understand that neither these Athenian "Machiavellians" and their "nation," nor any nation so conceived and so dedicated, can long endure.

Notes

This chapter was originally published as "Machiavellian *virtù* and Thucydidean *arete*: Traditional Virtue and Political Wisdom in Thucydides," in *The Review of Politics 51* (1989). Reprinted with permission. Thanks to Christopher Bruell, Patrick Coby, Clifford Orwin, and anonymous referees for helpful comments on earlier drafts.

1. G. Murray, *A History of Ancient Greek Literature* (New York: Appleton, 1897), 198.

2. J. B. Bury, *The Ancient Greek Historians* (London: Macmillan, 1909), 140-43, Bury's emphasis.

3. Ibid., 144-45.

4. See H. Gildin, *Political Philosophy: Six Essays by Leo Strauss* (Indianapolis: Pegasus, 1975).

5. J. Gunnell, "The Myth of the Tradition," *American Political Science Review 72* (1978): 133.

6. The critics include Q. Skinner, "Meaning and Understanding in the History of Ideas," *History and Theory 8* (1969): 3-53; J. G. A. Pocock, *Politics, Language, and Time: Essays on Political Thought and History* (New York: Atheneum, 1971); and *The Machiavellian Moment: Florentine Political Thought and the Atlantic Republican Tradition* (Princeton, N.J.: Princeton University Press, 1975); and, "Prophet and Inquisitor: Or, a Church Built upon Bayonets Cannot Stand: A Comment on Mansfield's 'Strauss's Machiavelli,'" *Political Theory 3* (1975): 385-405; Gunnell, "Myth of the Tradition"; and *Political Theory: Tradition and Interpretation* (Cambridge: Winthrop, 1979). The allies include H. C. Mansfield Jr., "Strauss's Machiavelli," *Political Theory 3* (1975): 372-84; and *Machiavelli's New Modes and Orders: A Study of the "Discourses on Livy"* (Ithaca, N.Y.: Cornell University Press, 1979); N. Tarcov, "Quentin Skinner's Method and Machiavelli's *Prince*," *Ethics 92* (1982): 690-709; and, "Philosophy and History: Tradition and Interpretation in the Work of Leo Strauss," *Polity 16* (1983): 5-29; N. Tarcov and T. Pangle, "Epilogue: Leo Strauss and the History of Political Philosophy," in *History of Political Philosophy*, 3rd ed., ed. L. Strauss and J. Cropsey (Chicago: University of Chicago Press, 1987), 907-38; W. R. Newell, "How Original in Machiavelli? A Consideration of Skinner's Interpretation of Virtue and Fortune," *Political Theory 15* (1987): 612-34.

7. C. Orwin, "The Just and the Advantageous: The Case of the Mytilenaian Debate," *American Political Science Review 78* (1984): 485.

8. L. P. S. de Alvarez, *Niccolo Machiavelli: The Prince: Translation, Introduction, and Notes* (Irving, Texas: University of Dallas Press, 1980), 93.

9. For some interesting reflection of Machiavelli *virtù* and Homeric *arete* see T. Ball, "The Picaresque Prince: Reflections on Machiavelli and Moral Change," *Political Theory 12* (1984): 521-36.

10. Alvarez, *Prince*, 51-55.

11. Ibid., 102, my emphasis.

12. See Leo Strauss, *Thoughts on Machiavelli* (Glencoe, Ill.: Free Press, 1958); and (in addition to Strauss's "allies" cited above in note 6) C. Orwin, "Machiavelli's Unchristian Charity," *American Political Science Review 78* (1978): 1219-28; H. C. Mansfield Jr., *The Prince: A New Translation with an Introduction* (Chicago: University of Chicago Press, 1985), vii-xxiv.

13. E. Bétant, *Lexicon Thucydideum* (Hildesheim: Georg Olms, 1961).

14. See Leo Strauss, *The City and Man* (Chicago: Rand McNally, 1964), 163-74. I am broadly and deeply indebted to Strauss's interpretation of Thucydides.

15. This is not to say that the speeches of Thucydidean characters can be ignored, in the end, or that Thucydides does not intend for us to learn important things from the speeches of his characters (1.22). And, in the end, analysis of the speeches must be essential to grasping Thucydides' understanding of things. But this is not the end; it is the beginning. I cite Thucydidean passages by the customary numbers: book, chapter, sentence (where relevant).

16. Ironically, the Athenians benefited from the lack of "virtue" of the "motherland" (myths of autochthony to the contrary notwithstanding).

17. Thucydides offers two assessments of Brasidas. They are sufficiently (apparently) redundant that "separatist" critics have claimed support here for their attempts to divine various stages of composition and (incomplete) revision of the narrative. But the passages are not, in fact, redundant. In this first (4.108), reference to Brasidas's "justice" is dropped. Among other things in the interim, Thucydides has "experienced," not merely "heard about," Brasidas. One might suggest that the Spartans' later betraying the cities that Brasidas liberated, for the sake of the "Peace of Nicias," prevented Brasidas's actions from being accounted "just" by Thucydides. But I believe Brasidas, had he lived, would not have permitted the betrayal of these cities; Thucydides hints that Brasidas's ambitions in Sparta rivaled those of Alcibiades in Athens. My argument, however, would require a paper of its own. Cf. W. R. Connor, *Thucydides* (Princeton, N.J.: Princeton University Press, 1984), 126-40.

18. See Connor, *Thucydides*, 205, for an important philological note and bibliography on the question of Nicias's *"areten nenomismenen,"* in which he directs us to, among other things, the important recent discussion of L. Edmunds, *Chance and Intelligence in Thucydides* (Cambridge, Mass.: Harvard University Press, 1975), 141-42; and A. W. H. Adkins, "The Arete of Nicias," *Greek Roman and Byzantine Studies 16* (1975): 379-91.

19. Murray, *History of Ancient Greek Literature*, 198.

20. Compare J. de Romilly, *Histoire et Raison chez Thucydide* (Paris: "Les Belles Lettres," 1956); R. Aron, "Thucydide et le récit des événements," *History and Theory 1* (1960-61); W. P. Wallace, "Thucydides," *Phoenix 18* (1964): 251-61; Strauss, *City and Man*, especially 163-74; V. Hunter, *Thucydides: The Artful Reporter* (Toronto: Hakkert, 1973); P. Pouncey, *The Necessities of War: A Study of Thucydides' Pessimism* (New York: Columbia University Press, 1980), 13-15, 165-67; H. R. Rawlings III, *The Structure of Thucydides' History* (Princeton, N.J.: Princeton University Press, 1981), especially 263-72.

21. These sorts of considerations are crucial for understanding many of the alleged defects of Thucydides' "history": his "unscientific" attention to acts of piety and impiety; his apparently pointless and cumbersome "digressions"; indeed, the dramatic structure of the narrative as a whole. Connor's *Thucydides* is such a marvelously successful study in part because he is so acutely sensitive to the nuances of Thucydides' narrative techniques. It is worthwhile to consult Connor on any passage in Thucydides.

22. A. W. Gomme, *A Historical Commentary on Thucydides*, vol. 1 (Oxford: Clarendon Press, 1945): 137, goes so far as to suggest that Thucydides would have eliminated this passage had he lived long enough to prepare a final revision of his "history."

23. For more of this "digression," and its larger context, see M. Palmer, "Alcibiades and the Question of Tyranny in Thucydides," *Canadian Journal of Political Science 15* (1982): 103-24; cf. S. Forde, "Thucydides on the Causes of Athenian Imperialism," *American Political Science Review 80* (1986): 440-42.

24. Cf. Strauss, *City and Man*, 200n65.

25. Similarly, in an inverted way, Machiavelli's calling the "inhuman cruelty" of Hannibal a "virtue" does not necessarily mean that Hannibal would have called it a virtue, or that Machiavelli thinks he would have.

26. Cf. what follows with discussion of the "archaeology" in Connor, *Thucydides*, 20-32, and Pouncey, *Necessities of War*, 45-53.

27. Thucydides notes that in Homer only those of the town of Achilles were called "Hellenes." I believe this is his way of suggesting that Homeric poetry was a key factor in the advent of "Greekness," or "Hellenization" of the world. As for how the name of Achilles' tribe might have been appropriated by others over the generations, consider the implication of the words Thucydides puts into the mouth of Alcibiades speaking before his fellow Athenians concerning how later generations of Athenians will speak of their relationship to him (6.16.5).

28. By way of contrast, the best regime that Athens ever had, at least in Thucydides' own explicit judgment, at least in Thucydides' own lifetime, the regime of the Five Thousand of 411, a measured blending of democracy and oligarchy that moved Athenians democracy in the direction of the Spartan regime, lasted but a few months (8.97.2).

29. Cf. Connor, *Thucydides*, 31; Pouncey, *Necessities of War*, 148.

30. It is remarkable, in view of many modern interpretations of the failure of the Sicilian expedition, that Thucydides takes the moment of the sailing of the second Athenian expeditionary force as an opportunity to remark not on Athenian overextension in Sicily, but on the world's underestimation of Athenian power and daring.

31. I borrow the epithet from the title of Hunter's book, cited above in note 20.

32. It is perhaps worth noting that in the middle of the "archaeology," Thucydides graphically anticipates modern archaeology: he bids his readers to imagine the day when all that will remain of Athens and Sparta will be ruins (1.10). And he puts the lesson into the mouth of Pericles: all things pass away (2.64.3). The description of Mycalessus before her tragedy recalls Thucydides' description of "old Athens," which had to be destroyed as a consequence of Pericles' strategy for defending Athenian imperialism (2.14-17), which Thucydides places immediately before the hubristic dazzle of the Funeral Oration.

33. An outstanding recent contribution to the literature on these passages is C. Orwin, "*Statis* and Plague: Thucydides on the Dissolution of Society," *Journal of Politics 50* (1988): 831-47.

34. On "*biaios didaskolos*," cf. Connor, *Thucydides*, 102n57; and Pouncey, *Necessities of War*, 182n5.

35. It is this, more than anything else, I believe, that separates Thucydides from modern authors such as Hobbes, whose description of the "state of nature" is virtually lifted from his own translation of Thucydides' account of the Corcyrean *stasis*. Connor, *Thucydides*, 104, remarks, "The illusion of progress is shattered. The constancy of human nature, the premise upon which much of the analysis of the Archaeology is based, remains, but its implications are deeply pessimistic. . . . No longer is there a suggestion that knowing the recurrence of events will enable us to draw useful inferences about the future (1.22.4). The past will recur, but that recurrence has become a threat, not a promise." Cf. Pouncey, *Necessities of War*, 43-44, 151-57.

36. Diodotus gives the most "Thucydidean" speech in the narrative, the speech that comes closest to expressing, if it is not identical to, Thucydides' own view of political life. Diodotus successfully opposes Cleon, the great political nemesis of Nicias before the advent of Alcibiades. This "Diodotus," the profoundest speaker in Thucydides' narrative, is otherwise unknown. His name might be translated "gift of Zeus," and he is said to be the son of "Euchrates" ("power well wielded"), another wonderful example, I believe of Thucydides' artfulness. Cf. M. Oswald, "Diodotus," *Greek Roman and Byzantine Studies 20* (1979): 5-13.

37. In the Corcyrean *stasis*, the Cleonian view of justice as vengeance rules supreme. On the heels of Cleon's destruction, in the Mytilenean Debate, of distinctions between enemies, allies, and subjects (3.38), comes the destruction of the distinction between enemies and fellow citizens at Corcyra. The democrats eventually slaughter the oligarchs at Corcyra, just as Cleon counseled the slaughter of democrats and oligarchs alike at Mytiene. On Diodotus's debate with Cleon, see Orwin, "The Just and the Advantageous," and, "Democracy and Distrust: A Lesson from Thucydides," *The American Scholar 53* (1984): 313-25; cf. M. Cogan, "Mytilene, Plataea and Corcyra," *Phoenix 35* (1981): 1-21, and *The Human Thing: The Speeches and Principles of Thucydides' History* (Chicago: University of Chicago Press, 1981), 50-65.

38. As the above note indicates, it is not unreasonable that "moderate" Athenians should prefer Cleon dead.

39. See M. Palmer, "Love and Glory and the Common Good," *American Political Science Review 76* (1982): 825-36, for elaboration.

40. Compare what follows with accounts of Nicias's career in Connor, *Thucydides*, 158-209, 236-37; Edmunds, *Chance and Intelligence*, 109-42; Pouncey, *Necessities of War*, 117-30; Strauss, *City and Man*, 200-209; and H. D. Westlake, *Individuals in Thucydides* (Cambridge: Cambridge University Press, 1968), chapters 6 and 11.

41. For the best brief elucidation of Thucydides' perspective, see C. Bruell, "Thucydides' View of Athenian Imperialism," *American Political Science Review 68* (1974): 11-17.

42. Connor, *Thucydides* suggests that Thucydides' point "is not whether Nicias's conduct is true *arete*, but that he acted in ways that he and his society considered to be *arete*. This is not malice, as J. B. Bury, *Ancient Greeks Historians* . . . [p.] 119 suggested, nor a sneer at Nicias's merely 'conventional' virtue, but a way of emphasizing the failure of Nicias's own expectations" (205n53). Edmunds' *Chance and Intelligence* maintains that "Thucydides' judgment on Nicias is . . . limited to the kind of death he died and is made from the point of view of Nicias's own expectations" (142). But Edmunds does not argue why Thucydides should wish to reflect or endorse this point of view.

43. Cf. Strauss, *City and Man*, 150.

Chapter 6

Machiavelli's Inhuman Humanism in *The Prince*

> *The doctrines of sovereign becoming, of the fluidity of all concepts, types and kinds, of the lack of any cardinal difference between man and animal—doctrines which I take to be true but deadly.*
>
> – Nietzsche

There is less to be said about the political philosophy of Machiavelli than has been said, and this essay adds a little more.[1] Indeed, the more one familiarizes oneself with the literature on Machiavelli, the more one realizes that there remains no position left to take on any major issue in his political philosophy that has not already been espoused.

Controversy has always attended Machiavelli's name. On the strictly political question, for example, is Machiavelli an advocate of tyranny and advisor to tyrants, or an ardent lover of republican liberty; essentially, the author of *The Prince*, or of the *Discourses on Livy*? Is he "scientifically" neutral? Was he initially an advisor to tyrants who became a lover of republican liberty, or initially an ardent lover of republican liberty who became an advisor to tyrants? Or was he a lover of republican liberty who understood the necessity of using tyrannical means, in the extraordinary situation of the founding of states, to secure republican liberty, or in the extraordinary situation of civil war, to maintain it? Perhaps he was a republican on domestic affairs and an imperialist in foreign affairs? Or was he is a lover of republican liberty who advised tyrants in such a way as to trick them into undermining their own power? Or, conversely, an admirer of tyranny who teaches tyrants how to trick republics into enslaving themselves?

On the politico-religious question, there is a similar spectrum of views.

There is Machiavelli the pagan versus Machiavelli the Christian. As for the pagan, he is a Greek or a Roman pagan, or a medieval believer in astrology. As for the Christian, he is antipapist, but not anticlerical; or antipapist and anticlerical, but of course not opposed to Christian principles, or at least Christian principles rightly understood; or antipapist, anticlerical, and opposed to Christian principles, however understood, but never anti-Christ. Finally, there is the Machiavelli who is neither pagan nor Christian, but an atheist, sometimes understood to favor the political use of religion, sometimes not.

But what is most astounding about this dizzying variety of views is that investigation reveals that almost all of them have been current in the debates on Machiavelli since the sixteenth century! There has been less to be said about the political philosophy of Machiavelli than has been said, for a very long time.[2]

What's a poor epigone to do? Choose one's side, and enter the fray. But intellectual probity impels one to raise one's Jolly Roger at the outset (mine, of course, being Leo Strauss's *Thoughts on Machiavelli*). To wit: I present a reading of *The Prince* that supports the view that Machiavelli is a radically revolutionary thinker who breaks with classical political thought in both its pagan and its Christian forms, breaks with so-called Renaissance humanism, and breaks with the so-called Atlantic republican tradition. My Machiavelli is an atheist. He is, moreover, more anti-Christian than antipapist, anticlerical, or antireligion; above all, he is radically anti-Christ. Machiavelli is the thinker who introduced the modern "truths" that Nietzsche takes to be so deadly: the sovereignty of becoming over being; the fluidity of all concepts; the lack of any cardinal difference between man and animal. I shall try to demonstrate how these Machiavellian doctrines are introduced in *The Prince*.

How Many Are The Kinds of Principalities and in What Modes They Are Acquired

That acquisition is a major theme of *The Prince* is revealed in the title of the very brief opening chapter, "How Many Are the Kinds of Principalities and in What Modes They Are Acquired." That "virtue" (*virtù*) is the paramount theme is somewhat obscured. This one-paragraph chapter presents several dichotomies: republics versus principates; hereditary principates versus new ones; new ones that are altogether new or only partly new, either accustomed to living under a prince or used to being free; either acquired with the arms of others or one's own, either by fortune (*fortuna*) or by virtue (*virtù*). But only the last—the fortune-versus-virtue dichotomy—proves to be fundamental to the deepest teaching of *The Prince*.

Because one's birth cannot be attributed to one's own virtue in any way, the second chapter of *The Prince*, "Of Hereditary Principalities," is also very brief. Its main point is that all hereditary principates were once new, i.e., acquired. So it is in the third chapter, "Of Mixed Principalities," that Machiavelli begins to teach his lessons in how to acquire. But more important than any lesson Machiavelli has to teach us about *how* we should acquire is the lesson he has to teach us about acquisition as such. Machiavelli's teaching calls for the liberation of acquisitive appetite (what later will be called "possessive individualism"[3]) *contra* Plato or Aristotle or classic Christian doctrine, so much so that this supposed Italian patriot would rather blame Louis XII of France for *failing*, twice, in his attempt to "acquire" Italian territory than blame him for trying; for "truly it is a very natural and ordinary thing to desire to acquire" (14).[4] The bulk of the chapter holds up the warlike Roman republic as the model city that knew how to acquire better than any, that knew especially the virtue of the preemptive strike: Machiavelli prefers "strike first, with deadly force" to "turn the other cheek." The Romans knew, because they could "foresee from afar," that war is inevitable, and is deferred only to the advantage of others. Machiavelli compares this to a physician's ability to diagnose consumption: "in the beginning of the illness it is easy to cure and difficult to recognize," but "when it has not been recognized and treated in the beginning, it becomes easy to recognize and difficult to cure" (12).[5]

This is not the place to demonstrate that the fourth chapter of *The Prince*, "Why the Kingdom of Darius Which Alexander Seized Did Not Rebel from His Successors after Alexander's Death," apparently concerned with the subject of its title, is in fact concerned with how Alexander VI (introduced at the end of chapter 3) had seized the papacy, but, above all, what can be learned from this concerning how to seize and maintain the papacy from his successors. Let us simply assert it.[6] Nor is it to our present purpose to investigate how chapter 5, "How Cities or Principalities Which Lived by Their Own Laws before They Were Occupied Should Be Administered," reveals the contemporary situation of the Medici in Florence.

Let us come immediately to the sixth chapter, in which the themes of acquisition and virtue unite, "Of New Principalities That Are Acquired through One's Own Arms and Virtue." Here Machiavelli introduces the "greatest examples" of acquisition: those principates in which the prince and the state alike are altogether new, those princes who have acquired altogether by virtue and not by fortune. The "most excellent" of these are Moses, the author, or I should say the propounder, of the Mosaic law, and hence the founder of the nation of Israel; Cyrus, the liberator of the Persians from the Medes, and founder of the Persian empire; Romulus, the founder of Rome; and Theseus, the founder of Athens. These men owed nothing to fortune, except the opportunity to display their mastering virtue. Moses is only an apparent anomaly on this list, should anyone assert that he was merely an executor of the things that had been ordered for him by God, hence did not acquire (to put it mildly) through his own arms and virtue. For besides the fact that he should have to be admired for the grace that made him worthy of direct communication with God, assuming he ever had any such communication, one can infer from the fact that the actions and the orders of the other three were identical with those of Moses, even without benefit of God's instruction, that, in fact, he did not. Machiavelli thus reveals, in the case of Moses, the stance that permits him to pass over in silence the miraculous or mythical elements in the ancient reports of Cyrus, and Romulus's being weaned by a she-wolf, and Theseus's slaying of the Minotaur. Machiavelli's first mention of God in *The Prince*, as does his last, serves only to eliminate God from consideration in examining human affairs.

In the penultimate paragraph of the chapter, Machiavelli makes his famous observation that "nothing is more difficult to handle, more doubtful of success, nor more dangerous to manage, than to put oneself at the head of introducing new orders" (23), followed by his even more famous observation that "all the armed prophets conquered and the unarmed ones were ruined" (24). "Unarmed" means lacking the ability to use force; it means having to beg, supplicate, or "pray" (*preghino*) for assistance. As the title and the entire chapter make clear, "armed" means "virtuous," for both prophets and princes. We have the examples of four "armed" princes or prophets—Moses, Cyrus, Theseus, and Romulus—to which is added a fifth, at the end of the chapter, Hiero ("prince" or "king") of Syracuse.[7] Of the "unarmed ones," Machiavelli names only one: Savonarola. Who may be the other "unarmed ones" whom Machiavelli has in mind is left to the reader's imagination.[8]

As the title of chapter 7, "Of New Principalities That Are Acquired by Others' Arms and Fortune," and the entire chapter make clear, acquisition by "fortune" is the contrary of acquisition by "virtue." And the example of acquisition by fortune *par excellence* in *The Prince* is Cesare Borgia. It is easy to miss the forest for the trees in this chapter, and most commentators have done so. The example of "virtue" in this chapter is Francesco Sforza (the sole person named in chapter 1, there as an "altogether new" prince [5]); the example of "fortune," Cesare Borgia.[9] But the true hero of the chapter is Cesare's father, the Borgia pope, Alexander VI, who "had very many difficulties, both present and future, when he decided to make his son the duke great" (27). In a digression from his account of Alexander's many difficulties, Machiavelli relates the unforgettable story of the use to which Cesare Borgia put Messer Remirro de Orco in the Romagna, leaving him in two pieces, in the piazza in Cesena, with a piece of wood and a bloody knife alongside, after he had no further use for him.[10] If we do not miss the forest for the trees, when Machiavelli bids us "return to where we left off," we understand that Cesare stands in relation to Alexander, in the main story, as Remirro stands to Cesare in the memorable digression. "Thus," says Machiavelli, "he [Cesare] should be put forward, as I have done, to be imitated by all those who have risen to empire though fortune and by the arms of others" (32). Machiavelli's real interest lies with Pope Alexander, who "showed how far a pope could prevail with money and forces. With Duke Valentino [Cesare] as his instrument and with the invasion of the French as the opportunity he did all the things I discussed above in the actions of the duke" (46). Cesare was neither "armed" nor "virtuous" in the decisive sense.[11]

Chapter 8, "Of Those Who Have Attained a Principality through Crimes," teaches us that Agathocles, another "king" (not "tyrant") of Syracuse (like Hiero, from chapter 6) *was* "armed" and "virtuous" in the decisive sense. Agathocles "kept to a life of crime at every rank of his career; nonetheless, his crimes were accompanied with such virtue of spirit and body [never 'soul' in Machiavelli's *Prince* or *Discourses on Livy*[12]]" that he ought, in Machiavelli's view, to be celebrated among the most excellent men, which is how Machiavelli, indeed, celebrates him. The distinction between crime and virtue breaks down in this chapter. For, Machiavelli tells us, "whoever might consider the actions and the virtue of this man will see nothing or little that can be attributed to fortune" (35). True, "one cannot call it virtue to kill one's citizens, betray one's friends, to be without faith, without mercy, without religion; these modes can enable one to acquire empire, but not glory" (35). Nonetheless, Machiavelli does call it "virtue" in the immediate sequel, and "does not see why [Agathocles] has to be judged inferior to any most excellent captain" (35). True, "his savage cruelty and inhumanity, together with his infinite crimes, do not permit (*non consentono*) him to be celebrated among the most excellent men" (35), but the key words are "permit" and "celebrated": Machiavelli's point is that Agathocles was, in fact, "virtuous," but the prevailing modes of moral discourse do not "permit" his virtue to be "celebrated." This mode of moral discourse is what Machiavelli intends to change.

To effect this change, Machiavelli must introduce a new mode of moral discourse to replace the prevailing modes.[13] This he begins to effect, later in chapter 8, when he returns to the story of Agathocles. How is it, one wonders, "that Agathocles and anyone like him, after infinite betrayals and cruelties, could live for a long time secure in his fatherland, defend himself against external enemies, and never be conspired against by his citizens . . . even in peaceful times, not to mention uncertain times of war" (37)? The answer is, "cruelties well used." "Those can be called well used (if it is permissible [*licito*] to speak well of evil) that are done at one stroke, out of the necessity to secure oneself, and then are not persisted in but are turned to as much utility for the subjects as one can" (37-38). But precisely what is *not* "permissible," of course, is "to speak well of evil." Indeed, for Christians, it is not even permissible to speak evil of evil (*Discourses on Livy* III.1.4). Machiavelli, nonetheless, insists on speaking well of evil, and even judges that those who use cruelty well "can have some remedy *with God* and with men, as had Agathocles" (38, my emphasis).[14] In chapters 6 and 8, then, Machiavelli conflates "one's own arms," "virtue," and "savage cruelty and inhumanity"; in chapters 7 and 9 ("Of the Civil Principality"), he conflates "the arms of others," "fortune," and "civility" or legality; for, as Thrasymachus had been made to observe long ago, by Plato in his *Republic*, to obey the laws is to serve the advantage of the stronger who made the laws.

In chapter 10, "In What Mode the Forces of All Principalities Should Be Measured," Machiavelli begins the transition to the second section of *The Prince*.[15] The general point of the chapter is to establish that the strengths of *all* principates should be measured by their ability to arm themselves, and the general point of the sequel ("Of Ecclesiastical Principalities")—a surprising chapter (not mentioned in the outline in chapter 1) on the papacy (especially that of Alexander VI)—is to establish that the papacy, too, is a principate—which brings us to the center of *The Prince*, Machiavelli's teaching on the various modes of being armed.

Chapter 6

The Prince of War

Military matters are at the center of *The Prince*, literally and figuratively: Machiavelli's prince is, above all, "the prince of war," the contrary, above all, of "the prince of peace." At the beginning of chapter 12, Machiavelli famously observes, "And because there cannot be good laws where there are not good arms, and where there are good arms there must be good laws, I shall leave out the reasoning on laws and shall speak of arms" (48). And he does so, too, no less rigorously than Plato's Socrates does the contrary in *The Republic* and *The Laws*. Indeed, as Berlin remarks, "Machiavelli does not so much as mention natural law, the basic category in terms of which (or rather the many varieties of which) Christians and pagans, teleologists and materialists, jurists, theologians, and philosophers, before and indeed for many decades after him, discussed the very topics to which he applied his mind."[16]

The lesson of chapter 12, "How Many Kinds of Military There Are and Concerning Mercenary Soldiers," is that Italy has been ruined by "mercenary soldiers"—literally, condottieri; figuratively, priests[17]—that is its "sin," which allowed Charles, king of France, to seize Italy "with chalk" (49), an expression elsewhere attributed to Pope Alexander VI, which source would probably have been familiar to Machiavelli's contemporary readers.[18] But in chapter 13, "Of Auxiliary, Mixed, and One's Own Soldiers," we come to the deepest heart of the matter, what it means to be "the total owner of one's own arms" (55). Here Machiavelli reverts to the story of Hiero of Syracuse, named at the end of chapter 6 (25), as "the like" of Moses, Cyrus, Romulus, and Theseus, the "greatest examples" of "armed prophets" who "acquired through one's own arms and virtue." What Hiero understood, when he was made head of the Syracusan armies, was that they were a mercenary militia, like Italian condottieri, so he had them all cut to pieces, which Machiavelli greatly admires, and recommends to whoever has to deal with "mercenary soldiers" (literal and figurative). Machiavelli wants further to recall to memory a figure from the Old Testament "apt (*fatta*, "made" in de Alvarez's translation[19]) for this purpose," David. As Mansfield remarks, "[Machiavelli's] account of this episode differs significantly from the biblical original" (56n5).[20] Indeed, the biblical story of David and Goliath is *made apt* for Machiavelli's purpose by Machiavelli: he drops God from the story and adds a knife to David's sling. In the Old Testament, the story teaches the paramount importance of human reliance on God; in *The Prince*, the story teaches the paramount importance of human independence from God. In his use of this biblical story in *The Prince*, Machiavelli borrows God's knife, we might say, to cut off His head. If "God is dead," as Nietzsche's Zarathustra says, who killed Him? Machiavelli's "confession of faith"[21] at the end of this chapter is ultimately an exhortation to human beings to assassinate—to decapitate—God.[22]

"Thus a prince should have no other object, nor any other thought, nor take anything else as his art but the art of war" (58), Machiavelli says in the opening sentence of chapter 14, "What a Prince Should Do Regarding the Military," as did Francesco Sforza, the "altogether new" prince of chapter 1, who is the prince of "virtue" contrasted with the prince of "fortune," Cesare Borgia, in chapter 7. Indeed, the prince's thoughts should be on the exercise of war even more in peacetime (*per impossible*, one might think) than in war, which he can do in two modes: with deeds and with the mind. The deeds consist of military exercises, or war games as we might call them. Exercise of the mind consists of reading histories for the examples of "the actions of excellent men" (60) to imitate; advice that recalls the opening paragraph of chapter 6, but with a new list of "excellent men," different from the list of the "greatest examples" of chapter 6: Alexander the Great, who imitated Achilles; Caesar, who imitated Alexander; and Scipio, who imitated "the life of Cyrus written by Xenophon." We must note the last, broken link in this chain, for only the last warrants comment from Machiavelli: "Whoever reads the life of Cyrus written by Xenophon will then recognize in the life of Scipio . . . how much in chastity, affability, humanity, and liberality Scipio conformed to what had been written of Cyrus by Xenophon" (60).[23] We will return to this later.

Chapter 15, "Of Those Things for Which Men and Especially Princes Are Praised or Blamed," opens with Machiavelli's emphatic insistence on the novelty of his ethical teaching:

> And because I know that many have written of this, I fear that in writing of it again, I may be held presumptuous, especially since in disputing this matter I depart from the orders of others. But since it is my intent to write something useful to whoever understands it, it has appeared to me more fitting to go directly to the effectual truth of the thing than to the imagination of it. And many have imagined republics and principalities that have never been seen or known to exist in truth; for it is so far from how one lives to how one should live that he who lets go of what is done for what should be done learns his ruin rather than his preservation. For a man who wants to make a profession of good in all regards must come to ruin among so many who are not good. Hence it is necessary to a prince, if he wants to maintain himself, to learn to be able to be not good, and to use this and not use it according to necessity.
>
> Thus, leaving out what is imagined about a prince and discussing what is true, I say that all men, and especially princes, since they are placed higher, are noted for some of the qualities that bring them either blame or praise. (61)

There following is a somewhat ambiguous list of pairs of traditional virtues and vices (not, however, called virtues and vices[24]) that Machiavelli proceeds to examine in successive chapters, but he unambiguously omits justice and injustice. He first examines "Of Liberality and Parsimony" (chapter 16). Toward the end of the chapter, he cites Cyrus, Caesar, and Alexander as exemplary practitioners of "Machiavellian" liberality, which implies that the true Cyrus, as opposed to the imaginary prince of Xenophon's "Life of Cyrus," is linked with Achilles, Alexander, and Caesar. In chapter 17, Machiavelli returns to the subject of "cruelty well used" of chapter 8. The chapter is titled "Of Cruelty and Mercy (*Pietate*), and Whether It Is Better to Be Loved Than Feared, or the Contrary."[25] We note, with Mansfield (65n1), that *pieta* may be translated "piety" as well as "mercy" (compare "pity"). And in fact, the chapter contrasts Machiavelli's teaching on the value of fear with Christ's teaching on the value of love, without, of course, naming names. "Among the admirable actions of Hannibal," Machiavelli writes, "is numbered this one: "

> that when he had a very large army, mixed with infinite kinds of men, and had led it to fight in alien lands, no dissension ever arose in it, neither among themselves nor against the prince, in bad as well as in good fortune. This could not have arisen from anything other than his inhuman cruelty which, together with his infinite virtues, always made him venerable and terrible in the sight of his soldiers; and without it, his other virtues would not have sufficed to bring about this effect. (67)

Hannibal's "inhuman cruelty" was not only a "virtue," in Machiavelli's view, it was his paramount virtue, without which his other virtues would have been ineffectual. And the writers have insufficiently considered this—hence Machiavelli's novel departure from their orders—for they admire Hannibal's action, but they condemn the principal virtue that effected it. In Machiavelli's new ethics, there will be no more of this hypocrisy. Machiavelli's contrast with Hannibal is Scipio, "whose armies in Spain rebelled against him. This arose from nothing but his excessive mercy" (68), which is one of the qualities he imitated from Xenophon's "Life of Cyrus" (60). Fortunately for Scipio, this damaging quality was not shared by the Roman Senate, and Scipio "lived under the government of the Senate" (68), of which we learn in Machiavelli's *Discourses on Livy* I.38, "in every fortune it always wished to be the one that was prince over the decisions that its own would have to make."[26]

Machiavelli brings his ethical teaching to its culmination in chapter 18, "In What Mode Faith Should Be Kept by Princes," and introduces the hero of *The Prince* in chapter 19, "Of Avoiding Contempt and Hatred." There are two kinds of fighting that must be mastered by Machiavelli's "Prince of War": with the laws and with force (note that both the laws and force are modes of fighting):

> Therefore it is necessary for a prince to know well how to use the beast and the man. This role was taught covertly to princes by ancient writers, who wrote that Achilles, and many other ancient princes, were given to Chiron the centaur to be raised, so that he would look after them with his discipline. To have as teacher a half-beast, half-man means nothing other than that a prince needs to know how to use both natures [*l'una e l'altra natura*]; and the one without the other is not lasting. (69)

We may now complete the list of linked imitators in the chain from chapter 14: Caesar imitated Alexander; Alexander, Achilles; Achilles, Chiron.[27] Thus, the alternative, as Machiavelli teaches covertly to modern princes, is to take as one's preceptor for imitation, the half-beast, half-man, imaginary "prince of war," Chiron the centaur; or the half-god, half-man, imaginary "prince of peace," Jesus of Nazareth. He leaves no doubt as to which the prudent prince ought to choose.

The prince of war must know well how to use two beasts in particular: the fox, to avoid snares; the lion, to frighten wolves.[28] Those who simply use the lion do not understand the importance of the fox, which means, especially, they do not understand the importance of being "a great pretender and dissembler" (70). This is what made Alexander VI such an admirable pope:

> Alexander VI never did anything, nor ever thought of anything, but how to deceive men, and he always found a subject to whom he could do it. And there never was a man with greater efficacy in asserting a thing, and in affirming it with greater oaths, who observed it [faith, *the* faith?] less; nonetheless, his deceits succeeded at his will, because he knew well this aspect of the world. (70)[29]

Thus, Machiavelli concludes, it is not necessary for a prince to have all the qualities listed above in chapter 15—traditionally called "virtues" by the writers—some of which have been analyzed in chapters 16 through 18. What is necessary is to *appear* to have them, "to appear merciful, faithful, humane [*umano*, "human" in de Alvarez's translation, 108], honest, and religious" (70). Above all, it is necessary for the prince to appear religious. (Pope Alexander VI, the keeper of the faith, appeared to keep the Christian faith, but in truth kept "Machiavellian" faith. This is what enabled him to show "how far a pope could prevail with money and forces" [46].)

Chapter 19, "Of Avoiding Contempt and Hatred," is the longest chapter of *The Prince*, and like the longest chapter of the *Discourses on Livy*, its theme is conspiracies: how to execute them, and how to avoid them. In this chapter, we are introduced to the hero of *The Prince*,[30] the Roman emperor, Severus (whose name could not be made more apt for Machiavelli's purpose; who is called a criminal, as Mansfield [77n16] points out, in *Discourses on Livy* I.10; and who, we might add, made the taking of the sacrament of the eucharist a crime in Rome, as Machiavelli's contemporary readers, no doubt, would have known). Severus was among the "very cruel and very rapacious" emperors of Rome, all of whom came to a bad end, except for Severus. And why not Severus? Because "in Severus was so much virtue" that he "was always able to rule prosperously because his virtues made him so admirable in the sight of his soldiers and the people that the latter remained somehow astonished and stupefied, while the former were reverent and satisfied" (78). Severus is identified as a "new prince," like the "greatest examples" of chapter 6, whose actions were "great and notable" (78). Above all, Severus knew well "how to use the persons of the fox and the lion, whose natures [*nature*] I say above are necessary for a prince to imitate" (78). But the fox and the lion are *not* precisely the "natures" Machiavelli says above are necessary for a prince to imitate. The "natures" Machiavelli says above are necessary for a prince to imitate are "the beast and the man" (69). Unless? Unless we recall and place due weight upon the significance of the intervening passage on the importance of appearances. There, at the center of Machiavelli's list of five qualities that it is necessary for the prince to *appear* to have is "human" (*umano*) (70). Is not Severus, then, the "new man," the man whose actions, to "whoever examines them minutely" will reveal "a very fierce lion and a very astutue fox" (79), Machiavelli's model of the prince of war? Strauss remarks, "The chief theme of the *Prince* is the wholly new prince in the wholly new state, that is, the founder. And the model for the founder as founder is the extremely clever criminal Severus."[31]

In sum, Machiavelli establishes a new model for humanity to imitate in *The Prince*. In a kind of inversion of the Docetist heresy, Machiavelli replaces the half-man, half-god, only apparently human, "prince of peace," Jesus of Nazareth, with the half-man, half-beast, only apparently human, "prince of war," Severus, a very ferocious lion and a very clever fox. In short, following Machiavelli, there is a lack of any cardinal difference between man and animal: apparent differences are merely appearances.

How Much Fortune and God Can Do in Human Affairs, and in What Mode Fortune May Be Opposed

A new vision of humanity calls for a new vision of the cosmos, with which the substantive teaching of *The Prince* reaches its culmination, in chapter 25.[32] After dehumanizing man in chapter 19, in the twentieth chapter, "Whether Fortresses and Many Other Things Which Are Made and Done By Princes Every Day Are Useful or Useless," Machiavelli, for the first time in *The Prince*, humanizes fortune: "she," when "she wants to make a new prince great" (85), makes enemies for him, so that they may serve as rungs on the ladder of his overcomings, climbing which, he rises to greatness. "Therefore," Machiavelli observes, "many judge that a wise prince, when he has the opportunity for it, should astutely nourish some enmity so that when he has crushed it, his greatness emerges the more from it" (85). In other words, a wise prince makes his own fortune. The next three chapters, "What a Prince Should Do to Be Held in Esteem," "Of Those Whom Princes Have As Secretaries," and "In What Mode Flatterers Are to Be Avoided," indicate (among other things) how Lorenzo de Medici could utilize Machiavelli to make his own fortune, were he only a wise prince.

Machiavelli prepares for the teaching of perhaps the most famous chapter of *The Prince*, chapter 25, "How Much Fortune Can Do in Human Affairs, and in What Mode It May Be Opposed," by drawing a sharp contrast between fortune and virtue, in the last paragraph of chapter 24, "Why the Princes of Italy Have Lost Their States." But in the first sentence of chapter 25, he makes it clear that the chapter deals not only with the role of the "ancient" Roman goddess, Fortuna, in human affairs, but also of the God of "modern" Rome. Machiavelli opens the chapter with a perfect summation of the teaching of classical political philosophy, in both its pagan and its Christian modes:

> It is not unknown to me that many have held and hold the opinion
> that worldly things are so governed by fortune and by God, that men
> cannot correct them with their prudence, indeed that they have no
> remedy at all; and on account of this they might judge that one need
> not sweat much over things but let oneself be governed by chance.
> (98)

They might judge, not, of course, Machiavelli[33]: "Nonetheless, in order that our
free will not be eliminated, I judge that it might be true that fortune is the arbiter
of half our actions, but also that she leaves the other half, or close to it, for us to
govern" (98). It *might* be true, it *could* be true, that Fortuna is the arbiter of
about half our actions; it could not possibly be true, then, that God, who is here
simply silently dropped from the argument, is the arbiter of *anything* in human
affairs.

As for Fortuna, she is like those violent rivers that, when they become en-
raged and flood, wreak destruction on human beings. Everyone flees before
them, but, Machiavelli reasons, "it is not as if men, when times are quiet, could
not provide for them with dikes and dams" (98), so that when they later rise, the
destruction will be minimized. It is similar with Fortuna: She "shows her power
where virtue has not been put in order to resist her and therefore turns her impetus where she knows that dams and dikes have not been made to contain her"
(98-99). For Machiavelli, "fortune" ultimately means nothing more than "lack of
virtue."

Machiavelli concludes his argument, and the philosophical argument of *The
Prince* as a whole, with the infamous image of the rape of the goddess[34]:

> I judge this indeed, that it is better to be impetuous than cautious, be-
> cause fortune is a woman; and it is necessary, if one wants to hold her
> down, to beat her and strike her down. And one sees that she lets her-
> self be won more by the impetuous than by those who proceed
> coldly. And so always, like a woman, she is the friend of the young,
> because they are less cautious, more ferocious, and command her
> with more audacity. (101)

To discuss this "from on high," to borrow a Machiavellian expression, not individual human beings, perhaps, but humanity as a whole, can indeed conquer
fortune, if sufficiently ferocious and audacious Machiavellian virtue is brought
to bear on her.[35]

The Prince ends with an ironical exhortation to Lorenzo de Medici, "Exhortation to Seize Italy and Free Her from the Barbarians" (chapter 26), just as it
began with an ironical dedicatory letter to Lorenzo.[36] For surely no discerning
reader will credit the claim in chapter 26, after reading chapter 25, that anyone
has been "ordered by God" to redeem Italy, but has been "repulsed by fortune";
although one may well believe that "she prays God to send her someone to redeem her" (102); that, indeed, is her sin, in Machiavelli's judgment.[37] Machia-

velli recalls for Lorenzo the "greatest examples" of chapter 6, but has the good taste to omit the Italian example of Romulus. And while he says that "extraordinary things without example" (103) have been seen to occur, the extraordinary things are not only *not* "without example," they are precisely the examples of Moses' miraculous leadership of the Israelites to the promised land, just before, as Mansfield points out (103n7), the revelation at Mount Sinai.[38] In another sense, of course, they *are* without example, since Machiavelli surely does not believe they ever happened to Moses and the Israelites. But if they never happened to Moses and the Israelites, are we to think that Machiavelli believes they recently happened to Lorenzo and the Florentines? Are we to imagine Lorenzo, sitting in his study, reading chapter 26 of *The Prince*, actually recalling the recent opening of the sea he witnessed, or the time a cloud escorted him along the way, or a stone poured forth water, or that it rained manna in Tuscany? God, indeed, does not want to do everything, no more for readers of *The Prince* than for princes.[39]

Machiavelli inaugurates a new "humanism," more radical than so-called Renaissance humanism. Machiavelli's "inhuman humanism" radically depreciates—indeed denies—any connection between the human and the divine—indeed, anything transcendent. The question is whether such a humanism can coherently articulate any meaningful distinction between the human and the bestial. Whether it does not inevitably lead to the doctrines of sovereign becoming, the fluidity of all concepts, the lack of any cardinal difference between man and animal—doctrines that are indubitably deadly, as Nietzsche understood, but perhaps not indubitably true.[40]

Notes

Thanks to Harvey C. Mansfield Jr. who graciously furnished me with a privately printed bilingual text of *The Prince*, with the Italian and his own translation on facing pages, which greatly facilitated the writing of this chapter.

1. I adapt the opening witticism of *The Collected Essays of J. V. Cunningham* (Chicago: Swallow Press, 1979), vii., Cunningham, poet and literary critic, continues, "What it adds is, or was when first published, new, though it would take a lifetime of bibliographical search to be sure." Silvia Ruffo-Fiore, *Niccolo Machiavelli* (Boston: Twayne, 1972), 144, remarks, "Anyone undertaking the study of Machiavelli is overwhelmed by the critical literature, particularly that of the twentieth century." I am, myself, an amateur (in what I hope is the best sense of the word); I aspire simply to present an interpretation of Machiavelli's teaching in *The Prince*, not a display of erudition. I am, of course, aware that *The Prince* is not all there is to Machiavelli's thought, but I am not persuaded that there is anything in *The Prince* that is inconsistent with the rest of Machiavelli. In this, I consign myself to Leo Strauss, *Thoughts on Machiavelli* (Seattle: University of Washington Press, 1958).

2. Ernst Cassirer, *The Myth of the State* (New Haven, Conn.: Yale University Press, 1946), 116, remarks, "From one century to another, almost from one generation to another, we find not only change but a complete reversal in the judgments about *The*

Prince." Isaiah Berlin, "The Originality of Machiavelli," *Against the Current: Essays in the History of Ideas* (New York: Viking, 1980), 25n2, noted that the bibliography of secondary literature on Machiavelli "now contains more than three thousand items"—and that was written in 1970. Berlin discusses the spectrum of interpretations of Machiavelli's political thought, beginning with Albericio Gentili and Cardinal Pole, in the sixteenth century, through to what he calls the latest of the many anti-Machiavels, Jacques Maritain and Leo Strauss. Berlin acknowledges his bibliographical survey's debt to Eric W. Cochrane, "Machiavelli: 1940-1960," *Journal of Modern History* 33 (1961): 113-36, which he calls "one of the best and liveliest accounts of the mass of conflicting theories" (36n3). Those who are interested in bibliographical searches may now consult Silvia R. Fiore, *Niccolo Machiavelli: An Annotated Bibliography of Modern Criticism and Scholarship* (Westport, Conn.: Greenwood Press, 1990). In addition to these bibliographical essays, see J. H. Whitfield, *Machiavelli* (Oxford: Basis Blackwell, 1947), 1-11, and Anthony Parel, "Machiavelli's Method and His Interpreters," in Anthony Parel, ed., *The Political Calculus: Essays on Machiavelli's Philosophy* (Toronto: University of Toronto, 1972), 3-28. I have found Giuseppe Prezzolini, *Machiavelli* (New York: Farrar, Straus and Giroux, 1967), to be informative, witty, and intelligent on the centuries of Machiavelli interpreters. While I do not, of course, agree with everything Prezzolini says about Machiavelli's thought, I find him full of good sense, and perhaps for that reason, underappreciated. On the sixteenth- and seventeenth-century readings of Machiavelli, Peter S. Donaldson, *Machiavelli and Mystery of State* (Cambridge: Cambridge University Press, 1988), is interesting and immensely informative. Claude Lefort, *Le travail de l'oeuvre Machiavel* (Paris: Gallimard, 1972) which analyzes eight of the leading Machiavelli interpretations, includes one of the few serious discussions of Strauss's *Thoughts.*

Berlin, "Originality," 79, remarks, "Where more than twenty interpretations hold the field, the addition of one more cannot be deemed an impertinence." His own contribution is that Machiavelli institutes a distinction between "two incompatible ideals of life, and therefore two moralities" (45), Christian and pagan, but that he does not judge one or the other good or bad, just that "to choose to lead a Christian life is to condemn oneself to political impotence" (47). "It is important to note," Berlin avers, "that Machiavelli does not formally condemn Christian morality" (48). Mark Hulliung, *Citizen Machiavelli* (Princeton, N.J.: Princeton University Press, 1983), argues emphatically that Machiavelli chooses pagan over any version of Christian morality, and that he consistently inverted Ciceronian Stoicism, and stood Renaissance humanism on its head. In place of Benedetto Croce's famous "autonomy of politics, of politics which are beyond good and evil," in his *Elementi di politica* (Bari, Italy: Laterza, 1925), 60, Hulliung suggests "the ubiquity of politics" (103). He quotes J. R. Hale's acute observation, from Hale's *Machiavelli and Renaissance Italy* (New York: Macmillan, 1960), contra Allan H. Gilbert, *Machiavelli's Prince and Its Forerunners: The Prince As a Typical Book* de Regimine Principum (Durham, N.C.: Duke University Press, 1938), "Because of its formal resemblance to old manuals *Of Princely Government,* Machiavelli's *Prince* was like a bomb in a prayerbook" (25). Hulliung's view is that Machiavelli is less concerned with republics versus principalities than he is with vigorous conquest. Hulliung's final chapter, "Interpreting Machiavelli" (210-57), is a valuable discussion of the twentieth-century Machiavelli debates. I should say, however, that while Hulliung is explicitly critical of Strauss's Machiavelli (238-41), it seems to me that his interpretation owes much to Strauss.

For recent collections of essays, see G. Bock, Q. Skinner, and M. Viroli, eds., *Machiavelli and Republicanism* (Cambridge: Cambridge University Press, 1990); A. R. Ascoli and V. Kahn, eds., *Machiavelli and the Discourse of Literature* (Ithaca, N.Y.: Cornell University Press, 1993); and the essays by Angelo M. Codevilla, William B. Allen,

Carnes Lord, and Hadley Arkes in Niccolo Machiavelli, *The Prince*, translated and edited by Angelo M. Codevilla (New Haven, Conn.: Yale University Press, 1997).

Published since Fiore's bibliography, Anthony J. Parel, *The Machiavellian Cosmos* (New Haven, Conn.: Yale University Press, 1992), has presented the Renaissance Machiavelli who believes in omens, medieval humors, astrology, and such with a vengeance; Maurizio Viroli, *Machiavelli* (Oxford: Oxford University Press, 1998), who agrees with Parel on the above questions of Machiavelli's "philosophy of life," has presented Machiavelli the lover of republican liberty, civic life, and the laws. Viroli's book reminds me of the remark of Prezzolini, *Machiavelli*, 224, concerning Alfieri's eighteenth-century exclusive emphasis on Machiavelli's republicanism: it was, he says, "like drawing a picture of a man with the thumb so large that the rest of the body is hardly visible." Viroli's Machiavelli is all thumb.

The only new interpretation in the twentieth century, so far as I can tell, is Strauss's *Thoughts on Machiavelli*. Strauss demonstrates that most of the "contradictions" in Machiavelli's thought, which his interpreters have labored to explain, are to be found in the presuppositions of the interpreters, not in Machiavelli, and he satisfactorily reconciles those that remain. Whitfield, *Machiavelli*, 75, points out, for example, that A. L. Burd "assured us that we should find the methods suggested in the *Discorsi* quite as unscrupulous as those of *The Prince*," whereas Whitfield "should prefer to make the opposite remark: that the healthy observations of the *Discorsi* find their counterpart in *The Prince*." Strauss shows how there is not a distinction in Machiavelli's thought between the "unscrupulous" and the "healthy." Strauss's interpretation is far too subtle and complex for me to summarize without severe distortion. Let me simply say that I have read the many criticisms of Strauss's reading of Machiavelli, and I do not find them convincing. In fact, I rarely recognize the Strauss I find being criticized. There are some especially egregious examples of such travesties in the most recent literature, but I do not wish to name names. It goes without saying that I am indebted, in many points, both general and particular, to Strauss's *Thoughts*; far too many to document in this essay. Harvey C. Mansfield Jr. has devoted much of his prodigious talent to developing Strauss's insights; see Mansfield, "Strauss's Machiavelli," *Political Theory* 3 (1975): 372-84, 402-5; *Machiavelli's New Modes and Orders: A Study of The Discourses on Livy* (Ithaca, N.Y.: Cornell University Press, 1979); *The Prince*, translated and with an introduction by Harvey C. Mansfield (Chicago: University of Chicago Press, 1985; 2nd ed., 1998); and *Machiavelli's Virtue* (Chicago: University of Chicago Press, 1996). I owe much to Mansfield, too, in this essay. See also W. R. Newell, "How Original Is Machiavelli? A Consideration of Skinner's Interpretation of Virtue and Fortune," *Political Theory* 15 (1987): 612-34; and Nathan Tarcov, "Quentin Skinner's Method and Machiavaelli's *Prince*," *Ethics* 92 (1982): 692-709. Vickie B. Sullivan, *Machiavelli's Three Romes: Religion, Human Liberty, and Politics Reformed* (Dekalb: Northern Illinois University Press, 1996), is especially good at demonstrating that Machiavelli's critique of religion runs deeper than any Renaissance anticlericalism, that it includes not only a critique of Christianity, but even of the Roman's political use of pagan religion. Machiavelli's "three Romes" are the ancient Rome of Livy, the modern Rome of the Christian Church, and the new "Rome," which is Machiavelli's political project.

3. C. B. Macpherson, *The Political Theory of Possessive Individualism: Hobbes to Locke* (Oxford: Clarendon Press, 1962), who does not, however, attribute the origin of this political theory to Machiavelli. Strauss originally did not trace it back far enough; see "Preface to the American Edition," *The Political Philosophy of Hobbes* (Chicago: University of Chicago Press, 1952; first published in 1936 by Clarendon Press, Oxford).

4. I quote from Mansfield's translation, except where otherwise noted.

5. These are the sorts of Machiavellian lessons that led Sheldon Wolin, *Politics and Vision* (Boston: Little, Brown and Co., 1960), 195-238, to advance his memorable thesis that Machiavelli teaches "the economy of violence."

6. See Strauss, *Thoughts*, 32, for hints.

7. Strauss, *Thoughts*, 25-26, explains why Machiavelli never says "tyrant" in *The Prince*.

8. Pierre Manent, *An Intellectual History of Liberalism*, trans. R. Balinski (Princeton, N.J.: Princeton University Press, 1994), 18: "There is, however, one 'unarmed prophet' who could be considered, especially by Machiavelli, as a 'conqueror': Jesus Christ. And what is Machiavelli himself, who writes tempting books instead of committing terrible deeds, if not an 'unarmed prophet'? Machiavelli is, in his own eyes, that unarmed prophet who is trying to disarm the teaching of the greatest of the unarmed prophets." See Strauss, *Thoughts*, 84, 171; Mansfield, *Virtue*, xi, 4; and Sullivan, *Three Romes*, 172. The Italian title of Prezzolini, *Machiavelli*, was *Machiavelli anticristo*.

9. For a brilliant reading of the use made of Cesare in the plot of *The Prince*, see John T. Scott and Vickie B. Sullivan, "Patricide and the Plot of *The Prince*: Cesare Borgia and Machiavelli's Italy," *American Political Science Review 88* (December 1994): 887-99. They elaborate a suggestion of Strauss, *Thoughts*, 68.

10. Cesare left Remirro in the town square, cut in half, with a piece of wood and a bloody knife alongside, as a Christmas present to Cesena! See Roberto Ridolfi, *The Life of Niccolo Machiavelli*, trans. C. Grayson (Chicago: University of Chicago Press, 1963), 62.

11. J. G. A. Pocock, *The Machiavellian Moment: Florentine Political Thought and the Atlantic Republican Tradition* (Princeton, N.J.: Princeton University Press, 1975), 173, observes that "in Cesare we see combined the maximum *virtù* with the maximum dependence on fortune."

12. See Strauss, *Thoughts*, 31, 200, 294, 333n59.

13. According to Frederico Chabod, *Machiavelli and the Renaissance* (Cambridge, Mass.: Harvard University Press, 1960), 142, "Nothing is further from Machiavelli's mind than to undermine common morality, replacing it with a new ethic." In a sense, this is correct; for it is, of course, true that Machiavelli does not mean to replace traditional virtue altogether with Machiavellian virtue, that the two must henceforth somehow coexist, as Mansfield, *The Prince*, xix, argues; see Strauss, *Thoughts*, 242. Machiavellian virtue could be practiced effectively by a prince, in fact, only in a context of traditional virtue, which means that most men are expected by Machiavelli to continue to practice traditional virtue. But what I am illuminating here is Machiavelli's presentation of "the effectual truth of the thing" for "whoever understands it" (*Prince*, chapter 15, 61). Whitfield, *Machiavelli*, 92-105, discusses Machiavelli's "anatomy of virtue." He believes "there is no consistent doctrine of *virtú* in Machiavelli's writings," but that "where he touches some such doctrine fleetingly it is a common (and I would add, a common-sense) inheritance," 99. I couldn't disagree more. J. G. A. Pocock, "Custom and Grace, Form and Matter: An Approach to Machiavelli's Concept of Innovation," in Martin Fleisher, ed., *Machiavelli and the Nature of Political Thought* (New York: Atheneum, 1972), comes close to contradicting himself, it seems to me, on this question. He admits that Machiavelli "employed the concept *virtù* in its purely formal sense of that by which order is imposed upon *fortuna* . . . in a way that separates it from the Christian and Aristotelian, moral and political contexts in which it ordinarily functioned," 169, but concludes that his "investigation of Machiavelli's thought . . . has shown it functioning, precisely where it is most original, within humanist, Aristotelian, and medieval limits," 173. This is a variation of the old thesis, for example in Felix Gilbert, *Machiavelli and Giucciardini:*

Politics and History in Sixteenth-Century Florence (Princeton, N.J.: Princeton University Press, 1965), 156, that "Machiavelli's theoretical assumptions . . . belong to the intellectual climate of the time." Mainstream scholarly opinions of Machiavelli's teaching on *virtù* are canvassed by John Plamenatz, "In Search of Machiavellian *Virtù*," in Parel, ed., *The Political Calculus*.

14. Virtually everyone would disagree with my reading of Machiavelli's judgment of Agathocles, although the view of Adam D. Danel, *A Case for Freedom: Machiavelli's Humanism* (Lanham, Md.: University Press of America, 1997), 265, comes close to mine, but with a different slant; cf. Strauss, *Thoughts*, 309-10n53. Where Berlin, "Originality," 52, says Agathocles is "excluded from the pantheon" in these passages, I say Machiavelli's radical innovation is to add him to it. The number of commentators who take Machiavelli's judgment, that Agathocles' methods won him imperium but not glory, as his final word on Agathocles is almost endless. To begin with the view furthest from my own, Whitfield, *Machiavelli*, who believes, in general, that "Machiavelli is inevitably and resolutely moderate," 156, even suggests that Machiavelli's "condemnation" of Agathocles is "Ciceronian" (80-81). For some of the recent commentators, see Sebastian de Grazia, *Machiavelli in Hell* (Princeton, N.J.: Princeton University Press, 1989), 314; Robert A. Kocis, *Machiavelli Redeemed: Retrieving His Humanist Perspectives on Equality, Power, and Glory* (Bethelem, Pa.: Lehigh University Press, 1998), 63, 88, 99, 119, 122-25; Viroli, *Machiavelli*, 38; and Wooton, *Political Writings*, xxi-xxii. Victoria Kahn, *Machiavellian Rhetoric: From the Counter-Reformation to Milton* (Princeton, N.J.: Princeton University Press, 1994), 26-39, gives an interesting and sophisticated reading of *The Prince*, chapters 7 and 8, highly recommended. She argues that "the aim of the passage . . . is to empty it [*virtù*] of any specific meaning," that "in the case of neither Borgia nor Agathocles can crime be called *virtù*, because *virtù* cannot be *called* any one thing" (31); and finally, most insightfully, "The rhetorical strategy that undermines the simple distinction between *virtù* and crime by stressing the rhetorical criterion of good usage (*'bene usate'*) also shows the link between tyranny and republicanism" (35). In general, the professors of literature, such as Kahn, who have recently investigated Machiavelli's philosophy, with emphasis on his rhetoric, have had many good insights. See, for example, Donaldson, *Machiavelli and Mystery of State*; Eugene Garver, *Machiavelli and the History of Prudence* (Madison: University of Wisconsin Press, 1987); Wayne A. Rebhorn, *Foxes and Lions: Machiavelli's Confidence Men* (Ithaca, N.Y.: Cornell University Press, 1988); and Nancy S. Streuver, *Theory As Practice: Ethical Inquiry in the Renaissance* (Chicago: University of Chicago Press, 1992), 147-81.

Pocock, *The Machiavellian Moment*, 550, summarizes his own work thus: "In terms borrowed from or suggested by the language of Hannah Arendt, this book has told part of the story of the revival in the early modern West of the ancient ideal of *homo politicus* (the *zoon politikon* of Aristotle), who affirms his being and his virtue by the medium of political action, whose closest kinsman is *homo rhetor* and whose antithesis is the *homo credens* of Christian faith." Cf. Viroli, *Machiavelli*, 112: "He practised political theory, not as the work of a philosopher, nor as the work of a scientist, but as the work of an orator"; Viroli suggests that this consideration might solve the old puzzle of the relationship between the *Prince* and the *Discourses on Livy*: "What would be contradictory for a philosopher . . . is perfectly permissible for an orator"; he acknowledges his debt to Quentin Skinner, *Reason and Rhetoric in the Philosophy of Hobbes* (1996); *Foundation of Modern Political Thought*, 2 vols. (1978); and *Machiavelli* (Oxford: Oxford University Press, 1981). See Mansfield, *Virtue*, 319n30, on the main fault of the interpretation of Machiavelli by Pocock and Skinner and their debt to Arendt; see also Newell, "How Original Is Machiavelli?" and Tarcov, "Quentin Skinner's Method."

15. See Strauss, *Thoughts*, 56-60, on the divisions of *The Prince* into four sections.

16. Berlin, "Originality," 36. H. Haydn, *The Counter-Renaissance* (New York: Scribner, 1950), distinguishes the classical, humanist, Christian renaissance from what he calls the counter-renaissance inaugurated by Machiavelli, which broke with all earlier ideals of moderation, harmony, and hierarchical order.

17. See Mansfield, *New Modes and Orders*, 251.

18. Mansfield, *The Prince*, 49n3, notes that "the expression is attributed to Pope Alexander VI by the French historian Philippe de Commines in his *Memoirs*."

19. *The Prince*, translation, introduction, and notes by Leo Paul S. de Alvarez (Irving, Texas: University of Dallas, 1980; reissued by Waveland Press Inc., 1989), 83.

20. Strauss, *Thoughts*, 45, remarks, "Machiavelli's examples are not always apt nor always true. I do not believe that we can infer from this that they are not always well chosen"; on the example of David and Goliath, see 329n10.

21. See de Alvarez, *The Prince*, 87n15.

22. Why it was that political modernity was not simply a prolonged and expanded renaissance, why it had to break with Aristotle and Cicero as well as Christianity, is lucidly explained by Manent, *Intellectual History of Liberalism*, 10-19.

23. As Mansfield, 60n5, notes, "The title of Xenophon's book is actually *Cyropaideia*, 'The Education of Cyrus.'" Machiavelli insists in his *Discourses on Livy*, too, on mistitling Xenophon's book, in his first and last references to it (*Discourses* II.13.1, III.39.1). Strauss, *Thoughts*, 161, remarks Xenophon's Cyrus is "a fictitious being." I suggest that Machiavelli's "mistake" permits readers to notice that "Life of Cyrus" could mean "Life of the Lord" for Christians, as in *Kyrie eleison,* "Lord have mercy." Cyrus is meant to call to mind, I suggest, another fictitious being.

24. See Clifford Orwin, "Machiavelli's Unchristian Charity," *American Political Science Review* 72 (December 1978): 1218. Orwin is very illuminating on *The Prince*, chapters 15-17.

25. According to Fiore, *Machiavelli*, 31, one of the last things Machiavelli did before his death was change the chapter titles of *The Prince* from Latin to Italian.

26. Machiavelli, *Discourses on Livy*, trans. Harvey C. Mansfield and Nathan Tarcov (Chicago: University of Chicago Press, 1996), 81. Machiavelli repeatedly contrasts Hannibal and Scipio. Mansfield, *The Prince*, 86n10, directs us to *Discourses on Livy* III.19-21. Hanna F. Pitkin, *Fortune Is a Woman: Gender & Politics in the Thought of Niccolo Machiavelli* (Berkeley: University of California Press, 1984), 75, emphasizes that this is an inversion of this standard pairing in Italian humanist literature. Wooten, "Introduction," xxxiv, notes that in *The Prince*, "All of the literary techniques of the humanist are brought to bear, but one of the chief casualties is intended to be humanism itself."

27. Ezio Raimondi, "The Politician and the Centaur," in Ascoli and Kahn, *Machiavelli and Discourse of Literature*, 153, observes that Machiavelli suggests a kind of "political equivalence between God and the centaur," with the "curious analogy between the pairing of the prophet [Moses] and his 'mighty teacher,' and the pairing of Achilles and Chiron"; this "in contrast with the Platonic-Christian approach of the humanist hermeneutic." Strauss, *Thoughts*, 204, makes this point; cf. Danel, *Case for Freedom*, 198, 246. On the "half-man, half-beast," see Strauss, *Thoughts*, 78, and Mansfield, *Virtue*, 37-38.

28. It is well known that Machiavelli derives his imagery of the lion and the fox from Cicero's *De officiis*, although Freccero's suggestion, "Medusa and the Madonna," in Ascoli and Kahn, *Machiavelli and Discourse of Literature*, 167, that he is echoing the words put into the mouth of Guido da Montefeltro by Dante in *Inferno*, Canto 27, is worth remarking. For comparison's between Cicero's text and Machiavelli's, see Marcia L. Colish, "Cicero's *De officiis* and Machiavelli's *Prince*," *Sixteenth Century Journal 9*

(1978): 81-93; she does not, however, appreciate the differences. Raimondi, "Politician and Centaur," 147, speaks of how Machiavelli uses "a cunning web of deceptions and denials that destroy the Ciceronian text without ever mentioning it," and he persuasively demonstrates, 153-56, how the line of thought of Machiavelli's Renaissance or humanist predecessors on Chiron, the "beast and the man," and the "lion and the fox," the thinking of figures such as Cristoforo Landino, Boccaccio, Coluccio Salutati, Marsilio Ficino, and Giovanni Pico della Mirandola, does not lead us to *The Prince*. Viroli, *Machiavelli*, 52, recognizes, "Most of the passages of the *The Prince* which have gained Machiavelli a sinister reputation are attacks on the main principles of Ciceronian political theory," but he believes that Machiavelli's attacks on that theory are "intended to restrict the range of its validity rather than to dismiss it altogether," 54.

29. Codevilla, *The Prince*, 65n287, points out that *della fede* means "of the Christian faith," as well as "trustworthiness."

30. See Strauss, "Niccolo Machiavelli" in Leo Strauss and Joseph Cropsey, eds., *History of Political Philosophy*, 3rd ed. (Chicago: University of Chicago Press, 1987), 302. On the connection between the "greatest examples" of chapter 6 and Severus in chapter 19, see Strauss, *Thoughts*, 60.

31. Strauss, "Machiavelli," 277. Fiore, *Machiavelli*, 43, finds resemblances to Nietzsche's *übermensch* in Machiavelli's "new prince."

32. Mainstream scholarly opinions on Machiavelli's teaching on fortune are canvassed by Thomas Flanagan, "The Concept of *Fortuna* in Machiavelli," in Parel, ed., *The Political Calculus*, 127-56; and Pitkin, *Fortune Is a Woman*, passim, but especially her chapter 6, "Fortune," 138-69. Kocis, *Machiavelli Redeemed*, 46-55, makes interesting observations on *fortuna* and *virtù*.

33. De Grazia, *Machiavelli in Hell*, 199, mistakes this for Machiavelli's own view, one of de Grazia's many mistakes.

34. *The Prince* celebrates the rape of Fortuna by force; *Mandragola*, the rape of Lucrezia by fraud: the virtues of the ferocious lion and the clever fox, respectively. Freccero, "Medusa and the Madonna," 164, calls this "a brutal figure for the refusal of Christian resignation."

35. Cf. Strauss, *Thoughts*, 216, 292.

36. Prezzolini, *Machiavelli*, 117, maintains that Machiavelli wrote the Dedicatory Letter after completing *The Prince*, and that chapter 26 is "an addendum."

37. Pitkin, *Fortune Is a Woman*, 43, observes, "Machiavelli often makes use of Christian terms for his own secular or anti-Christian purposes, speaking of 'redemption,' 'rebirth,' and 'sin.'" For a more comprehensive statement of Machiavelli's use of Christian doctrines for secular purposes, see Harvey C. Mansfield Jr., *Taming the Prince: The Ambivalence of Modern Executive Power* (New York: Free Press, 1989), 121-49.

38. Strauss, *Thoughts*, 83, remarks, "The ancient miracles happened on the way from the house of bondage to the promised land: they happened immediately before the revelation on Mount Sinai. What is imminent, Machiavelli suggests then, is not the conquest of a new promised land, but a new revelation, the revelation of a new code, of a new decalogue." See also 71-74, where Strauss notes, among other things, that Machiavelli does not call these extraordinary events "miracles."

39. Whitfield, *Machiavelli*, 84-85, speaks of "those closing passages of the *Prince*, where Machiavelli used with great naturalness, and with obvious conviction the same prophetic fervor, and the same Old Testament rhetoric" as Savonarola. For Frederico Chabod, *Machiavelli and the Renaissance*, 147, "This is the imagery of one whose emotion is still tempered by faith." For Ridolfi, *Life of Machiavelli*, 149, "the famous final exhortation redeems the book from its impious and cruel maxims," but then Ridolfi is

also impressed with Machiavelli's "religious and Christian conscience" (102). Fiore, *Machiavelli*, 49, speaks of "the ironic if not sarcastic assertion" of Machiavelli in chapter 26, that "God does not want to do everything." But Pocock, *The Machiavellian Moment*, 180-82, finds no irony in chapter 26; similarly, he thinks Machiavelli's comment, in chapter 11, that ecclesiastical principalities are exalted and maintained by God, is "perhaps not wholly ironical," 191, and he finds Machiavelli's language about Moses, in chapter 6, "irritatingly orthodox," 176. Berlin, "Originality," 55, thinks, "The last chapter of *The Prince* is scarcely the work of a detached, morally neutral observer." Viroli, *Machiavelli*, 23, seems impressed with Machiavelli's references to God in this chapter; according to Viroli, "Machiavelli's patriotism is not antireligious and not even antichristian; it is just anticlerical, as Florentine patriotism had been since the end of the fourteenth century," 165; and that "without patriotism . . . Machiavelli's thought becomes utterly unintelligible," 7; thus chapter 26 "is not an extravagant addition to *The Prince*, but its necessary completion," 6. De Grazia, *Machiavelli in Hell*, 101, believes that Machiavelli believes "Moses did talk with God," that he "discourses about God always in the conventional reverent attitude," 59; that "Niccolo cannot be found to speak irreverently of God," 87; that for "Niccolo," "all religions great and small are false; the exception is Christianity," 89. For this sort of thing, one is awarded a Pulitzer Prize.

40. "Even if, and precisely if we are forced to grant that his teaching is diabolical and he himself a devil, we are forced to remember the profound theological truth that the devil is a fallen angel. To recognize the diabolical character of Machiavelli's thought would mean to recognize in it a perverted nobility of a very high order." Strauss, *Thoughts*, 13.

Chapter 7

The Master Fool: The Conspiracy of Machiavelli's *Mandragola*

Introduction

Machiavelli is the master of conspiracy. He is both a master theoretician and master practitioner of conspiracy. He may have been the most ambitious conspirator in the history of political philosophy—if, that is, one assumes that modern political thought emerged around the turn of the sixteenth century as a revolutionary reaction against ancient thought in both its pagan and its Christian forms, and that Machiavelli is the architect of that revolution. Machiavelli announces the revolutionary nature of his teaching in both *The Prince* (chapter 15) and *Discourses on the First Ten Books of Titus Livius* (book 1, introduction), the two books that contain or comprise, by his own confession, everything he knows (*Prince,* dedicatory letter; *Discourses,* dedicatory letter).

It is certainly true that the theme of conspiracy plays a paramount role in Machiavelli's political thought. The longest chapters in *The Prince* and *Discourses* each deal with conspiracies. *The Prince,* chapter 19, "Of Avoiding Contempt and Hatred," discusses, among other things, how the Roman emperors executed and avoided conspiracies. It is here that we learn that the "bad" emperor, Severus, is the one who above all others combined the ferocity of a lion and the cleverness of a fox to gain and then secure sole possession of the empire and subsequently to frustrate every attempt to take it away from him. Severus is, indeed, the hero of *The Prince.*[1] *Discourses* 3.6, "On Conspiracies," provides an exhaustive analysis of no less than five baker's dozen conspiracies from ancient and modern times: how they were executed, how they succeeded, how they failed, how they could have succeeded, and what lessons aspiring conspirators should learn from these examples. Perhaps the most memorable passages in *Florentine Histories* are those dealing with the conspiracy against the Sforza, reported at the end of book 7, and the Pazzi conspiracy against the Medici, recounted in book 8, both of which were executed and involved executions, surely to Machiavelli's delight, in a church. Indeed, in the midst of relating these conspiracies, in the opening sentence of book 8 of *Florentine Histories*, Machiavelli writes, "Since the beginning of this eighth book lies in the middle of two conspiracies—one already narrated and taking place in Milan, the other yet to be narrated and occurring in Florence—it would appear the proper thing, if we want to follow our custom, to reason on the qualities of conspiracies and their importance. This would be done willingly if I had not spoken of it in another place or if it were a matter that could be passed over with brevity."[2] "Another place" where the qualities of conspiracies and their importance are discussed (and certainly not "passed over with brevity") is *Discourses* 3.6 (see also *Prince*, chapter 19). And, of course, there is *Mandragola*, a comedy about conspiracies. Its plot, much of which accords with Machiavelli's lessons about conspiracies in *The Prince* and *Discourses*, is nothing but a series of interrelated conspiracies. It should not be surprising, in light of Machiavelli's conspiratorial lessons, that *Mandragola* has elicited a variety of interpretations, for we submit that *Mandragola* is not only a play *about* conspiracies, it is a play that is, itself, a conspiracy.

We get indications of this in what are the most satisfying interpretations of *Mandragola* to date, those of Carnes Lord and Theodore Sumberg.[3] Lord manages to read *Mandragola* both as a self-contained comedy about a group of characters, all of whom are conspiring against each other, and as a somewhat cryptic, allegorical commentary on the politics of Machiavelli's Florence, that includes an esoteric confession on the part of Machiavelli that he was involved in a conspiracy in or about the year 1504 (the dramatic date of the action of *Mandragola*), against his political patron, Piero Soderini, who had by 1504 served for two years as chief executive for life of the Florentine republic. We do not wish to dispute Lord's suggestions about the political parallels in his allegorical reading of the play. But we have doubts about his reading of the play within the play's own horizon. In the end, the direction in which Sumberg points may prove more satisfactory. Sumberg suggests—and we intend to pursue this point—that Machiavelli has the last laugh, and at the expense of his audience:

> Machiavelli puts a mask on himself as well as his cast. The masked dramatist covers the face of the arch-conspirator. Against whom does he conspire? Against his audience, of course. While the audience laughs at the play, Machiavelli laughs at the audience. He puts horns on the audience laughing at the cuckoldry of Nicia. By making them laugh he disarms them, and amidst their laughter he and his associates go about busily uprooting the established order. He has the last laugh.[4]

Just as the characters within the play put on masks and conspire against each other, Machiavelli puts on a mask, as playwright, and conspires against us.

Sumberg's observation is one of the utmost importance; indeed, Sumberg, him-self, does not take it seriously enough. Thus Sumberg's interpretation, too, has its limitations, as will be discussed below.

Most of the play's interpreters have acknowledged that the spirit of the comedy is in harmony with the moral-political teaching that is found in Machia-velli's more overtly political writings.[5] Many have attempted to sort out the var-ious conspiracies that constitute the plot of the play in order to determine who is "The Prince" of *Mandragola*; that is, who ultimately is the master conspirator who dupes all others while never being duped in turn, the consummate "Machia-vellian"? Who best exemplifies Machiavellian *virtù*, the ability to act alternately in accord with traditional virtue and traditional vice, to be both human and bes-tial, to combine the fox and the lion most efficaciously in the pursuit of his per-sonal ambition, who has the audacity to flout traditional morality and piety but the political prudence not to flaunt it? The many interpretations of *Mandragola* have sought to discover the character with true Machiavellian designs. As a re-sult, the honor of chief conspirator has been granted to most of the leading char-acters of the play. We contend, however, that despite all the attention that has been paid to it, this question is yet to be answered satisfactorily. Interpreters have yet to expose fully the conspiracy *within Mandragola* because they have failed to notice the conspiracy that *is Mandragola*. "L'audace, toujours l'audace!" This is the proper motto for interpreters of Machiavelli. But it is not the best mode for expostulators to present their interpretations. In a more appro-priately Machiavellian conspiratorial mode, we do not wish to expose our own plot until the moment is ripe for its execution.

Callimaco, "the miserable lover"

At the beginning of *Mandragola* we learn that a "young woman" is to be tricked, and that Machiavelli's "Prologue" "would wish that [we the audience] might be tricked, as she was."[6] The romantic lead of the play, Callimaco, is burning with desire for the beautiful Lucrezia Calfucci, a married woman. He has traveled with his servant, Siro, all the way from Paris to his native Florence after hearing of Lucrezia's charms from a relative of Messer Nicia Calfucci, her husband.[7] Sadly for him, she is "extremely honest" and "in all ways alien to the things of love" (1.1). If Callimaco is to satisfy his lust, he will need to use ex-traordinary means, even if they are "dangerous, harmful, scandalous" (1.3). Two things give him hope: he believes that although Messer Nicia is very rich and a doctor of law (*dottore*), he "is the simplest and most stupid man in Florence," and he knows that both the Calfuccis yearn to have children, although they seem unable to produce any (1.1). Callimaco's beliefs serve to set the plot in Florence into motion. In the end, Callimaco gains the object of his lust through an out-landish ploy that tricks Lucrezia into compliance, with the willing acquiescence of her impotent husband.

The first and most obvious candidate for "Prince" of *Mandragola* is Calli-maco. Although Callimaco has given his life over to "studies," "pleasures," and "business," he seems to have the nature of a lion, or at least he is brave enough to risk everything to possess Lucrezia (1.1). Of course, strong erotic desire need not conduce to martial valor and may even militate against it (for the past ten years Callimaco found that he could live "more securely" in Paris than in his native Florence), but Callimaco says that he will risk death to satisfy his yearnings (1.1, 3). His passions are the kind that "men and gods alike dread" ("Song" after the first act). His enthusiasm rouses others to follow; it binds his conspiracy together by giving his accomplices, Ligurio and Siro, a vicarious share in the thrill of accomplishing a difficult feat (1.3; 2.4).

Salvatore Di Maria sees "Callimaco as both a Machiavellian and a social hero exploiting and exposing Messer Nicia as a social misfit"; for Di Maria, "Callimaco's major strength lies in his propensity to assess and act upon the situation at hand." His success in finally seducing Lucrezia is "not fortuitous," for it indicates the value that Machiavelli places on *virtù,* or boldness of action combined with adaptability of means.[8] Lord, too, maintains that "Callimaco is the natural or 'virtuous' prince in the Machiavellian sense." According to his allegorical reading of the play, "Only a prince of this kind is capable of satisfying the most fundamental longing of the people of Florence—the longing not for freedom but for security and efficient government."[9]

But Callimaco has serious shortcomings; too serious to cast him in the role of "Machiavellian prince." For one, he is unable to control his passions: He cannot sleep, eat, converse, or take pleasure in anything because of his lust for Lucrezia. More important, he is willing to risk something "scandalous" and thereby to expose himself to unnecessary danger to gratify his desires. Ligurio has to remind Callimaco not to speak so intemperately and to curb his rushes of desire (1.3). Indeed, Callimaco is quite inept without his guide. As Mera Flaumenhaft points out, when "Callimaco's *'animo'* fails, it is Ligurio who always thinks of the 'remedy.'"[10] Callimaco is in fact completely dependent on Ligurio for concocting, adapting, and executing the scheme that leads to his conquest of Lucrezia. "But," as Augustus Mastri remarks, "if a prince puts himself entirely in the hands of someone else, he will eventually lose his state to his underling."[11] In *The Prince,* chapter 22, Machiavelli presents this lesson under the heading, "Of Those Whom Princes Have As Secretaries." He argues that there are three kinds of brains: "one that understands by itself, another that discerns what others understand, the third that understands neither by itself nor through others; the first is most excellent, the second excellent, and the third useless."[12] Callimaco certainly lacks a "most excellent" brain, as can be seen by the tenor of the questions he poses to Ligurio: "But what can I do? What course can I take? Where can I turn? How will this serve us? What are you saying?" (1.3). Callimaco may not have the second sort of brain either; for example, even after the plot begins to unfold he asks Ligurio, "Where do you want me to go now?" (2.6). It is, we believe, Callimaco's lack of a "most excellent" or even an "excellent" brain that disqualifies him as "Machiavellian prince." It is what prompts Sumberg to depict Callimaco and Ligurio together in council as "the complete statesman," and

Lord to assign Ligurio the honor of Machiavelli's "self-portrait."[13]

Ligurio, "the darling of malice"

Mark Hulliung proffers the view of many interpreters of the play when he claims that "Ligurio is the perfect Machiavellian."[14] After all, Ligurio apparently originates the ploy, organizes the cabal, and directs the intrigue that surmounts the major stumbling block to Callimaco's wish: Lucrezia's reluctance to commit adultery. He tests his cunning against her virtue and employs the *mandragola*— the ersatz potion that is supposed to cure her alleged infertility—to win victory. (Since the *mandragola* is to be drunk by the man who copulates with Lucrezia, it is obviously another "potion" that effects her impregnation.)

Yet for all his cunning, Ligurio, too, does not quite fit the role of "Machiavellian prince." As Hanna Pitkin points out, Ligurio thinks that Lucrezia is "fit to rule a kingdom";[15] but would Machiavelli himself have such regard for a woman who is so easily seduced? Sumberg remarks that Ligurio is not a passionate person, and argues that he would never have instigated this (or any other) plot without the urging of an ardent person such as Callimaco.[16] In fact, it is difficult to understand exactly what interest Ligurio has in aiding Callimaco. Callimaco claims that Ligurio will gain "a good sum of money" if the conspiracy succeeds, and "a lunch and supper" if it fails. But Ligurio will gain more than money from Callimaco and a few dinners with Messer Nicia: he will acquire the status of social respectability; he will be granted free access to Messer Nicia's house and thereby gain entry into a social circle that has been denied him in the past. Are such plebeian motivations worthy, however, of a true Machiavellian prince? Other than the obvious fact that some people can use their calculating cunning to ascend the social ladder, what point would Machiavelli be teaching if the satisfaction of Ligurio's desires were the lesson of the play?

There is another, and more serious, problem with the theory that Ligurio is the master conspirator. At the crucial moment when Lucrezia discovers that Callimaco is her lover, and he proposes that he be so perpetually, Ligurio has no control over events. Indeed, unlike the *three* in the bedroom, he is not present and must leave her decision to chance. Would a true Machiavellian be absent when Lady Fortuna was being conquered?

Lucrezia, "a shrewd young woman"

Shall we dare to suggest Lucrezia—a woman—is the "prince"?[17] We are not the first to have suspicions about Lucrezia. Susan Behuniak-Long argues that it "may well be that readers have indeed been tricked as Machiavelli warned" (more correctly, as the "Prologue" says), because Lucrezia, who is so widely understood to be an honest and pious woman who experiences a "fall" from goodness during the play, is in fact of questionable character from the start.[18] "Most of what we know of Lucrezia is not from first hand information but from what others say about her throughout the play."[19] According to Behuniak-Long, if we examine Lucrezia's actions, however, a different picture of her character emerges; according to Behuniak-Long, her virtue is more imagined than real: she willingly consents, for example, to a plan that involves murder. Once the deception is uncovered, she accepts a stranger—one who has essentially just raped her—as her lover, and assents to conceive his child.[20] Does this not demonstrate, Behuniak-Long asks rhetorically, that "Lucrezia is the key to reaching the deeper level of the play"?[21]

We think that Behuniak-Long is on to something and offer our own, even more censorious, suspicions. Clearly, Lucrezia realizes what has happened on the night of her seduction and readily acquiesces. She does not resist the advances of Callimaco, yet she does not respond to his proposal of marriage. She takes Callimaco as her lord, master, guide, father, and defender, but not her husband. The most telling evidence, however, of Lucrezia's possible involvement in the conspiracy is that she mysteriously, indeed inexplicably, knows *in advance* that Messer Nicia will make Callimaco his close friend and godfather to the child, that Callimaco will go to the church as a member of the family later that morning, that he will be invited to dinner that evening, and that he will come and go from the Calfucci house "without suspicion" (5.4). It is indeed startling to realize that Callimaco's report of Lucrezia's instructions to him in the early morning hours after the satisfaction of his desires are identical to Messer Nicia's instructions to him given later that morning (5.4; 5.6). This leads us to recall that it is not Callimaco but Ligurio who suggests that Callimaco perpetuate the liaison with Lucrezia, which leads us to wonder, was it Ligurio's idea in the first place, or someone else's? Does Callimaco succeed in seducing Lucrezia with the aid of his advisor or does Lucrezia succeed in seducing Callimaco with the aid of her advisor?

Messer Nicia, "the not-very-astute *dottore*"

Messer Nicia is universally judged a simpleton. He is easily taken in by a ludicrous ruse and thereby cuckolded. His desire for children, his need to keep up social appearances, and his unfailing ability to be duped make him the object of contempt and derision. "Nicia is comical precisely because he considers himself shrewd and socially aware, when, in fact, his behavior not only offends social decorum, it also exhibits a clear lack of *virtù,* since he is unable to discern fact from fiction. In Machiavellian terms, he is laughable essentially because he fails to perceive actual truth (*realtà effettuale della cose*), allowing himself to be taken in by appearances."[22]

Messer Nicia has many traits that have made it difficult for commentators to draw a clear picture of him. Their interpretations are either self-contradictory or do not square with the text. For instance, Lord argues that Messer Nicia represents the "political simplicity and the frivolity of princes" in Italy; nevertheless, he has somehow acquired "a certain awareness of the defects of his class."[23]

Flaumenhaft asserts that "Italian Christianity, along with Nicia's indolent bourgeois life, has made him impotent in more than one way and, therefore, subject to the deceits of more vigorous men," but she admits that "Nicia is not a devout practicing Christian."[24] Sumberg reasons that Messer Nicia "will kill a man to have an heir"; however, this same "man, who is an accomplice in a planned murder, could not be more law-abiding. Nicia pleads repeatedly with the fellow-plotters not to transgress the law, even in its most picayune detail."[25] But, far from being "a pillar of respectability in the community," as Sumberg suggests,[26] Messer Nicia states that his Florence does not "appreciate any *virtù*," especially his kind: he has never held a political position, and although clearly he covets "status," he cannot "find a dog to bark at him" (2.3).[27]

Di Maria avers that "Nicia is so engrossed in attempting to enforce social etiquette that he is hardly alarmed by the curious familiarity existing between a marriage-broker turned parasite and a renowned doctor."[28] But why would a person "engrossed in attempting to enforce social etiquette" associate with "a marriage-broker turned parasite" at all? Di Maria asserts that Messer Nicia is easily beguiled by "Maestro" Callimaco's use of Latin, and thus accepts Callimaco's authority as a doctor of medicine: "Since Callimaco's medical elucidation is altogether meaningless and outright idiotic, the *bene ragionare* which wins Nicia's admiration does not refer to the doctor's science, but to the Latin rhetoric informing it."[29] Again we ask, could the man who read the works of Boethius, which were written in Latin ("Prologue"), really be so easily charmed by a few Latin phrases? Messer Nicia's alleged inability to comprehend Latin, despite his claim to Siro that he studied it (2.3), is supposedly indicated by his failure to understand "Maestro" Callimaco's diagnosis of his impotence, when spoken in Latin. He objects to Callimaco's claim only when it is repeated in Italian. This proves to Di Maria that Messer Nicia did not understand the Latin. But we suggest an alternative: Might not Messer Nicia be luring Callimaco into his web? Messer Nicia does not protest until the diagnosis is made in Italian because he is willing to abide the truth about his impotence when it is uttered by "Maestro" Callimaco in Latin, that is, in private; however, he is unwilling to have it repeated in Italian, in front of others, that is, publicly. This would lead the "real" Callimaco to conclude that Messer Nicia is a fool, easily impressed by a few high-blown Latin phrases, who is desperately trying to conceal his inadequacies from the public, here represented by Ligurio. But perhaps Messer Nicia maintains a public facade of virility, and at the same time plays the fool before the "Maestro," because he wishes to present himself to the "real" Callimaco as someone easily duped. It should be remembered that for the plot to succeed two things must happen: Messer Nicia must apparently be duped by Callimaco and the plot must never be uncovered. Clearly, Messer Nicia does not want his double deception of Callimaco revealed. He demands that Callimaco tell no one of their plan involving the *mandragola*: "Above all," he implores him, "don't let it be known" (2.6).

Readers of Machiavelli's conspiratorial comedy ought not be so easily deceived by appearances as Messer Nicia always seems to be. We propose a reconsideration of the obvious folly of Messer Nicia. In Machiavelli's terms, we ask, what is the "effectual truth" (*Prince*, chapter 15) of Messer Nicia's folly?

Messer Nicia, the Master Fool

It is often asserted that Machiavelli is a teacher of political means. He is scientific in the modern sense of the word because he has no teaching about the purpose or end of political life. Instead, he examines and offers advice on the most efficient means of attaining whatever objects people desire. If Callimaco's desire were the only catalyst within *Mandragola*, that claim might satisfactorily express the teaching of the play. We must not forget, however, that there are two desires in the play that give impetus to the grand fraud: Callimaco's lust for Lucrezia and Messer Nicia's longing for children, or to put it formally, a new foundation of his family.

Messer Nicia Calfucci is a wealthy doctor, "a *dottore* who learned in Buethius a great deal of law" ("Prologue").[30] Boethius was a scholar and principal minister to Theodoric, the Ostrogothic king of Italy. His major work, *The Consolation of Philosophy*, was written while he was in prison for plotting to overthrow Theodoric in an attempt to restore the Roman Senate and to reestablish the ancient liberties of Rome. He died without revealing his part in the plot.[31] Among his other scholarly achievements, Boethius was a translator of Aristotle. Moreover, although he never avowed Christianity, he was honored as a Christian martyr. His two sons became consuls of Rome.[32] Now if Messer Nicia learned a great deal from Boethius, not only might he know the classical Greeks and value being honored by the Christians, he would also understand the importance of refoundations or new foundations. And just as Boethius was denied political activity while in prison, Messer Nicia (like Machiavelli, himself) is kept from political opportunity in Florence. Boethius was unable to create or re-create a political order, while Messer Nicia lacks the power to create or re-create his family, at least by nature.

Messer Nicia is married to the most beautiful woman in Florence, who is much his junior. What is his problem? He is apparently deficient in two ways: he cannot produce children and he cannot fully control his wife on account of her piety. Yet, Lucrezia's impeccable propriety is important to Messer Nicia, as are all appearances of being law-abiding and respectable. In order for Messer Nicia to overcome his natural deficiency and lay a new foundation for his family, he must locate an appropriate stud for his wife and find a way around his wife's religious scruples, all the while maintaining appearances. Moreover, if fortune is to be mastered, the liaison must be perpetuated over time to insure him the son or sons that he desires. To see how Messer Nicia seeks to achieve his twin goals one must investigate his relationship with Callimaco and Ligurio.

Messer Nicia remarks that Ligurio and Callimaco live like beasts (5.6). In *The Prince* (chapter 18), Machiavelli counsels that a prince should act like two particular beasts, the lion and the fox. Lions are fearless and foxes are cunning.

These qualities are rarely found in the same individual; still, for difficult ventures to succeed, both are necessary. To facilitate his scheme, Messer Nicia needs the boldness of Callimaco and the shrewdness of Ligurio. But is it not Messer Nicia, himself, who knows his own nature—including his impotence—and thus knows when he must change his nature, combining or prudently alternating the lion and the fox in personae that enable him to master his (ill) fortune?

Callimaco is a brash young man whose parents died in his youth. His intense passions have not been tamed by parental instruction. Love of tradition, devotion to religion, or respect for authority loom small in Callimaco's life. Rather, his untamed erotic impulse drives him to pursue above everything the satisfaction of his lust for Lucrezia. His *eros* is a propelling force of the play. But Callimaco cannot control it. He has the perfect kind of soul to be ruled by someone who possesses self-control and can therefore control others. Is not Callimaco, as Aristotle suggests of people who cannot rule their passions, the natural slave to the person who can (*Politics*, 1254b1-1255a1)? We dare to suggest that Callimaco does not have to suppress his *eros* because Messer Nicia has his own plans for it, plans that depend on its full vigor. Callimaco is the perfect live-in lover for Messer Nicia's beautiful young wife; that is, as Messer Nicia himself says, Callimaco is the perfect "staff" of his old age (5.6). Callimaco is Messer Nicia's lion.

Ligurio is a "marriage broker" with whom Messer Nicia maintains an acquaintance that involves giving him money (1.1). Despite a long-standing relationship, however, Ligurio is never admitted into Messer Nicia's home—that is, not until after Callimaco's conquest of Lucrezia. Messer Nicia needs the assistance of a man like Ligurio to accomplish his grand design. Ligurio is Messer Nicia's fox. But the fox must not be allowed too near the lamb. Ligurio thinks that Lucrezia is not only "beautiful," but "wise, well-mannered, and fit to govern a kingdom" (1.3). Given the opportunity, this fox might himself lie down with the lamb. This, however, would foil Messer Nicia's designs, for Lucrezia would never accept as her lover a man of Ligurio's vulgar status, certainly not over the long term necessary to produce Messer Nicia's sons. Furthermore, Ligurio lacks the aristocratic seed Messer Nicia wants from his "staff."[33]

As we have seen, Ligurio is often taken to be Machiavelli's "Machiavellian" character. Yet Ligurio is instructed and scolded by Messer Nicia on a number of occasions, particularly concerning the best means of carrying out the conspiracy. It is Messer Nicia who tells Ligurio that he is "wrong," that he has "a mouth full of milk," when he rejects Ligurio's scheme of going to the baths to consummate the seduction, probably because Messer Nicia fears that at a public place there is no way to control who could approach Lucrezia (1.2). It is Messer Nicia who first subtly introduces the idea of a doctor of medicine, the scheme that is later adopted as the means of gaining intimate access to his wife (1.2): "The *Dottore* has commissioned me to find a doctor," Ligurio tells Callimaco (1.3). It is Messer Nicia who directs Ligurio to call Callimaco *maestro* so that he can effectively masquerade as a doctor (2.1). It is Messer Nicia who points out that for the intrigue to go forward, Lucrezia's piety must first be circumvented by "way of her confessor" (2.6). He castigates Ligurio, calling him "really dumb," for not informing him of all parts of the plan, even picayune details (4.9).

It is true, of course, that once Ligurio gets hold of the plot he uses his shrewdness to overcome Lucrezia's resistance, her moral reservations. He enlists a priest who will absolve her of any sin. But she is hesitant to see her confessor; it seems she had suffered sexual harassment at the hands of a priest. To triumph over this reluctance, Ligurio appeals to an authority, the most natural of all authorities, the parental. Parents command dominion over their children because parents claim to guide children to what is good for them. Parents are able to direct children toward what is good for them because parents have more wisdom than children. Wisdom comes with age. Thus, parents acquire authority by being old. The old, in other words, is synonymous with the good. But Sostrata, Lucrezia's old mother, used to be "good company," as Callimaco remarks, when she was not so old (1.1). Sostrata quickly becomes part of the conspiracy and convinces her daughter to see the priest, Frate Timoteo. In Machiavelli's world the old may not always teach the young to be good, but they may teach the young how to have a good time.

How can Ligurio undermine Lucrezia's religious conviction? Again he appeals to an authority to corrupt her, this time the authority of the Church. First, he entraps Frate Timoteo into joining the conspiracy with a bribe. Timoteo agrees to sanction an abortion in exchange for a donation to his parish, on the ground that it "will do good for the greatest number" (3.4). Then, when the need for the abortion turns out to be entirely fictitious, he induces the frate to cooperate in the plot against Lucrezia. The frate agrees to sanction the abortion both under his own authority and that of the abbess, suggesting that the Church is so badly in need of donations that it will act against its own moral canons. He admits that the Church is becoming corrupt and that its influence is declining (5.1).

When we first meet Frate Timoteo he is talking with a woman about her deceased husband. She complains that he mistreated her, perhaps in a sexual way, but that the Church could do nothing about it. She then asks if the Turks will invade Italy—she fears the impaling she might suffer. The frate assures her that the Turks will not invade if she keeps up her devotions (3.3).[34] Lucrezia too fears that sin will cause her death (3.11). She is pious because of the dread of retribution both in this life and in the afterlife. From these examples we can infer that in the play religion claims to deliver both earthly felicity and eternal salvation. But since it derives its ultimate strength from being other-worldly, it cannot truly satisfy worldly desires. To be effective in the visible world, it must counsel taking "a certain good" over "an uncertain evil" (3.11).

Eventually the inconsistency of religion will cause its doom. Another faith will have to take its place. In a way, the *mandragola*, which is supposed to cure Lucrezia's alleged infertility, is a new kind of faith, a new mode: outwardly, everyone professes to believe in its powers; it allows them all to maintain their propriety. But the new mode is merely instrumental (2.1; 3.12; 4.2). Its function is to satiate the temporal appetites of human beings—as, of course, it does for every character in the play (with the possible exception of Siro). Just as the *mandragola* sanctifies an adulterous sexual union by joining it to generation, so the new ethical mode disguises human desires by acknowledging them as moral actions (later called rights). The new ethical mode rests on a conspiracy in which each person gets what he or she wants, but each is fearful of admitting his or her complicity (4.6). Mutual complicity in crime is the ground of Machiavellian trust; indeed, it establishes the "common good" and is the basis of citizenship in Machiavelli's new political order. To establish the new order, the remnants of the old must be swept away. This involves an inversion of standards. (Thus Callimaco's beauty is turned to ugliness by his preposterous disguise [5.1].) Eventually the new order can be institutionalized, as Callimaco and Lucrezia are joined in quasi-matrimony by Messer Nicia himself (5.6). If Lucrezia is tricked into committing adultery it is because she mistakes a new mode for her old religion (5.4). She does not abandon her husband, rather she "lives to enjoy continued sexual infidelities with an untroubled conscience, but is careful to preserve her reputation, that is, the appearance of honor."[35] The old forms are maintained although they contain "new matter" (see *Discourses* I.25).

During the change from old to new, the founder must insure that nothing is overlooked (5.2). For example, on the night that the disguised comic band goes out to ensnare a "victim" to copulate with Lucrezia, Messer Nicia is the only one carrying a weapon (4.8). Sumberg argues that there "is no show of force in the play. No one carries a weapon with the exception of Nicia who puts on a small sword upon joining the plotters to find the young man to drag to Lucrezia. But he never unsheathes the sword and its uselessness is emphasized by the irony of his buckling it on the moment before he loses his wife. . . . The action of the play consequently gives the lie to the statement of the *Prince* (chapter 6) that the armed prophets win and the unarmed lose."[36] But seen in a different light Messer Nicia's behavior seems prudent. He carries a sword in case something goes awry with the intricate and potentially embarrassing plot, a scheme that could come to the attention of the Florentine magistrates (3.6).[37] Even a small sword can be quite effective when no one else is armed.[38] He does not use the weapon because the intrigue unfolds according to his wishes and his plan calls for the use of the sword only if something goes wrong. Messer Nicia is not losing his wife; he is gaining a son. Prophets succeed best when they can use fraud as well as force (*Prince*, chapter 18).

Although Messer Nicia's activities on the evening of the conspiracy's culmination are made to look ridiculous, appearances can be deceiving; they take on a far different complexion if we entertain the possibility that he is aware of what is going on. The apparent deception of Messer Nicia rests, for example, on his inability to recognize people. He fails to identify the frate disguised as Callimaco and Callimaco masquerading as a street musician with a twisted face and a large nose (4.2; 4.8). But are Messer Nicia's powers of perception that flawed? As Lord points out, "In spite of his comic ignorance of the world outside his native city, Nicia boasts of having visited Pisa, and he promptly recalls for Ligurio the correct name of a fort in the vicinity (the Verrucola) recently occupied by the Florentines in the long war against their former subjects."[39] He is also able to detail its size (1.2). Furthermore, consider Callimaco's disguise. Are a twisted face and a fake nose really sufficient concealment to fool even a child? The features of the face, no matter how contorted, are readily distinguishable. In fact, children and childish people are often the most difficult to fool with such games. It is true that Messer Nicia professes not to have recognized Callimaco (5.2), but the supposedly childish Messer Nicia has an interest in acquiescing in this charade, because he is childless.

But Messer Nicia more than acquiesces, he insists "that nothing . . . [be] done under a hood": As the plot is about to reach its climax, so to speak, he uses his own hands to make certain that things are proceeding according to plan (5.2). Unlike Ligurio, who is absent, Messer Nicia takes the advice of Machiavelli's *Prince* (chapter 18):

> Men in general judge more by their eyes than by their hands, because seeing is given to everyone, touching to few. Everyone sees how you appear, few touch what you are; and these few dare not oppose the opinion of the many, who have the majesty of the state to defend them; and in the actions of all men, and especially princes, where there is no court to appeal to, one looks to the end. So let a prince win and maintain his state: the means will always be judged honorable, and will be praised by everyone. For the vulgar are taken in by the appearance and the outcome of a thing, and in this world there is no one but the vulgar.

So thoroughly does Messer Nicia wish to conquer chance that he allows Callimaco unlimited access to his wife in case the couple's first union does not produce a child, or the first child is not a boy, or the first boy is not possessed of the right character.[40] But we should not be surprised if the new union lasts but a few years.

Callimaco and Sostrata knew each other some time in the past (1.1). Perhaps the old woman told Messer Nicia about Callimaco, and Nicia somehow influenced his relative, Cammillo, to entice the aristocratic Florentine back to Italy. Only a handsome and passionate young man, preferably a Florentine nobleman, could overcome Lucrezia's reluctance to commit adultery. Messer Nicia complains throughout the play of his difficulties controlling his wife. But, in what way does he wish to control her? Perhaps he has asked her to undergo the sixteenth-century equivalent of artificial insemination, but her propriety compelled her to refuse. Once she has seen the beautiful Callimaco, however, and tasted the fruit, she becomes an accommodating participant in Messer Nicia's scheme. Yet, if this orphaned Florentine expatriate, without family to avenge him—not even the young sons he has sired—were to meet with some ill fortune or accident after some years—say, he died in the arms of another woman and thereby alienated Lucrezia's affections—no one would raise too much of a disturbance.[41]

Conclusion

Mandragola is a play about conspiracies, and *Mandragola* is, itself, a conspiracy. All of the various conspiracy theories put forward by the interpreters of *Mandragola* have a certain credence, and it is clear that Machiavelli wanted his audience to wonder about who was at the center of the plot's intrigue. Machiavelli hoped to stimulate his readers to think the way skillful conspirators should: trust no one fully, including, if not the playwright himself, at least his "Prologue" and "Songs." Machiavelli both conspires with and against his audience; he tests his audience; and those who pass the test, he trains. He can make accomplices of the best of his audience only if the play's conspiracy is similar to real-life conspiracies: complex, intricate, and full of false leads. Among his friends, Machiavelli referred to his play as "Messer Nicia";[42] it is called *La Mandragola* by his "Prologue." Machiavelli certainly knew enough not to call attention to his true intentions, not to give his conspiracy away by naming names.

The key to *Mandragola* can be found in *Discourses* 3.2. There Machiavelli recounts the famous story of the Roman maiden Lucrezia who chose to commit suicide rather than live with the dishonor of having been raped. The rape of *Mandragola*'s Lucrezia by fraud cannot help but bring to mind the rape of the historical Lucrezia by force, and Machiavelli surely chose the name in order to bring the incident to mind. The project of Brutus was the overthrow of the Tarquins and the establishment of Roman republican liberty. He used the "accident" of the rape of Lucrezia as a means to his political end. To effect his scheme, he played the fool. Machiavelli's lesson is revealed in the title of *Discourses* 3.2: "At the Right Time It Is the Highest Wisdom to Simulate Folly."[43] This lesson Messer Nicia, too, learned, perhaps from reading Livy in Latin (as Machiavelli did), as well as Boethius.

Messer Nicia never prays to heaven for children. He takes matters into his own hands. He overcomes the defects of his nature by playing the fool and by allowing others to believe that he has been deceived by the *mandragola* scheme. Not only does Messer Nicia wish to have progeny, he hopes to control the future, if you will, to conquer chance.

Messer Nicia is aware that his Lucrezia aspires to the same sort of reputation for virtue as her ancient Roman namesake. If he is to safely cajole her into engaging in a dishonorable act, he must do so by means of the wisdom gained from both Boethius's and Brutus's examples. Lucrezia cannot be publicly humiliated; her reputation must be maintained. Moreover, the plot can never be revealed if Messer Nicia is to be the acknowledged father of Lucrezia's offspring. He must overcome his defective nature, but he must conceal the consequent artificial or conventional character of his relationship to his children. To found his family he must conquer his ill fortune; to do so, he knows, as does

Machiavelli, that to overcome his ill fortune, it is the highest wisdom to feign folly at the right time, "and this is sufficiently done by praising, speaking, seeing, and doing things contrary to your way of thinking" (*Discourses* 3.2).[44]

Machiavelli is surely a serious student of politics, yet he is the author of this funny play. Like Messer Nicia, Machiavelli plays the fool. As Sumberg argues, "Only as a fool can a wise man mingle unmolested with the people. Machiavelli understood Socrates' fate as well as anyone. Playing the clown is even more necessary for Machiavelli than for earlier philosophers, for he starts a new and more dangerous kind of philosophy."[45] Both Machiavelli and his incredible "fool," Messer Nicia (who, as has often been suggested, may be named after Nicias, the leader of the ill-fated Athenian expedition to Sicily), teach us to what lengths human beings must go to subdue an otherwise hostile nature.[46] If they are shrewd enough and learn the correct lessons, Machiavelli's students can avoid the fate of Nicias, avoid being victims of ill fortune. To become shrewd enough, they must understand the human condition, the things of this world: that whatever possible order exists among the chance occurrences of the universe is humanly created.[47]

Notes

This chapter, co-authored with James F. Pontuso, was originally published in *Perspectives on Political Science 25* (1996). Reprinted with permission of Heldref Publications. I have made some revisions. Thanks to Harvey C. Mansfield Jr. for graciously providing a transcript of a lecture on *Mandragola*.

1. Leo Strauss, "Machiavelli," in L. Strauss and J. Cropsey, eds., *History of Political Philosophy*, 3rd. ed. (Chicago: University of Chicago Press, 1987), 302. Compare the ingenious reading of Machiavelli's treatment of Cesare Borgia, who is often identified as the hero of *The Prince,* in John T. Scott and Vickie B. Sullivan, "Patricide and the Plot of *The Prince*: Cesare Borgia and Machiavelli's Italy," *American Political Science Review 88* (1994): 887-900.

2. Machiavelli, *Florentines Histories*, trans. Laura F. Banfield and Harvey C. Mansfield Jr. (Princeton, N.J.: Princeton University Press, 1988), 317.

3. Carnes Lord, "On Machiavelli's *Mandragola*," *Journal of Politics 41* (1979): 806-27; Theodore A. Sumberg, "*La Mandragola*: An Interpretation," *Review of Politics 23* (1961): 320-40.

4. Sumberg, "*La Mandragola*," 337.

5. Mark Hulliung, "Machiavelli's *Mandragola*: A Day and Night in the Life of a Citizen," *Review of Politics 40* (1978): 32-57, represents this position most clearly: "The true link between seduction and conspiracy, as understood by Machiavelli, is that they are virtually interchangeable phenomena, to be conducted according to identical rules" (39).

6. All quotations are from Machiavelli, *Mandragola*, trans. Mera J. Flaumenhaft (Prospect Heights, Ill.: Waveland Press, 1981). Citations in the text of this essay are by act and scene number, in parentheses (e.g., 1.1)

7. One of Sumberg's errors is to argue that Messer Nicia is the ideal object of a con-

spiracy because he has no relatives to avenge him (Sumberg, *"La Mandragola,"* 332). He forgets about Cammillo Calfucci. Indeed, everyone forgets about Cammillo Calfucci, who plays a critical role in the architectonic conspiracy within *Mandragola*.

8. Salvatore Di Maria, "The Ethical Premises for the *Mandragola*'s New Society," *Italian Culture 7* (1986-89): 19, 21, 25-26.

9. Lord, *"Mandragola,"* 812-13. Sumberg, *"La Mandragola,"* 332, also argues that Callimaco has political ambition, but he gives no textual evidence for his assertion. Mera Flaumenhaft, "The Comic Remedy: Machiavelli's *Mandragola*," *Interpretation 7* (1978): 33-74, points out that "Machiavelli goes out of his way to emphasize that the protagonist of his play is an *unpatriotic* man" (42). We note that Callimaco had never intended to return to Florence (1.1).

10. Flaumenhaft, "Comic Remedy," 39.

11. Augustus Mastri, "Machiavelli's *La Mandragola*: A Political and Personal Statement," *Ball State Review 28* (1987): 3-15, 9; see also Sumberg, *"La Mandragola,"* 331-32; Hulliung, "Day and Night," 44; Joseph A. Barber, "The Irony of Lucrezia: Machiavelli's *donna di virtù*," *Studies in Philology 82* (1985): 450-59, 453; and Wayne A. Rebhorn, *Foxes and Lions: Machiavelli's Confidence Men* (Ithaca, N.Y.: Cornell University Press, 1988), 54.

12. Machiavelli, *The Prince*, trans. Harvey C. Mansfield Jr. (Chicago: Chicago University Press, 1985), 92.

13. Sumberg, *"La Mandragola,"* 332; Lord, *"Mandragola,"* 87.

14. Hulliung, "Day and Night," 44; see also Barber, "Irony of Lucrezia," 453; Lord, *"Mandragola,"* 817; and Mastri, "Political and Personal Statement," 10-11.

15. Hanna Pitkin, *Fortune Is a Woman: Gender and Politics in the Thought of Machiavelli* (Berkeley: University of California Press, 1984), 112.

16. Sumberg, *"La Mandragola,"* 324, 332.

17. "Prince" is a technical term in Machiavelli's works, not reserved for a single male, but used to designate whoever holds final executive power in the state. At one point in the *Discourses*, for example, Machiavelli calls the Roman Senate "prince" of Rome (1.38), and at another, the Decemvirs "absolute prince of Rome" (1.40). In *The Prince*, chapter 20, he claims that "in our times fortresses have not been seen to bring profit to any prince, unless to the Countess of Forli, when Count Girolamo, her consort, died; for by means of a fortress she was able to escape a popular uprising, to await help from Milan, and to recover her state," i.e., the countess is a "prince."

18. Susan Behuniak-Long, "The Significance of Lucrezia in Machiavelli's *La Mandragola*," *Review of Politics 51* (1989): 264-83, 265.

19. Ibid., 267-68.

20. Ibid., 268-70.

21. Ibid., 279; see also Jack D'Amico, "The *virtù* of Women: Machiavelli's *Mandragola* and *Clizia*," *Interpretation 12* (1984): 261-73, 268-70.

22. Di Maria, "Ethical Premises," 27. Even Machiavelli's "Prologue" and "Songs" join in to belittle Messer Nicia, calling him "a not-so-astute *dottore*" (*una dottore poco astuto*) and stating that he "would believe an ass would fly" ("Prologue" and "Song" after the first act). The same "Prologue"—which we are suggesting should be treated as a character in the play, one whose views are not necessarily identical to Machiavelli's— notes that Lucrezia is shrewd (*una giovane accorta*), Callimaco a miserable lover and a monster (*un amante meschino, monstro*), Timoteo an ill-living frate (*un frate mall vissuto*), and Ligurio a parasite, the darling of malice (*un parassito, di malizia li cucco*). But are any of those fully accurate descriptions of the characters portrayed? They seem to be at odds with at least some aspect of their behavior. Perhaps we should heed Machiavelli's

advice and "not pay attention to words." The "Prologue" states explicitly that Machiavelli would wish that we (the audience) would be tricked as she (Lucrezia) was. The "Prologue" also states that these characters are "yours," meaning the audience's, or perhaps Francesco Guiccardini's. The "Prologue" and "Songs," which were not originally in the play, were written at the request of Guiccardini. In a letter in which Machiavelli responds to some questions that Guiccardini had about the play, he quotes the second decade of Livy to him, which was not extant (*The Letters of Machiavelli*, ed. Allan Gilbert [Chicago: University of Chicago Press, 1961], 213). In another letter to Guiccardini, Machiavelli writes, "For a long time I have not said what I believe, nor do I ever believe what I say, and if indeed sometimes I do happen to tell the truth, I hide it among so many lies that it is hard to find" (Machiavelli, *The Chief Works and Others*, trans. Allan Gilbert, 3 vols. ([Durham, N.C.: Duke University Press, 1989]), 2: 973.

23. Lord, "*Mandragola*," 817.

24. Flaumenhaft, "Comic Remedy," 48. We note, in fact, that it is "more than ten years" since he has even spoken to the Frate (3.2).

25. Sumberg, "*La Mandragola*," 329.

26. Ibid., 320.

27. See Harvey C. Mansfield Jr., *Machiavelli's Virtue* (Chicago: University of Chicago Press, 1996), 281-94, on *stato* and *status*.

28. Di Maria, "Ethical Premises," 27.

29. Ibid., 27-28.

30. Boethius is misspelled, and this could be taken as a sign of Messer Nicia's incompetence. But it is not Messer Nicia speaking here; it is Machiavelli's somewhat deceptive "Prologue."

31. If Lord, "*Mandragola*," is correct that the play is Machiavelli's retrospective, esoteric confession of his own part in a conspiracy against Soderini in 1504, the parallel here between Boethius and Machiavelli is striking. Both our own and Lord's reading of the play may be correct. Not that we wish to subscribe to literary theories that permit myriad "readings" of "texts," but we believe Machiavelli capable of constructing a plot that, on the comic level, calls for our reading, and on the allegorical level, calls for Lord's. The two readings need not be mutually exclusive: nor, for that matter, need they exclude a third: Machiavelli's writing is polysemous.

32. Paul Edwards, ed., *The Encyclopedia of Philosophy*, vols. 1 and 2 (New York: Macmillan, 1967), 328-30.

33. Messer Nicia desires sons of the correct sort. Unlike Callimaco, Ligurio lacks the lion's heart; as Sumberg, "*La Mandragola*," 324, says, Ligurio is "aloof." Perhaps Messer Nicia wants children with the spiritedness that Ligurio lacks.

34. We think the lady doth protest too much! On the basis of the frate's implied threat, she might abjure her religious devotions and hope for the best. At any rate, her belief that her religion can affect her individual fate is steadfast.

35. Flaumenhaft, "Comic Remedy," 46.

36. Sumberg, "*La Mandragola*," 322. Sumberg, 327, argues that "Callimaco unchallenged will very much be master of the new order;" adding that this "new state rests on force, as do all political orders." But Messer Nicia is the only character in the play who is capable of employing force, since he is the only one armed.

37. Cf. *Discourses* 3.5, in which Machiavelli explains that "Tarquin was driven from Rome, not because his son Sextus had violated Lucrezia, but because he had disregarded the laws of the kingdom. . . . Princes should remember, then, that they begin to lose their state from the moment when they begin to disregard the laws and customs under which

people live contented for a length of time." See also *Discourses* 3.26.

38. As Sostrata points out in Machiavelli's other great comedy, *Clizia* (4.12), which involves some of the same characters as *Mandragola*.

39. Lord, "*Mandragola*," 816.

40. We know that the scheme was successful. In *Clizia* (2.3), Frate Timoteo is said to have worked a miracle in helping Lucrezia to have a child.

41. Sumberg, "*La Mandragola*," 326, suggest that Callimaco might hasten Messer Nicia's death since Lucrezia will then marry him. All the more reason for Messer Nicia to rid his family of the outsider after two or three years. As we noted earlier, Sumberg mistakenly asserts that it is Messer Nicia who is without family to avenge him, forgetting about Cammillo Calfucci, the very man who first approached Callimaco in Paris.

42. Rebhorn, *Foxes and Lions*, 67.

43. Pitkin, *Fortune Is a Woman*, 38, understands how important playing the fool was for Machiavelli, but her interpretation of *Mandragola* overlooks the great master of foolery in the play.

44. Our imaginary sixth act of *Mandragola* goes something like this: The scene is Messer Nicia's house, three years hence. Messer Nicia reminds Ligurio of their meetings in the Lucelli Gardens in 1503-1504, where Nicia's friend, Niccolo Machiavelli, discoursed on the lessons to be drawn from Brutus's conspiratorial activities in founding Roman liberty. Now Messer Nicia and his lieutenant, Ligurio (who was on Messer Nicia's payroll before the opening of the play), must bring their conspiracy to its end: they must "make sure" of Callimaco. Nicia now has two sons. As for Callimaco, he is no longer so enamored of Lucrezia, but he is devoted to the young boys, especially Niccolo, the first born (perhaps his paternal ardor is enhanced by his own orphaned youth). Messer Nicia is no longer in need of a "staff" to sustain his old age; Callimaco has become, rather, a dangerous rock. Messer Nicia's self-interest and Callimaco's no longer coincide; they no longer share the same "common good." Callimaco, not Messer Nicia (contra Sumberg), is without family to avenge him.

45. Sumberg, "*La Mandragola*," 338.

46. Lord, "*Mandragola*," 815; Rebhorn, *Foxes and Lions*, 83.

47. Strauss, *Thoughts on Machiavelli*, 198, 200, 203.

Chapter 8

Hobbesian and Thucydidean Realism

Thomas Hobbes found in Thucydides' *History of the Peloponnesian War* confirmation of his own views of human nature, which became the foundation for his mature political teaching. Hobbes believed that his contemporaries could learn valuable lessons from Thucydides. Thus he helped inaugurate a long tradition of modern thinkers who have claimed an affinity between their own political theories and what they purported to find in Thucydides. In the twentieth century, international relations theorists of the various "realist" schools, in particular, have traced their intellectual pedigree to Thucydides' *History* via the political philosophy of Hobbes. But these twentieth-century realists, who have read Thucydides through lenses ground by Hobbes, have fundamentally erred in their understanding of Thucydides (and, incidentally, never really got the intricacies of Hobbes's political theory straight, either).

This, at least, is the central contention of Laurie Johnson's *Thucydides, Hobbes, and the Interpretation of Realism*: Hobbes's tendentious reading of Thucydides may support the Hobbesian view of political life, but no genuinely philosophical reading of Thucydides can. Johnson's intention is to furnish us with such a reading, in order to construct a hypothetical debate, an "experiment" (xiii), in which Thucydides (anachronistically) responds to Hobbes, corrects Hobbes's reading of his narrative, and thus Hobbes's understanding of both political life and the role of theory in political life; thereby, Johnson corrects the realist and neorealist schools on both Hobbes and Thucydides, and thus their understanding of both international relations and the proper tasks and modes of international relations theory.

Johnson compares Thucydides' narrative and Hobbes's political theory in three chapters, each examining an important question over which the two could hypothetically debate: human nature, justice, and leadership and regimes. In each chapter, the same procedure is followed: first, a presentation of the teaching of Hobbes, summarizing arguments of major relevant texts, especially *De Cive* and *Leviathan*, usually followed by examples of how Johnson's reading of Hobbes is confirmed in Hobbes's account of the English civil wars in *Behemoth*; second, analysis of key passages of Thucydides from which one can infer what Thucydides' response to Hobbes's theories would be; third, a comparison.

Thucydides is invariably the winner in these debates. Consequently, in the concluding chapter of the book, Johnson offers the authentic Thucydides as an alternative to both Hobbes and the realist and neorealist schools of international relations. (She claims that these schools are, unbeknownst to themselves, in agreement with one another on the deepest questions.) Johnson acknowledges, "Of course, to do justice to the issue of the realist/neorealist paradigm in international relations would require another book, not just a concluding chapter" (xiii), but the reader doubts that she really means it—that is, that were Johnson to write such a book, her conclusions would be any different: If the neo/realists properly understood Hobbes and Thucydides they would abjure misinformed Hobbesianism and become genuine Thucydideans.

The first chapter of the book, on human nature, provides Johnson's fundamental argument, and is the key to the other two substantive chapters: the "Athenian thesis" on human nature, developed by Thucydides through the speeches of those Athenians who attempt to excuse or defend their imperialism, becomes Hobbes's position, which is in turn the twentieth-century neo/realist position: "Human beings are universally selfish and always motivated by fear, honor, and interest. Since they are compelled by their passions, they are not to be blamed for their actions" (3). But Hobbes and contemporary realists failed to consider that, "In order to identify Thucydides' position, as opposed to the Athenian position, which is in its essence the realist position, one must ask whether and how Thucydides' view differs from this Athenian thesis and how and for what purpose Thucydides uses this thesis within the overall *History*" (212). Should one do so, one will realize that Thucydides' analysis "rightly understood, insists that none of the passions compel or force people to act, even though they may be very strong" (27).

Johnson's book has much to offer that is useful and instructive. She raises numerous intelligent questions of interest to political theorists, students of international relations, and political scientists generally. I believe, however, that she tends to overstate her case. This is all the more unfortunate because the main thesis of her book in its various forms—"Hobbes misread Thucydides or robbed him of his subtleties in many places" (196); "Hobbes, despite his pessimistic assumptions about human nature, is not realistic" (201); "If by realistic . . . we mean reflecting reality and being useful, the Thucydidean account of political behavior is more realistic" than the Hobbesian (202)—does not require the overstatement. Furthermore, while I agree with her main thesis, I frequently disagree with her "close textual analysis" (xiii).

With Hobbes, Johnson tends to press his arguments to the point of either absurdities or contradictions that Hobbes himself would recognize; which means, of course, that they are not simply Hobbesian absurdities or contradictions. For example, Johnson claims that "Hobbes had no use for statesmanship and absolutely no use for political rhetoric. . . . The only language needed is the language of science and scientific method" (142). Given, however, that *Leviathan* contains a Hobbesian indictment of the use of metaphorical language as one of the abuses of speech, while the commonwealth as "the great leviathan" is, of course, the titular and thematic metaphor of the entire work, one suspects that there might be a Hobbesian rhetoric; that Hobbes knows it, and expects us to know it; and that it might account for, among other things, Hobbes's professed devotion to the language of science and scientific method.

As for Johnson's reading of Thucydides, I find much with which to agree and much with which to disagree. A few examples of the latter will suffice. Johnson is too conventional in her view of the failure of the Sicilian expedition as punishment for Athenian *hubris* (133); rather, what is so remarkable about the Sicilian expedition is not its failure, but just how close it came to succeeding; even though the Athenians in general failed to appreciate the enormity of the task they had undertaken; even though Alcibiades was imprudently deprived of his generalship; even though the ever-cautious Nicias was left in command of their most daring enterprise; and even though the Athenians were hard-pressed, after the Spartan fortification of Deceleia, fighting two large wars at once.

I disagree, too, with Johnson's claim that "Nicias was correct in his estimation of Alcibiades" (55). I think, rather, that Thucydides' own assessment of Alcibiades is more sympathetic than Nicias's or Johnson's. Nor do I think that Alcibiades failed to understand how difficult it would be to conquer Sicily (60), although I can well understand why he should insist, in the debate on the Sicilian expedition, that it would be easy. (Do we think Alcibiades above telling a fib?) Nor am I persuaded of the cogency of Johnson's argument concerning the Melian Dialogue, that "the Athenians at Melos choose the form of a dialogue to *eliminate* true argumentation" (137, Johnson's emphasis).

In only one case, however, does my disagreement run the risk of posing a threat to the central arguments of Johnson's book. She makes much of the Hobbesian roots of neo/realism's structuralism, and rightly so, but in radically contrasting Thucydides with Hobbes on this point, she goes too far. For example, she overemphasizes Pericles' personal qualities as the key to his success in democratic Athens, or, rather, she depreciates the importance of the fortuitous circumstances in which Pericles found himself able to rule Athens, virtually uncontested, as its de facto monarch. Similarly, she thinks that "Thucydides shows that war between Athens and Sparta had nothing to do with Athens's insecurity and fear, as the [Athenian] envoys claim" (29), while I do not.

But the greatest error that Johnson's enthusiasm to downplay any "structuralist" tendencies in Thucydides' teaching leads her into, is that she utterly discounts what is his insistence upon the importance of Sparta's concerns about the Helots (the conquered Messenians whom the Spartans held in subjection in the Peloponnese) in determining Spartan domestic and foreign policy, and even what Johnson calls the "national character" of Sparta. In fact, in her first chapter, Johnson constructs her entire case concerning Thucydides' emphasis on "national character" as an important determinant of Athenian versus Spartan behavior without so much as acknowledging the existence of the Helots. Thus it was "national character" that caused Sparta to be "conservative, calculating and sometimes vicious" (27-28), and "the Spartans acted out of a chosen inwardness and reticence that the Corinthians were later to criticize" (31) when they acquiesced in Athenian expansionism in the decades before the outbreak of the war. Thucydides, however, repeatedly indicates how important a determinant the fear of Helot uprisings was for Spartan behavior; yet this fear does not figure even in Johnson's otherwise intelligent discussion of events at Pylos and Sphacteria (46-51).

In her treatment of justice, in her second chapter, Johnson notes Thucydides' comparison (at 8.24.4) of the Chians and the Spartans as moderate in prosperity (99), but she fails to note his remark, shortly thereafter (at 8.40.2), that the Chians held more slaves than any other city, except for Sparta, and were consequently most severe in their punishments of them. The Helots are mentioned for the first time by Johnson more than half way through her book (117), and only in passing. (There is no entry for the Helots in Johnson's index.) To be fair, she nods in the direction of the point I am pressing in her concluding chapter: "While Thucydides mentions that fear of a slave uprising made the Spartans less willing to extend themselves at times, it is far from clear that Thucydides would attribute to this one factor the difference in the two national characters" (213). And, of course, the way she states it, she is correct: Thucydides would unlikely attribute *anything* to any *one* factor. Nevertheless, this is too little, too late, on the importance of the Helots.

Johnson's concluding chapter, in which she discusses contemporary scholarship in international relations theory, could serve as a chapter in the late Herbert Storing's edited volume, *Essays on the Scientific Study of Politics*[1] (1962), by which reference I intend high praise. In sum, regardless of my own disagreements with portions of it, Johnson's book will be valuable to anyone interested in the political thought of Hobbes and Thucydides, and especially the twentieth-century schools of realism and neorealism.

Notes

This chapter was originally published as "Hobbes's Thucydides and Thucydides Himself," a review of Laurie M. Johnson: *Thucydides, Hobbes, and the Interpretation of Realism* (DeKalb: Northern Illinois University Press, 1993), in *The Review of Politics 57* (1995). Reprinted with permission.

1. New York: Holt, Rinehart and Winston, 1962.

Chapter 9

The Citizen Philosopher: Rousseau's Dedicatory Letter to the *Discourse on Inequality*

Introduction

It was not Jean-Jacques Rousseau's practice to write dedicatory letters for his philosophic works. He made one exception: the *Discourse on the Origin and Foundations of Inequality among Men (Second Discourse).*[1] In his *Discourse on the Arts and Sciences (First Discourse)*, Rousseau had attacked what the Enlightenment extolled. His thesis, in a sentence, was that developments in the arts and sciences, far from generally improving human life, had actually corrupted mankind, and were paving the way for the greatest of political evils: despotism. At the same time, the new understanding of human wisdom that culminated in the "progressive" views of the *philosophes* of the Enlightenment was actually destructive of philosophy.

But it was the *Second Discourse*, according to Rousseau, that revealed his principles "completely," which made it "a work of the greatest importance."[2] And the *Second Discourse* is not merely an attack on the Enlightenment view of progress in the arts and sciences, but on civil society as such. It apparently leads to the conclusion that all civil societies stand on illegitimate foundations, thus anticipating the famous beginning of the *Social Contract*: "Man is born free, and everywhere he is in chains." The picture of human society presented in the *Second Discourse* certainly gives cause for deep pessimism. It is a picture of man's decline from his natural beginnings, complicated by Rousseau's admission that the "happiest and most durable epoch" in human history, the age that was "best for man," and "the veritable prime of the world," was a social condition.[3] This is the *Discourse*, paradoxically, to which Rousseau affixed his only dedicatory

121

letter, addressed to the city of his birth, the republic of Geneva.

Controversy over Rousseau's intention arose immediately, and has never abated.[4] The controversy concerns whether Rousseau wrote the letter to pay "honor to the ideal Citizens of the ideal State" of Geneva, at least the Geneva of his dreams,[5] or whether this "flattering image" is meant "to teach the Genevans a lesson" concerning their political deficiencies.[6]

Jean Guéhenno suggests Rousseau may have written the dedicatory letter simply to expedite the restoration of his Genevan citizenship, lost years earlier, at the age of sixteen, when he had fled the city of his birth and converted to Catholicism in Turin.[7] James Miller has adequately responded by showing the letter was not published until months after Rousseau left Geneva, his citizenship already recovered, and that while at Geneva he showed the manuscript to almost no one.[8] Indeed, Rousseau notes in his *Confessions* that when he read the manuscript of the *Second Discourse* to Jean Jallabert, a professor of mathematics and experimental physics at Geneva (later Councillor and Syndic), he omitted reading the "Dedication."[9]

I hope to demonstrate that the key to understanding Rousseau's letter to the Genevans is an appreciation of its rhetorical context. How can the virtuous "Citizen of Geneva" of the *First Discourse* justify publishing a philosophical essay revealing "completely" the truth about the origins of humanity and the illegitimate foundations of civil society? This dilemma was present, implicitly, even for the author of the *First Discourse*, and was resolved, implicitly, in that essay. Rousseau there distinguished the classical understanding of philosophy, grounded on a radical distinction between knowledge and opinion, and exemplified by the Platonic Socrates, from the pursuits of his own fellow Encyclopedists who aspired to reconcile philosophy and politics, knowledge and opinion, and to become public educators in the name of progress.[10]

I maintain that the "Dedication" to the *Second Discourse*, addressed explicitly to the citizens of Geneva, is simultaneously addressed implicitly to the *philosophes* of Enlightenment Europe, with the intention of enlightening them, by the exemplary method, concerning how *philosophes* should address *citoyens*. Rousseau demonstrates how a *political* philosopher must address non-philosophic citizens—politically—that *political* philosophy is as much the political treatment of philosophic questions as the philosophical treatment of political ones.

To understand properly the letter to Geneva is not to determine whether Rousseau is sincere or saucy, whether his "eulogy" to Geneva is zealously hyperbolic, or even "couched in terms sufficiently extravagant to permit one to question its sincerity."[11] The letter is, in fact, both, and more. It is Rousseau's public presentation of his understanding of the relationship between the Republic of Geneva and his philosophic thought. The letter reveals that Rousseau's thinking about the deepest questions can be presented, and may be understood, without reference to Geneva, because his philosophizing is free of any limitations the brute facts of his birth and childhood in Geneva might have imposed on him. Rousseau qua philosopher (as he understands the philosopher) distances himself from Geneva. Indeed, he states explicitly in the introductory section of the *Second Discourse* that he will use a language that suits all nations, or, rather, will forget time and place altogether to think only of the men to whom he speaks. And are these the Academicians of Dijon? No. Rousseau rather imagines himself in the Lyceum of Athens, with Plato and Xenocrates for judges, and the human race for his audience.[12]

But Rousseau intends also to relate his philosophical concerns and the political concerns of the Republic of Geneva. The "Dedication" lightens the "pessimism" of the picture of human society found in the *Second Discourse* by offering these thoughts to a fatherland that gives some ground for optimism: modern republican optimism. It reveals both how the philosopher's true fatherland must remain his own philosophical "ideal," and how the philosopher can responsibly address his concerns to the citizens of the fatherland of his birth. Rousseau's praise of Geneva thus displays both philosophic irony and patriotic sincerity.[13] Geneva is flawed, but attachment to it is reasonable because it keeps alive the possibility of republican government amidst the general monarchical corruption of eighteenth-century Europe. Rousseau intends neither simply to flatter nor insult the Genevans, but to instruct them, and at the same time to instruct the *philosophes*. The Genevans are (or should be) citizens; the *philosophes* are cosmopolites. Rousseau is essentially a philosopher, not a patriot. (Or, we might say, he is a philosophical, that is, a critical, patriot.) But he refuses to parade himself before the country of his birth as a cosmopolitan sophisticate. He wishes to demonstrate the superiority, both philosophical and political, of his "patriotic" social criticism to the *philosophes'* cosmopolitan social criticism. He instructs the Genevans concerning patriotism, and the *philosophes* concerning philosophy.

What follows takes the form of a commentary on Rousseau's letter.[14] Rousseau's letter consists of an opening salutation, twenty-two paragraphs, and a closing.[15] The letter is divided neatly in half. After the opening salutation, Rousseau devotes eleven paragraphs to a portrait of the society into which he would have chosen to be born had he been (*per impossible*) free to choose. Examination reveals it is not Geneva but what I call "the philosopher's fatherland." After repeating the opening salutation in the twelfth paragraph, in the second half of the letter Rousseau presents to his "distant fellow citizens" an idealized portrait of Geneva, which serves to promote political reconciliation on the ground of love of country. This I discuss under the rubric, "the citizen's fatherland."

Between my discussions of the two halves of the letter, I digress to comment briefly on Rousseau's epigraph to the *Second Discourse* in order to indicate the philosophic ground on which Rousseau establishes his ideal fatherland and from which he offers patriotic criticism of his real one.

The Philosopher's Fatherland

Rousseau begins his letter "TO THE REPUBLIC OF GENEVA" with the salutation "MAGNIFICENT, MOST HONORED, AND SOVEREIGN LORDS." His contemporaries must have been startled to discover this salutation, of such aristocratic tenor, directed to the Genevan people, not the magistrates—an indication of the republican thrust of Rousseau's intention. Rousseau begins by addressing, and for most of the letter speaks to, the Genevan people as a whole.[16]

The opening sentence asserts "only the virtuous citizen may properly give his fatherland those honors that it may acknowledge." Rousseau himself has worked for thirty years to deserve the appellation "virtuous citizen," but in vain. Rather than by the right that ought to be his authorization to pay public homage to his fatherland, Rousseau is rather prompted by "zeal." He very zealously praises the Genevans. They seem to "possess society's greatest advantages and to have best prevented its abuses." They have combined "the equality nature established among men" and "the inequality they have instituted . . . in the manner most approximate to natural law and most favorable to society." (Genevan society has achieved only an approximation of what would be in accordance with natural law.) Even had he not been born in Geneva, Rousseau would have felt himself "unable to dispense with offering this picture of human society" to the Genevans.[17]

Having noted the historical fact of his birth within the walls of Geneva, in the immediate sequel Rousseau liberates his mind from those confining walls, and describes the society into which he would have chosen to be born, had he been free to choose. In this section of the letter—his vision of his true fatherland—Rousseau never deigns to mention, nor even allude to, Geneva.

Rousseau's freely chosen birthplace would be "a society of a size limited by the extent of human faculties—that is, limited by the possibility of being well governed"; one where "all the individuals knowing one another, neither the obscure maneuvers of vice nor the modesty of virtue could be hidden from the notice and judgment of the public." In short, Rousseau would have chosen to live in a society modeled on the ancient *polis*, a city restricted in size by the natural limits of the human capacity for trust and a truly common good. Perhaps more than any other writer in the modern period, Rousseau understood and appreciated the virtues of the ancient city;[18] his model society, however, is not the ancient city as it understood itself, as we shall see.

In addition to preferring a *polis*, Rousseau would have chosen to be born in a democracy, "wisely tempered," where the sovereign and the people would have "only one and the same interest, so that all movements of the machine always tended only to the common happiness." And this is not possible "unless the people and the sovereign [are] the same person." Democratic government is the only government that can secure the "common happiness," thus the only desirable government. (What is meant by the qualification "wisely tempered" will emerge below.[19])

Rousseau "would have wished to live and die free." To "live free" means to live in a particular relation to the laws, not to live without the constraint of laws. It is to bear their "honorable . . . salutary and gentle yoke" proudly, the condition being that everyone do so equally.

Rousseau is especially concerned "that no one in the state could declare himself above the law and that no one outside could impose any law the state was obliged to recognize"—a wish laden with significant political implications. No man—no king, priest, or pope (not even a messiah?)—is to be above the law. And no one outside, no power temporal or spiritual, is to be able to impose any law—especially "divine" or religious law—upon the state. The reason? It is "impossible," writes Rousseau, for both a "national chief" and a "foreign chief" to be well obeyed "whatever division of authority they may make": even to render unto Caesar what is Caesar's and unto God what is God's. In short, Rousseau opposes the "modern" dualism of the earthly and heavenly fatherlands. (By "modern," I mean here what Machiavelli and his followers meant: Christian as opposed to pagan.)

The central and longest of the eleven paragraphs between Rousseau's first and second salutations to his "MAGNIFICENT, MOST HONORED, AND SOVEREIGN LORDS" provides the key for understanding the letter as a whole. The paragraph addresses the problem of the founding of a free republic, one where all are equal before the law; the work to which the letter is attached is devoted to the question of the origin and foundations of inequality among men. What is most striking is that here in the middle of this address to the Genevan people, Rousseau calls not the Genevans but the early Romans "the model of all free peoples."

Rousseau "would not have wished to live in a newly instituted republic, however good its laws might be." The difficulty with newly instituted republics is that the government may have to be constituted differently than one in a long-established republic. Indeed, there is an initial period of indeterminate duration in which the people and the government may prove incompatible, a period in which the state would be subject to disturbances, even destruction. The characteristic of republics is freedom, but freedom is not for all peoples: "once peoples are accustomed to masters, they are no longer able to do without them." Rousseau adds a strikingly antirevolutionary statement: in attempting to shake off the yoke of their masters, a people moves *farther* from freedom, "mistaking for freedom an unbridled license which is its opposite." Peoples' revolutions "almost always deliver them to seducers who only make their chains heavier."

Here we get an intimation of how the author of the *Second Discourse*—a work that profoundly calls into question the foundations of all civil society—could at the same time speak of revolution in so guarded and even discouraging a manner. Whatever truth there is in the view that Rousseau is the father, or grandfather, of the modern revolutions of the left, for "Man is born free; and everywhere he is in chains," to become "Workers of the world unite; you have nothing to lose but your chains," something had to be added to Rousseau's thought, something non-Rousseauan, perhaps anti-Rousseauan. What had to be added, and what the author of the *First Discourse* would not have added, is the modern belief in a univocal history of social progress. Rousseau knew a revolution was coming, that the *ancien régime* was finished. But he did not share, as Marx did, the modern faith in progress. He consequently was very much bothered by what seems to bother Marx very little: the problems that shall have to be faced *after* the revolution.[20]

Peoples' revolutions "almost always" deliver them to seducers—yet the debased, slavish, stupid mob that emerged from the oppression of the Tarquins eventually became the most respectable of all peoples. What the Roman mob needed was to be guided through the transition period with great wisdom, and then, once their origins had been "in a way lost in the night of time," they could become the constituent element of the kind of republic into which Rousseau would have wished to be born, the home of the most respectable of all peoples because of their "severity of morals" and "spirited courage"—a people "not only free but worthy of being so."

Rousseau does not share the characteristically modern conviction that fundamental political problems can be solved by institutional means. A republic's government and laws, "however good," cannot assure the freedom of its citizens: severity of morals and spirited courage are necessary. Rousseau thus adopts something like the ancient view, but not simply the ancient view. The ancients considered the most important thing politically to be the question of the regime, the *politeia*: is the regime democratic or oligarchic? From the regime everything else follows. For Rousseau, the question is narrower. It is transformed into a question about the "government" as opposed to the "society," a distinction that would scarcely have been understood in antiquity, and which is, in fact, incompatible with the classical conception of *politeia*.[21]

In addition, for Rousseau, "freedom," not "virtue," is the standard by which to judge political life. The Romans are the "most respectable of all peoples" because they are the "model of all free peoples." One might think the most respectable of all peoples would be the most moderate, most pious, justest, or wisest: the most virtuous of all peoples. Not Rousseau. Rousseau's model may be the ancient *polis*, but he understands it differently than it understood itself. Rousseau understands virtue as a means toward the higher end of freedom. (But once we have accepted an instrumental view of virtue, is it not legitimate to look for other, perhaps surer, means to freedom?) To put it differently, Rousseau appears to reduce virtue to freedom. In any case, just as it had long been understood that not all peoples are capable of virtue, Rousseau maintains that not all peoples are capable of freedom.[22]

Having observed that Rousseau's model republic is not Geneva but ancient Rome (albeit understood in a special way), we are struck that the next condition he places on his chosen fatherland is that it be "diverted by fortunate impotence from a fierce love of conquests." As everybody knows, the Roman republic was the conquering republic *par excellence*. Rousseau appeals from the Genevan to the Roman republic, but here is another indication that his standards are not those of antiquity.[23]

Coupled with its fortunate impotence, the city would have an "even more fortunate location," which would relieve it from any fear of being conquered. In a word, the city would desire, like the "wise" Otanes of Rousseau's sole footnote to the letter, neither to rule nor be ruled. The citizens would be trained in the use of arms in order to maintain that "warlike ardor and spirited courage which suit freedom so well and whet the appetite for it, rather than from the necessity to provide for their own defense."

In the next four paragraphs, Rousseau indicates what he had in mind when he stated, "I would have wished to be born under a democratic government—wisely tempered." The right of legislation would be common to all citizens. But Rousseau would not have approved plebiscites like those of the Romans, because they excluded from the deliberations on the safety of the state those who were most interested in its preservation, absurdly depriving the magistrates of the rights enjoyed by common citizens. Rousseau would prefer that only the magistrates had the power to propose new laws. Even then he would have it used cautiously, and hope, in addition, that on those rare occasions the people would hesitate to give its consent to any changes in its constitution, for "it is above all the great antiquity of laws that makes them holy and venerable." Rousseau adopts the "ancient" view, what may properly be called the "conservative" position, that all but the most necessary changes in a regime tend to undermine its stability, and that even necessary changes (for example, changes dictated by the exigencies of military policy) are not necessarily without harm.[24] But note how Rousseau follows Machiavelli's "modern" reading of the Bible in attributing the "holiness" of laws to their antiquity—and to nothing else. (Machiavelli would insist, of course, that Moses' "executive" modes after he descended Mount Sinai had more than a little to do with the success of his Decalogue!)

Rousseau "would have fled as necessarily ill-governed" a republic where the people augmented its legislative power by retaining the administrative and executive functions in its own hands—one of the vices that in his view ruined (democratic) Athens. Rather, they should merely sanction the laws and important decisions proposed and reported by the city's magistrates. The latter would be elected on the ground of merit alone, annually, to administer justice and govern the state. Rousseau concludes these remarks with comments on the "fatal misunderstandings" that may beset republics, and the requisites for "sincere and perpetual reconciliation"—comments that are usually taken to be allusions, albeit ironic, to certain events in the history of eighteenth-century Geneva.[25]

Such are the advantages Rousseau would have sought in the fatherland of his choosing. He again addresses his "MAGNIFICENT, MOST HONORED, AND SOVEREIGN LORDS." He avers that if Providence smiled on his fatherland in a few other respects, for example, if it were granted a fertile countryside (as Geneva was not), he would have happily enjoyed these things "living peacefully in sweet society with my fellow citizens, practicing toward them . . . all the virtues; and leaving behind me the honorable memory of a good man and a decent and virtuous patriot." We cannot help reminding ourselves that Rousseau did not reside in Geneva.

In this first half of the letter, Rousseau has indicated to the Genevans why he is addressing them, and has described the kind of society he would have chosen for his birthplace, had he been free to choose. To casual readers, it appears to be a description of Genevan society. To less casual readers, like the former First Syndic Du Pan (see my note 4), it appears to be a zealously exaggerated, if well-meaning, description of Geneva's virtues. In fact the letter has (thus far) not been about Geneva at all.

Careful readers should not be surprised, then, to find Rousseau *now*, after a dozen paragraphs, saying that if he were reduced to living in other climes than those of his (actual) fatherland (as he was, in fact, by an "imprudent youth"), he would, "moved by tender and disinterested affection" for his "distant fellow citizens," address to them "approximately the *following* discourse" (my emphasis), that is, *not* the preceding one.

What, then, was the *preceding* description? Starobinski calls the description *following*, "*Discours dans le discours.*"[26] I should think it is rather the other way around. We have already had what might helpfully be called a "*discours dans le discours*" (a "discourse within the discourse")—Rousseau's tendentious eulogy to the ancient *polis*—and *now* we are going to get Rousseau's zealously exaggerated, if well-meaning (or not), description of Genevan society.

But why two "discourses" within the letter? In the last sentence of the first paragraph, Rousseau writes: "[E]ven had I not been born within your walls, I should have believed myself unable to dispense with offering this picture of human society to that people which, of all others, seems to me to possess society's greatest advantages and to have best prevented its abuses." What picture of human society? Rousseau never refers explicitly to the *Second Discourse* in the letter. Is it possible the "picture of human society" Rousseau has in mind is as much the one we find in the immediate sequel, the succeeding eleven paragraphs of the letter, as the one we find in the *Second Discourse* itself? Does Rousseau even purport to describe Geneva, however hyperbolically, in the paragraphs between his first and his second salutations to his "MAGNIFICENT, MOST HONORED, AND SOVEREIGN LORDS"? Is the picture of human society Rousseau felt himself unable to dispense with offering to the Genevans the picture of the fatherland he would have chosen instead of Geneva, had he been free to choose?

Cranston offers this judgment concerning the letter as a whole:

> It was not unnatural that some readers should even suspect Rousseau of having intended all the time to attack the Genevan regime by the device of praising it where it least deserved praise and of showing how far it had fallen from its principles by expounding the principles which it had most conspicuously betrayed. But this, I believe, is to impute to Rousseau a more devious sophistication than he possessed as a polemicist.[27]

I believe Cranston underestimates both Rousseau's talents as a "polemicist," and his propensity for "devious sophistication." Rousseau describes two fatherlands in the "Dedication" to the *Second Discourse*: the one of Rousseau the philosopher; the other of the citizen of Geneva. To clarify the relation between the philosopher's fatherland and the citizen's, not so much to dedicate the *Second Discourse*, is the *philosophic* purpose of Rousseau's letter to the republic of Geneva. Starobinski correctly suggests the letter is meant "to teach the Genevans a lesson," but Rousseau also intends to teach a lesson to the *philosophes* of Enlightenment Europe.

Digression on an Epigraph

Rousseau's model for political life is the ancient *polis*, but he "improves" upon it. He follows Machiavelli in admiring antiquity as against modernity, but "nature"—as Rousseau understands it in the *Second Discourse*—is the standard by which he criticizes both. Rousseau's disagreement with both the early moderns and Aristotle stems from their disagreements about "nature." It is helpful here to reflect for a moment on the only writing other than the dedicatory letter that Rousseau places between the title of the *Second Discourse* and the discourse itself: the epigraph from Aristotle. This is not the place for an extended interpretation, but I digress to adumbrate one.

The epigraph is a Latin translation of a sentence from Aristotle's *Politics* (1254a 36-38). In English it reads: "Not in corrupt things, but in those which are well ordered in accordance with nature, should one consider that which is natural."[28] It calls to mind the famous statement from Rousseau's introduction to the *Second Discourse*: "The philosophers who have examined the foundations of society have all felt the necessity of going back to the state of nature, but none of them has reached it."[29] Rousseau uses the quotation from Aristotle to indicate his criticism of the modern "state of nature" theorists, most obviously Hobbes and Locke. He appeals to classical political philosophy to begin his critique of modern political philosophy, just as he appeals from modern Geneva to ancient Rome. But if we turn to the context of the quotation in the *Politics*, we find that it implies, when juxtaposed with its context on the title page of Rousseau's *Second Discourse*, a critique of classical political philosophy as well. (Note how Rousseau invites us to compare the contexts by supplying the citation to Aristotle; he did not supply the citation for the epigraph on the title page of the *First Discourse*.)

The context in the *Politics* is Aristotle's discussion in the first book of the "first pairing" of human beings forming the household from which the *polis*, the association most salubrious to the development of human virtue and the good life, will emerge. This first pairing includes that of "female and male for the sake of generation," and that of "ruler by nature and ruled by nature for the sake of preservation," that is, it appears that some being enslaved by others is as natural a human phenomenon as procreation. Aristotle deals with the immediate objection, that slavery is merely conventional and not at all natural, in a perplexing manner: he discusses property and the art of acquisition (1253b 23ff.). We learn that the just acquisition of slaves is a kind of hunting, and that man's hunting is natural and just and should be used against "wild beasts and that part of mankind which is meant by nature but is unwilling to be ruled" (1256b 25-27). It is in the middle of this discussion—a demonstration that the distinction of ruler and ruled pervades all of nature—that we find Aristotle's remark about corruption and nature that Rousseau cites.

The *Second Discourse* is Rousseau's work on man's origin and nature, especially the origin of inequality among men. This inequality is inextricably linked with the unjust origins of private property. It is not a frolic in the esoteric garden to suggest Rousseau chose his epigraph carefully, and that reflection on his choice may be a helpful entry point to his philosophic teaching.

Citing the authority of Aristotle on the title page of the *Discourse*, Rousseau appears to be appealing to Aristotle's understanding of nature, according to which the nature of a being is best seen in its perfection, but he manifestly rejects that teleological understanding, as well as the crypto-teleology of Hobbes and Locke (the substitution of a *summum malum* for a *summum bonum*). Rousseau's natural man is peaceable, herbivorous, solitary, and asocial. Aristotle's is a hunter of wild beasts and other men, naturally part of a household, and intended by nature for life in a *polis*: a man without a city is like a beast or a god. According to Rousseau, the city is always unnatural, although we may observe that for Rousseau, too, a man without a city is like a beast or a god: consider his "natural" man, and his dreaming, solitary walker, respectively. In particular, for Rousseau slavery is unnatural and wholly unjust, but the ancient city was impossible without slavery. Rousseau may appeal from modern to ancient political philosophy, from the modern to the ancient city, but he appeals from ancient political philosophy and the ancient city to nature, understood in a new, radically modern way in the *Second Discourse*.[30] But let us return to the letter.

The Citizen's Fatherland

The second half of Rousseau's letter "TO THE REPUBLIC OF GENEVA" can itself be divided into sections corresponding to its various addressees. Rousseau speaks directly to three classes of Genevans: his "dear fellow citizens" or rather his "brothers"; the "MAGNIFICENT AND MOST HONORED LORDS" of Geneva, her magistrates; and the "*aimables et virtueueses Citoyennes*" of Geneva, that is, the women or, we might say, his "sisters." In the course of his address to the magistrates of Geneva, Rousseau speaks about, but does not directly address, a fourth element of Genevan society: the clergy. It is in these passages that Rousseau will (to echo the words of Du Pan) represent the Genevans as they ought to be, not as they are—and what they *all* ought to be is *citizens*.

Rousseau begins his address to his "brothers" sounding very much like he did in the first paragraph of the letter: "The more I reflect upon your political and civil situation, the less I can imagine that the nature of human things can admit of a better." But between the first paragraph and its echo, here, Rousseau has precisely imagined and described in some detail a better political and civil situation. The two complementary sentences serve as something like bookends for the "*discours dans le discours*" that comes between them.[31]

What makes Rousseau and his dear fellow citizens "brothers"? "The bonds of blood as well as the laws unite almost all of us." In addition to the explicit qualification ("almost"), we should note that while Rousseau may be united with a portion of Geneva's population, an extremely small portion, by bonds of blood, he is actually united with none by Geneva's laws, neither the first nor last time he draws our attention to this fact.

Essentially, what Rousseau has to say to his dear fellow citizens is that their lot is a very good one, for which they may claim no credit. The full and universal recognition of their sovereignty, their excellent constitution, their precious freedom—all are due to the efforts of their ancestors; their happiness is "all established." The only precaution left for them to take is to remain united, obey the laws, and respect their magistrates. Rousseau queries rhetorically: "Does anyone among you know a more upright, more enlightened, more respectable body in the universe than that of your magistracy? Do not all its members give you the example of moderation, of simplicity of morals, of respect for the laws, and the most sincere reconciliation?" Masters notes the irony of this passage;[32] it should also be remarked that Rousseau's rhetorical question precludes the answer that Geneva's Calvinist clergy might be such a body. This is all the more striking since Rousseau has just bid the Genevans to look deep into their hearts and consult that specifically Christian phenomenon: "conscience."

Rousseau's address to those "MAGNIFICENT AND MOST HONORED LORDS," Geneva's magistrates, may be divided into four parts: a praise of the Genevan people in general; a praise of Rousseau's father in particular; advice to the magistrates concerning the people; and praise of Geneva's clergy. Rousseau addresses the magistrates as "MAGNIFICENT AND MOST HONORED LORDS": they are not sovereign.[33] Rousseau reminds the magistrates that they have been raised to their position by their fellow citizens, and by no one else. He speaks of the magistrates' "talent," "virtue," and "merit," but their particular superiority to magistrates of other cities derives from their relation to the free people of Geneva, "men capable of governing others," who have chosen magistrates "in order that they themselves be governed." It is the character of the people of Geneva that adds special luster to the magistracy of these magnificent and most honored lords. In his letter to Perdriau (see my note 16), Rousseau defends having addressed his letter to the Genevans as a whole, rather than the magistrates, by claiming he reserved his eulogies in the letter for the magistrates, and his exhortations for the citizens. It is perhaps more helpful to observe that Rousseau eulogizes the rulers when speaking to the ruled, and the ruled when speaking to the rulers, but leaves no question where sovereignty lies. Political strife in eighteenth-century Geneva consisted essentially of quarrels between democrats and oligarchs. Rousseau does not try to adjudicate the rival claims to rule; he emphasizes, rather, the good the two factions possess in common: the fatherland.[34]

Rousseau wishes to speak of one "virtuous citizen" of Geneva in particular: his father, Isaac Rousseau. Anyone who knows anything about Rousseau's father must find these passages rather hilarious.[35] There is no question, Isaac Rousseau was "not distinguished among his fellow citizens." But was he really "only what they all are"? And what are they all? Why, the equals "by education, as well as by the rights of nature and of birth" of the magistrates, inferior to them only by their own will, for which the magistrates owe them a debt of gratitude. Suffice it to say, as much as Rousseau may claim to wish better records remained of the example his father set for the Genevan people, he was fortunate they did not! That Rousseau's father is the only Genevan named in the letter who is said to deserve the cherished appellation "virtuous citizen" adds ironic insult to injury.[36]

Rousseau discusses but does not directly address the clergy of Geneva. Would it be inappropriate to address members of the clergy in a letter to a "republic"? Is their status different from that of the citizens, male and female, and the magistrates of Geneva? Are they somehow excluded from the body constituting Rousseau's "MAGNIFICENT, MOST HONORED, AND SOVEREIGN LORDS"? Does it not go without saying that Rousseau would never address the clergy, even hyperbolically, as "SOVEREIGN LORDS"?

The clergy, Rousseau tells us, are "those who consider themselves as the magistrates, or rather the masters, of a more holy and sublime fatherland." But Geneva's are a "rare exception": they love the glory and happiness of the Genevan republic, and may be placed in the ranks of its "best citizens." What is the ground of this eulogy? In Geneva, these "venerable pastors of souls" are the "zealous trustees of the sacred dogmas authorized by the laws," that is, *not* zealous trustees of any dogmas *not* authorized by the laws. Just as Geneva's magistrates are superior to other magistrates especially because of their relation to the Genevan people, her clergy are superior to other clergy especially because of their relation to the Genevan, and precisely no other, laws. "I note, with a pleasure mixed with astonishment and respect," Rousseau writes, "how much they abhor the atrocious maxims of those sacred and barbarous men of whom history provides more than one example, and who, in order to uphold the pretended rights of God—that is to say their own interests—were all the less sparing of human blood because they flattered themselves that their own would always be respected." Rousseau does not hesitate to call such men, despite their barbarity, and the atrociousness of their maxims, "sacred"! (This is more shocking than the "Machiavellian" understanding of the "holy" that emerged in the first half of the letter.) And who are these "sacred and barbarous men" who uphold the "pretended rights of God"? Starobinski dares to suggest that this remark may apply to Calvin himself [37] (but Rousseau may have in mind even greater examples— biblical ones, such as Moses and David). The clergy are, indeed, those most prone to disturb the public repose: they may regard themselves as masters of another fatherland, or rather servants of another master, and Rousseau has already insisted there must be no "foreign chief" in a good regime.

Finally, Rousseau has a few words for the women of Geneva. Addressing them as "*aimables et virtueuses Citoyennes*," he indicates he considers them as worthy of the appellation "virtuous citizen" as the men. He demonstrates, in addition, his willingness to grant Genevan citizenship to others as well as to himself: not only does he refer to himself in the letter, and sign it, as a citizen of Geneva, which at that time he was not, but he also calls Geneva's women "citizens," which at that time they were not. (Miller asserts that "the question of Rousseau's patronizing attitude toward women" is uncontroversial.[38] I controvert him. I rather think Rousseau may be counted in some respects, along with Locke, among the founders of the women's liberation movement.[39])

According to Rousseau, women commanded at Sparta by means of their "chaste power," and thus do they deserve to command at Geneva. The "power" here is the granting of sexual favors, the "chastity" of which appears to consist in its being "exercised solely in conjugal union." Cranston notes the irony: "Notwithstanding these words in praise of chastity, Rousseau set off for Geneva in the company of his mistress, Therese," and he humorously reports how the "virtuous aunts" who helped raise Rousseau wielded their "chaste power."[40] It is interesting that Rousseau should claim that the primary effect of female command will be to teach the men of Geneva to "despise vain luxury." According to ancient authorities, the exercise of their "chaste power" by the Spartan women resulted precisely in the Spartan men becoming lovers of luxury (consider, for example, Aristotle's *Politics* 1269b 12ff). Rousseau is not blind, however, to bad effects that may result from the rule of women over men. Indeed, the "extravagances" of the young people of Geneva, their "childish tone and ridiculous airs," their admiration for "pretended grandeurs, frivolous compensations for servitude, which will never be worth as much as august freedom," are due to their having come under the influence of "debauched women."

Is Rousseau suggesting these problems could be obviated by granting the women of Geneva citizenship, as he does in his salutation to them? (Presumably, this would entail the kind of civic education Aristotle suggests might have mitigated the problems created by the position of women at Sparta.) In any case, Rousseau's flattery of the women of Geneva is in the same ironic voice as the rest of the letter. To correct the "extravagances" of the youth, Geneva's women need only be always what they are, "the chaste guardians of morals and the gentle bonds of peace; and continue to exploit on every occasion the rights of the heart and of nature for the benefit of duty and virtue." Consistent with his reinterpretation of the ancient *polis* in the first half of the letter, Rousseau emphasizes the importance of peaceableness, and the role women can play in promoting it. Note that the women of Geneva, not Calvinist religion, are praised for making the city austere. The women, in a way, replace the clergy as the city's moral guardians, and attach the citizens to the fatherland through the family.

To whom is the penultimate paragraph of the letter addressed? There is no salutation, yet Rousseau clearly is no longer speaking solely to Geneva's women. He expresses hopes for the "happiness of the citizens and the glory of the Republic." "It will not shine," he admits, "with the brilliance that dazzles most eyes." "Dissolute youth" will find no satisfaction here, nor will "the supposed men of taste" find anything to admire: "all the refinements of softness and luxury" will be absent. There will be only men, a spectacle possessing a value surpassing that of all others.

What sort of glory is this? In the first half of the letter Rousseau cites the Romans as the model of all free peoples, and the most respectable of all peoples. Sparta and Athens have also been mentioned, but it is the Spartan women who are praised and the Athenians are an example not to be emulated. Historically, Sparta's glory—like Rome's—was based on her outstanding military prowess, and Athens' lasting glory on her intellectual virtues, or, we might say, her achievements in the arts and sciences. Neither Rousseau's freely chosen fatherland nor his reformed Geneva will shine for its accomplishments on the battlefield, and there are not even allusions made, except proscriptively, to achievements in the arts and sciences.

But do Rousseau's actions not speak louder than his words? We may be reminded in this respect of Thucydides. While Thucydides nowhere in his narrative discusses the intellectual life that thrived at Athens, the accomplishments of which have brought her more everlasting glory than anything Pericles praises in the funeral oration, Thucydides does not fail, subtly but powerfully, to indicate Athens' superiority over Sparta in this sphere: he begins his narrative, his "possession for all time," with, "Thucydides, *an Athenian*, wrote the war of the Peloponnesians and the Athenians" (my emphasis). On the title page of Rousseau's discourse we find, "By Jean-Jacques Rousseau, Citizen of Geneva." Rousseau's picture of Geneva may be closer to Sparta than to Athens; Rousseau, himself, is more Athenian than Spartan.[41]

In the final paragraph, Rousseau again addresses his "MAGNIFICENT, MOST HONORED, AND SOVEREIGN LORDS." He begs pardon for any "indiscreet excess" of which he may have been guilty. He refers again to himself as a "patriot," and again also to his "zeal," which in this last paragraph as opposed to the first, is called "legitimate."

The closing reads: "I remain, with the most profound respect, MAGNIFICENT, MOST HONORED, AND SOVEREIGN LORDS, Your most humble and most obedient servant and fellow citizen, Jean-Jacques Rousseau." The letter is dated from Chambéry on June 12, 1754. Rousseau officially returned to the Protestant religion, and regained his Genevan citizenship (which was afterwards again revoked, permanently), on August 1, 1754. On the date the letter is signed, then, Rousseau was neither a member of the Genevan church, nor a Genevan citizen, nor a Genevan resident. We can only conclude that he consciously chose to leave a permanent record of these facts.[42]

Conclusion

Rousseau's letter "TO THE REPUBLIC OF GENEVA" must be seen to consist of two distinct parts. In the first half, Rousseau addresses the question of the society into which he would have chosen to be born, had he been free to choose—the timeless question of "the best regime." Einaudi remarks that the letter contains "the most complete outline of Rousseau's theory of the state before the *Social Contract*."[43] What are its main features?

Rousseau's political ideal is a *polis* with a democratic *politeia* (regime). This requires a social approximation to the equality of human beings in nascent civil society, consequently the abolition of the radical social inequality that developed historically. Both that nascent social condition and the history of the emergence of radical inequality are described in detail in the *Second Discourse*. Social equality—indeed, virtue entire—serves the political goal of freedom. Among the requisites of freedom are "severity of morals" and "spirited courage," not in the service of conquest, but of independence: the ideal is neither to rule nor be ruled.

The democracy must not be participatory, plebiscitory democracy; there must be no doubt where sovereignty resides—in the will of the people—but the democratic regime must be "wisely tempered." This requires, among other things, what we call the separation of church and state, or rather, the subordination of divine authority to civil authority, and what we call separation of powers, at least between the legislative and executive functions; magistracy must be elective, and for brief tenure.

In the second half of the letter, Rousseau presents a portrait of Genevan society that ironically praises the Genevans for virtues they do not possess, or rather, insufficiently possess, in light of the ideal. The letter as a whole is Rousseau's public presentation of the relation, in his own mind, between the timeless concerns of political philosophy and the temporal concerns of political life.[44] The view of Cranston, that "we must remember that at the time he was working on the *Discourse on Inequality* he had not looked far behind the splendidly republican facade" of Genevan society,[45] is untenable. The "picture of human society" Rousseau finds himself unable to dispense with offering to the city of his birth is as much the picture of the society into which he would have wished to be born instead of Geneva as it is the picture found in the *Second Discourse*. Republican Geneva of the eighteenth century is not Rousseau's model for "the best regime." Rather, Rousseau's reflections on "the best regime" permit him to correct the deficient politics of eighteenth-century republican Geneva.

Rousseau exhorts the Genevans to put aside their differences—especially class differences—and devote themselves to the common good of their fatherland. He emphasizes, indeed, exaggerates the equality that reigns among them. He wishes to reconcile the oligarchs and the democrats, the magistrates and the clergy, the men and the women. Perhaps most noteworthy (today) are Rousseau's remarks concerning women: he calls for female citizenship, and he certainly appreciates the political importance of women. He highlights the critical role they can play in nurturing the "severity of morals" and "spirited courage" that are requisites of political freedom. It is above all the mediation of the women, as moral guardians, that will conduce to the unprecedented combination of martial virtue and peaceableness that is to characterize Rousseau's new regime.

Rousseau also indicates in the letter how the "political philosophy" of the Enlightenment *philosophes* is insufficiently political, that is, politic. His famous quarrel with the *philosophes* concerned (among other things) the goodness of an enlightened citizenry, and how the latter could be produced. Rousseau abjures all displays of cosmopolitan sophistication before the Genevan citizenry. In the *Second Discourse*, he questions the origin and foundations of political society more radically than any Enlightenment *philosophe*. But he does not revel in flaunting the politically dangerous aspects of his teaching before the unenlightened. He rather speaks to them—ironically—as one of them. He is the self-deprecating "citizen of Geneva" who has labored for three decades to earn the appellation "virtuous citizen," but who lacks sufficient virtue.

The letter "TO THE REPUBLIC OF GENEVA" serves as a bridge between the

First Discourse and the *Second Discourse,* and indicates how the "Citizen of Geneva" of the former can publish the latter. In the light of the "Dedication," the radical teaching of the *Second Discourse* is perceived to be in the service of civil society. This is precisely the manner in which Socrates, the founder of political philosophy, introduced philosophy into the city (*Republic* 471c-472a). Following Socrates, whom he praises so highly in the *First Discourse,* Rousseau gives *philosophes* of all times and places an exemplary lesson in how to speak to citizens—a lesson of more than "historical" interest.

Notes

This chapter was originally published in *Interpretation: A Journal of Political Philosophy 17* (1989). Reprinted with permission. I am grateful to several anonymous referees, and especially to Professors David Lowenthal and Daniel Cullen for their generous and painstaking criticisms of earlier drafts. While preparing this essay for original publication, I was saddened to hear of the death of Robert Horwitz (1923-1987), of whose generosity I was more than once the beneficiary. I dedicated it to his memory. For this reason more than any other, I wish it were better.

Not long after this essay was originally published, I received correspondence from Dr. Heinrich Meier, director of the Carl Friedrich von Siemens Foundation, Munich, which contained detailed and scrupulous criticisms of my argument. I wish to thank Dr. Meier for his comments. In general, he thinks that my essay does not sufficiently appreciate the numerous allusions in Rousseau's letter to the contemporary political situation in Geneva. Here, I am happy to direct the reader to Dr. Meier's definitive, critical edition of the *Second Discourse: Diskurs über die Ungleichheit / Discours sur l'inegalité. Kritische Ausgabe des integralen Textes. Mit sämlichen Fragmenten und ergänzenden Materalien nach den Originalausgaben und den Handschriften neu ediert, übersetzt und kommentiert von Heinrich Meier,* 3rd, revised edition (Vienna and Zurich: Schöning, 1993).

1. In 1753, Rousseau dedicated his opera *Le Devin du Village* to M. Duclos, and declared it would be his only dedication. The exception of the dedicatory letter to the republic of Geneva was made with Duclos's permission. See *Oeuvres Complètes de Jean-Jacques Rousseau,* vol. 1, Gagnebin and Raymond, eds. (Paris: Gallimard, 1959), 382. In this essay, I have followed the translation in Jean-Jacques Rousseau, *The First and Second Discourses,* R. D. Masters, ed. (New York: St. Martin's Press, 1964), with only occasional alterations, and used the French text in J. Starobinski, *Oeuvres Complètes de Jean-Jacques Rousseau,* vol. 3 (Paris: Galllimard, 1964). Where I quote Rousseau in English, but the citation is to the French text, translations are mine.

2. Gagnebin and Raymond, *Oeuvres Complètes,* 388.

3. *First and Second Discourses,* 150-51.

4. The best-known comment on the letter is that of Du Pan, a former first syndic of Geneva, writing to Rousseau shortly after its publication: "You have followed the movements of your heart in the Dedicatory Epistle, and I fear it will be found to flatter us too much; you represent us as we ought to be, not as we are." (*First and Second Discourses,* 229; for this and other contemporary reactions in Geneva, see Starobinski, *Oeuvres Complètes,* 1286-89.)

5. James Miller, *Rousseau: Dreamer of Democracy* (New Haven, Conn.: Yale Uni-

versity Press, 1984), 25.

6. Starobinski, *Oeuvres Complètes*, xlix.

7. Jean Guéhenno, *Jean-Jacques Rousseau*, 2 vols., trans. J. and D. Weightman (London: Routledge and Kegan Paul, 1966), vol. 1, 304.

8. Miller, *Dreamer of Democracy*, 25. For more on the adventures in Geneva of the manuscript of the letter, see M. Launay, *Jean-Jacques Rouseau: écrivain politique (1712-1762)* (Grenoble: L'A. C. E. R., 1971), 233-34. The view of Cranston, *Jean-Jacques*, 9, 52, that at the time of writing the letter, Rousseau was "an uncritical patriot" who had not yet been "robbed . . . of his illusions about his native city," or its variation in Miller, *Dreamer of Democracy*, 25, that Rousseau "safeguarded his ignorance" of the real Geneva by completing the letter to his "ideal republic" before his actual return to Geneva, is untenable, as I hope my reading of the letter demonstrates. On this point, I follow Roger Masters, *The Political Philosophy of Rousseau* (Princeton, N.J.: Princeton University Press, 1968), 192-95. For Masters, too, the "Dedication" concerns Rousseau's teaching about the "best regime," and he indicates that Geneva, or any Christian regime, must fall short of the best for Rousseau.

9. Gagnebin and Raymond, *Oeuvres Complètes*, 394.

10. For a brief discussion of this thesis, see Masters, *First and Second Discourses*, 7-14; for a fuller treatment, see Leo Strauss, "On the Intention of Rousseau," *Social Research 14* (1947).

11. Masters, *First and Second Discourses*, 15.

12. Ibid., 103.

13. On "philosophic irony," see Leo Strauss, *The City and Man* (Chicago: Rand McNally, 1964), 51; cf. Plato, *Erastai* 133d-e, 134c.

14. As such, it may be compared with the similar effort of M. Einaudi, *The Early Rousseau* (Ithaca, N.Y.: Cornell University Press, 1967), 150-65. Miller writes extensively on the letter, but analyzes it on the basis of assumptions very different from mine: "I will attempt to reanimate and give fresh force to the whole of Rousseau's Alpine fantasia. . . . My primary guide in this task will be Rousseau's own dedication of his *Second Discourse* to Geneva, although supplementary material will be drawn from the passages on Switzerland and Geneva in the *Letter to D'Alembert* (1758), *La Nouvelle Héloïse* (1761), and a few other sources. The goal is to restore for the purposes of study the Alpine city of Rousseau's reveries: a model of harmony, a world of perfection" (*Dreamer of Democracy*, 26). Miller has written an informative and imaginative book, but fails to understand the letter to Geneva correctly; for one thing, in his speculations on Rousseau's "Alpine fantasia" he treats various writings of Rousseau, from the *Social Contract* to letters to Mme. Dupin, without discrimination, despite his professed awareness that the question of Rousseau's "audience" is an important one to consider when reading him (67-68). Throughout my commentary, I have followed the laconic suggestions of Leo Strauss, *Natural Right and History* (Chicago: University of Chicago Press, 1953), 253-54.

15. These are consistent in Starobinski, *Oeuvres Complètes*; Masters, *First and Second Discourses*; and M. Cranston, ed., *Jean-Jacques Rousseau: A Discourse on Inequality* (New York: Penguin, 1984).

16. Rousseau was well aware how unorthodox it was to address his dedicatory letter to the republic of Geneva rather than its magistrates; see Cranston, *Early Life and Work*, 349, who cites Rousseau's response to a letter of Jean Perdriau ("Pedriau" throughout Cranston), a pastor, and one of Rousseau's associates in Geneva, who had raised this objection. Rousseau's letter to Perdriau in its entirety can be found in R. A. Leigh, *Correspondence complète de J.-J. Rousseau* (Geneva: Institut et Musée Voltaire, 1965-), vol. 3,

55-64. In my commentary, I will usually omit references for quotations because I will follow Rousseau so closely as to render frequent citation superfluous.

17. Starobinski, *Oeuvres Complètes*, 1289, interprets Rousseau's statement to mean he would freely choose citizenship in Geneva even had he not been born there. This view is held, explicitly or implicitly, by all Rousseau's commentators. Miller, *Dreamer of Democracy*, 43, states it forcefully: "How emphatically Rousseau approves of this society is made clear by the rhetorical device that structures the early paragraphs of the dedication. . . . . Geneva is not simply the *patrie* of Rousseau's birth. That is a contingent fact of his existence. More significantly, Geneva is his city of choice, an emblem of his self-conscious freedom, the essence of what human society ought to be—an eidetic intuition achieved by his inability, in the free play of his reveries, to 'imagine that the nature of human things could admit of a better one.'" But neither Starobinski's view that Rousseau makes his actual past the object a wish (Jean Starobinski, *Jean-Jacques Rousseau: la transparance et l'obstacle* [Paris: Plon, 1958], part 1), nor Miller's variation, that Rousseau is swept away in an Alpine reverie, is adequate. In this first half of the letter, Rousseau reveals a standard for political life utterly unrestricted by accidents of time and place. For an interesting discussion of the roles played by "Geneva" and "Switzerland" in Rousseau's intellectual odyssey, see Benjamin Barber, "How Swiss is Rousseau?" *Political Theory 13* (1985): 475-95. Barber chronicles Rousseau's disenchantment with Geneva; I am suggesting Rousseau was never as enchanted as he led the Genevans, and others, to believe.

18. See Strauss, *Natural Right and History*, 254.

19. Miller, *Dreamer of Democracy*, 41, remarks, "This is the kind of democracy Rousseau imagined in Geneva: this is the homeland of his dreams." It is precisely "the kind of democracy Rousseau imagined in Geneva," and "the homeland of his dreams," that Rousseau distinguishes in the letter.

20. Cf. Hilail Gildin, "Revolution and the formation of political society in the *Social Contract*," *Interpretation 5* (1976): 247.

21. See H. Jaffa, "Aristotle," in L. Strauss and J. Cropsey, eds., *The History of Political Philosophy*, 2nd. ed. (Chicago: Rand McNally, 1972), 65-67, for a clear statement distinguishing the classical conception of *politeia* from the modern conceptions of "state" and "society."

22. On the difficult question of the meaning of "freedom" in Rousseau's thought, see Strauss, *Natural Right and History*, 277-82; cf. Marc Plattner, *Rousseau's State of Nature: An Interpretation of the Discourse on Inequality* (DeKalb, Ill.: Northern Illinois University Press, 1979), 12-13.

23. Concerning Rousseau's tendentious presentation of the character of the ancient city, consider the observation of N. D. Fustel de Coulanges, *The Ancient City* (Garden City, N.Y.: Doubleday, 1956 [First publication: *La Cité Antique*, 1864]), 11: "In our system of education, we live from infancy in the midst of the Greeks and Romans, and become accustomed continually to compare them to ourselves, to judge of their history by our own, and to explain our revolutions by theirs. What we have received from them leads us to believe that we resemble them. . . . Hence spring many errors . . . not without danger. . . . Having imperfectly observed the institutions of the ancient city, men have dreamed of reviving them among us. They have deceived themselves about the liberty of the ancients, and on this very account liberty among the moderns has been put in peril." The "ancient city" must be distinguished not only from interpretations of it made by the modern philosophers, but as well from the "city of the philosophers" of antiquity; see Strauss, *City and Man*, 240-41. Does Rousseau, himself, not appeal from ancient philosophy to ancient practice? Is this not implied, for example, by the comparison between

Cato and Socrates in *Political Economy* (*Jean-Jaques Rousseau: On the Social Contract with Geneva Manuscript and Political Economy*, R. D. Masters, ed. [New York: St. Martin's, 1978]), 219? Cf. the extended treatment of Rome in book 4 of the *Social Contract*.

24. Consider Aristotle, *Politics*, 1268b 22-1269a 29, 1274b11-23.

25. See, for example, Masters, *First and Second Discourses*, 229-30.

26. Starobinski, *Oeuvres Complètes*, 1291.

27. Cranston, *Discourse on Inequality*, 52.

28. Masters, *First and Second Discourses*, 229.

29. Ibid., 102.

30. See Strauss, *Natural Right and History*, 252-94; cf. Plattner, *Rousseau's State of Nature*. In challenging slavery, Rousseau could also be said to accept the ancient tradition according to which society arose from a contract, an ancient tradition that denied "natural slavery," above all Lucretius' account of the genesis of civil society in *De Rerum Natura*, which serves, according to Strauss, 271n37, as the "model" for Rousseau's own account in the *Second Discourse*. We have already remarked that it is ancients—Plato and Xenocrates—whom Rousseau accepts explicitly as his judges. Illuminating discussions of Aristotle's understanding of the "naturalness" of the family, acquisition, and slavery are Wayne Ambler, "Aristotle on Acquisition," *Canadian Journal of Political Science 17* (1984): 487-502; "Aristotle's Understanding of the Naturalness of the City," *Review of Politics 47* (1985): 163-85; "Aristotle on Nature and Politics: The Case of Slavery," *Political Theory 15* (1987): 390-410; Mary P. Nichols, "The Good Life, Slavery, and Acquisition: Aristotle's Introduction to Politics," *Interpretation 11* (1983): 171-83; and Catherine Zuckert, "Aristotle on the Limits and Satisfactions of Political Life," *Interpretation 11* (1983): 185-206.

31. Note how Miller's judgment (see note 17) begins by quoting from the first sentence of the second paragraph of the letter, and ends with a quotation from the fourteenth paragraph, conflating the two "discourses." This is symptomatic of his failure to recognize correctly the significance of what he calls Rousseau's "rhetorical device."

32. Masters, *First and Second Discourses*, 230.

33. Everyone remarks this implication: see, for example, Cranston, *Early Life and Work*, 51-52, and *Discourse on Inequality*, 349; and S. Ellenburg, *Rousseau's Political Philosophy: An Interpretation from Within*, 256. Note Ellenburg's remark that this anticipates the important distinction between sovereign and government in the *Social Contract*; on which distinction, see Gildin, *Rousseau's Social Contract*.

34. The republic of Geneva was in fact a functioning oligarchy in the eighteenth century; see Cranston, *Early Life and Work*, 13-17, 340-41. It was Machiavelli who taught us how to manage the conflicts between the popular and princely "humors." Rousseau strives rather to eradicate them by encouraging a common love. Rousseau, in concert with all the "moderns," shares Machiavelli's perspective on many things political, but where Machiavelli in the end relies on fear, Rousseau does not.

35. See Masters, *First and Second Discourses*, 230-31, and F. C. Green, *Jean-Jacques Rousseau: A Critical Study of His Life and Writings*, 1-12.

36. L. G. Crocker, *Jean-Jacques Rousseau: The Quest* (New York: Macmillan, 1968), 251, remarks the insolence of this "exhaltation of a citizen who had been in bad odor until he was finally forced into exile." For a "historical" portrait of Isaac Rousseau, see Cranston, *Early Life and Work*, the first chapter, and 37-38, 50, 93-94, 114, 192, 255.

37. Starobinski, *Oeuvres Complètes*, 1293.

38. Miller, *Dreamer of Democracy*, 222n60.

39. Cf. Joel Schwartz, *The Sexual Politics of Jean-Jacques Rousseau* (Chicago: University of Chicago Press, 1984); and Mary P. Nichols, "Women in Western Political

140   *Chapter 9*

Thought," *Political Science Reviewer 13* (1984): 241-60.

40. Cranston, *Early Life and Work,* 319, and 19.

41. This is why, in fact, it was practically out of the question that Rousseau should settle at Geneva after recovering his citizenship (consider Cranston, *Discourse on Inequality,* 51). The most recent detailed account of Rousseau's "exile" from Geneva is Miller, *Dreamer of Democracy,* 52-54. For a commentary on Pericles' praise of Athens in his famous funeral oration, and Thucydides' judgment of Pericles, see Michael Palmer, "Love of Glory and the Common Good," *American Political Science Review 76* (1982): 825-36.

42. It was in Chambéry that Rousseau spent his early adult life after his flight from Geneva. Miller, *Dreamer of Democracy,* 25, suggests that Rousseau's completing the dedicatory letter at Chambéry "safeguarded his ignorance" of Genevan reality. In his *Confessions* (Gagnebin and Raymond, *Ouevres Complètes,* 392), Rousseau claims he dated the letter at Chambéry to avoid quibbling in France or Geneva. Cranston, *Early Life and Work,* 323, suggests Rousseau wished to avoid embarrassment in France or Geneva.

43 *Early Rousseau,* 158; cf. R. Grimsley, *Jean-Jacques Rousseau* (New York: Barnes and Noble, 1983), 121, and Miller, *Dreamer of Democracy,* 72.

44. Rousseau's major writings may be distinguished, like the two halves of this letter, according to whether they deal primarily with the permanent question of the best regime, or with Rousseau's assessment of contemporary political life. A prime candidate for the former category is the *Social Contract*; for the latter, *Letters Written from the Mountain.* For discussion of Rousseau's critique of Geneva, and argument that the society of the *Social Contract* is not Geneva, see Ellenburg, *Interpretation from Within,* 239-40, Starobinski, *Ouevres Complètes,* 1664-65, and their references; cf. Judith Shklar, *Men and Citizens: Rousseau's Political Theory* (Cambridge: Cambridge University Press, 1969), the first chapter.

45. Cranston, *Discourse on Inequality,* 13.

Chapter 10

On Leo Strauss's "Jerusalem and Athens"

Susan Orr's *Jerusalem and Athens: Reason and Revelation in the Works of Leo Strauss* is one of a relatively small but rapidly increasing number of attempts to read and understand the writings of Leo Strauss as Strauss read and understood the writings of political philosophers before him. The first genuinely philosophical reading of Strauss was Alexandre Kojève's, half a century ago in postwar Paris. The most recent commendable attempt is Laurence Lampert's *Leo Strauss and Nietzsche*,[1] a remarkably thoughtful book.

Orr's book is a paragraph-by-paragraph, even sentence-by-sentence, commentary on Strauss's 1967 lecture, "Jerusalem and Athens: Some Preliminary Reflections." Orr says in her introductory chapter that she limits herself to only one essay because the subject of reason and revelation in Strauss's thought is so complex that a discussion of it in all of his works "could lead us to incorrect assumptions" (18). How a discussion of the theme in all of Strauss's works, as opposed to just one, leads to incorrect assumptions is not specified. Orr nevertheless insists on the importance of, and makes liberal use of, five other works of Strauss: "Progress or Return? The Contemporary Crisis in Western Civilization"[2] and "The Mutual Influence of Theology and Philosophy",[3] both from lectures delivered in 1952; "On the Interpretation of Genesis",[4] a lecture from 1957; the "Introductory Essay" Strauss wrote for the English translation of his *Spinoza's Critique of Religion*;[5] and *Natural Right and History*.[6] She refers to other writings, too. Orr's protestations to the contrary notwithstanding, then, we believe that she presents what is, to the best of her ability, a comprehensive interpretation of reason and revelation in the thought of Leo Strauss. Mimicking Orr mimicking Strauss, we might suggest that this is the esoteric intention behind the fact that the cover page of her book refers to "the *Works* of Leo Strauss" while the title page within reads "the *Work* of Leo Strauss" (my emphases), which would appear to more casual readers to be an obvious mistake. (Similarly, we wonder how much we are supposed to read into the subtle revisions of the translation of God's Hebrew name, "Ehyeh-Asher-Ehyeh," which appears in four slightly different versions in five successive paragraphs of her book (93-95), sometimes quoting Strauss, sometimes not; and a startlingly new version, later, quoting Harry V. Jaffa quoting Strauss (119).

Orr's central theme is to demonstrate how Strauss restores the Bible ("Jerusalem") as a serious alternative to classical political philosophy ("Athens") even, or especially, for philosophically minded contemporary readers. This is all to the good. But she situates her commentary in the context of the debate between so-called "West Coast Straussians" and "East Coast Straussians," especially Jaffa and Thomas L. Pangle as champions of the former and the latter, respectively. This is not the place to elaborate on this debate, but it must be remarked that Orr's presentation of it is suspect. In her acknowledgments, she thanks Jaffa for his "unflagging support and inspiration" (ix). She also thanks Jaffa for clarifying Pangle's position for her (160n21) in the very note in which she provides the citation for her approving quotation from Jaffa that "Pangle's account . . . has nothing whatever in common with anything that might be attributed to Leo Strauss" (10). There is, of course, no indication that she sought clarification of Jaffa's account from Pangle. Thus her "conclusion" that Jaffa's Strauss is superior to Pangle's cannot surprise (although she quotes Strauss, elsewhere, explicitly stating what appears to be Pangle's allegedly fantastic distortion of Strauss's view [27]).

Orr says that she follows "all the rules" that Strauss said were necessary for understanding difficult and important texts (33). Both the strengths and some of the weaknesses of the book follow from Orr's obedience to these "rules." Strauss warned that there could really be no such rules, that part of what makes a great book great is that it teaches its readers how to read it, and that the rigid application of his own discoveries about how to read Machiavelli, for instance, could lead to fallacious results if applied to someone else. Orr makes myriad discrete observations on Strauss's text in the course of following her rules, many of which are thoughtful and insightful, many of which are not. The net result is a book that sometimes reads more like preparatory notes for an interpretation of Strauss than an interpretation. Orr's repeated observations about which paragraphs are at the center of sections, or which sentences are at the center of paragraphs, or the number of sentences that a paragraph contains, are sometimes apt: that the middle sentence of the first of Strauss's two paragraphs on the six-day story in Genesis is the ironic remark that only God was an eyewitness to the beginning of the universe (65); or that the middle sentence of the second paragraph contains the lesson of the first creation account, that "Heaven is lower than earth" (67). But they are also frequently inapt: Does it really matter that the paragraph on Hesiod, the twenty-sixth, also has twenty-six sentences (100; therefore, we note, no middle sentence)?

A general problem with Orr's discussion is that she insists on precise distinctions when they suit her case, but glosses over them when they do not; for example, she warns that in reading Strauss we must recognize that there are differences between Zeus and Yahweh, not to mention Zeus and Christ (14, 41), which "East Coast" Straussians allegedly insufficiently appreciate (154). But she does not hesitate to speak of the "the Judeo-Christian God" (13), as if Strauss might not also have something to say about any differences between Christ and Yahweh. Indeed, Orr's book homogenizes Judaism and Christianity, throughout. She claims that she is careful to note exactly what Strauss writes, the order in which he considers items, and what he fails to mention (18)—she even notes his emphatic failure to mention Christianity (28)—but she pays little more than lip service to the difficulties that follow, simply asserting whenever she wishes that Strauss includes Christianity in his defense of Jerusalem (150, 154). An important piece of evidence in support of her assertion is supposed to be that Strauss's use of the Christian term "Bible" throughout his lecture is significant, since he treats exclusively the Old Testament in the lecture without using the term "Hebrew Bible," as he does elsewhere (29). Yet Orr later quotes another writing where Strauss does use "Bible" and "Old Testament" synonymously (45). She even cites one where Strauss reminds us "that there is no *biblical* word for doubt" (54, my emphasis), and supplies a footnote in which she reminds us that this cannot apply to the New Testament (164n57). Her commentary proper ends on an especially confused note, attributing to Strauss a position that her quotation from him makes clear is not his own (145). And the power of her summary conclusions is vitiated by the fact that the conclusive ones are admittedly obvious (147), the intriguing ones admittedly borrowed (150), and the rest admittedly inconclusive. Orr does take serious questions seriously, however, and many readers will benefit from the exercise of contending with her reading of Strauss's important essay, even if that reading is questionable. An unqualified good is that the book contains, in addition to a reprint of "Jerusalem and Athens," Strauss's "On the Interpretation of Genesis," previously difficult to obtain.

Notes

This chapter, a review of Susan Orr, *Jerusalem and Athens: Reason and Revelation in the Works of Leo Strauss* (Lanham, Md.: Rowman & Littlefield, 1995), was originally published in the *American Political Science Review 90* (1996). Reprinted with permission.

1. Laurence Lampert, *Leo Strauss and Nietzsche* (Chicago: University of Chicago Press, 1996).

2. Leo Strauss, "Progress or Return: The Contemporary Crisis in Western Civilization," *Modern Judaism 1* (1981): 17-45.

3. Leo Strauss, "The Mutual Influence of Theology and Philosophy," *The Independent Journal of Philosophy 3* (1979): 111-18.

4. Leo Strauss, "On the Interpretation of Genesis," *L'Homme: Revue Française d'anthropologie 21* (1981): 5-20.

5. Leo Strauss, *Spinoza's Critique of Religion* (New York: Schocken, 1965).

6. Leo Strauss, *Natural Right and History* (Chicago: University of Chicago Press, 1953).

Chapter 11

On George Grant's *English-Speaking Justice*

Reading George Parkin Grant is nothing if not refreshing. And now, with the publication of *English-Speaking Justice* (*ESJ* hereafter) by the University of Notre Dame in "Revisions: A Series of Books on Ethics," Americans are more readily given the opportunity to refresh themselves. (*ESJ* was published relatively obscurely in Canada in 1978.) As Stanley Hauerwas and Alasdair MacIntyre, general editors of the series, remark in their introduction, "About George Parkin Grant's writings on moral and political theory two things need be said at the outset. They are among the most interesting North American work to be produced in that area since 1945; and they are almost entirely unknown in the United States." This is attributed, on the one hand and in part, to the "philistine parochialism" of American intellectuals so far as things Mexican and Canadian are concerned, but on the other hand only in part, because it is acknowledged that "Grant has considerably directed what he has to say to the contemporary concerns of his own political and cultural milieu, that of English-speaking Canadians."

Readers of *The American Review of Canadian Studies*, however, can scarcely be accused of philistine parochialism so far as things Canadian are concerned, nor of an inability to appreciate the contemporary concerns of English-speaking Canadians. They may nevertheless have their own difficulties with *ESJ*, for however apt the above observations may be regarding Grant's writing in general, they are quite inapt regarding *ESJ*. And this poses something of a problem in reviewing the book for "Canadianists": Grant's concerns in *ESJ* are not "Canadian" in any meaningful sense, no, not even peculiarly "North American"; Grant is concerned, rather, with nothing less than the fate of western civilization. He understands this fate, and therewith the fate of Canada, to be enframed within the fate of "technology," the unique fusion of knowing and making that manifests itself most clearly, but not exclusively, in "modern mastering science." True, *ESJ* is dedicated to Alex Colville and Dennis Lee, respected Canadian artists, but the names we run into in the first pages of the book are Kant, Heisenberg, Einstein, Descartes, Rousseau, and Nietzsche, not a native English-speaker among them. This is a far cry, or so it appears, from the George Grant of *Lament for a Nation*, his most widely known book. (As fate would have it, *ESJ* is the written version of the Wood Lectures, delivered in 1974 at Mount Allison University, New Brunswick. Grant was obliged to step in for the ailing Lester Pearson, whose government received such sustained criticism in *Lament*.)

The primary task for thinking in our time, according to Grant, is to ponder the question concerning technology—"to think what technology *is*: to think it in its determining power over our politics and sexuality, our music and education" (1). This question has been left unthought by English-speaking people; in particular, the political consequences of the fact that technology "is increasingly directed toward the mastery of human beings" have been left unthought. The great difficulty is that "the heartlands of the English-speaking empire," where these developments are being most vigorously pursued, are also the heartlands of modern "liberalism"—"the belief that political liberty is a central human good." Why is this a great difficulty?

> The practical question is whether a society in which technology must be oriented to cybernetics can maintain the institutions of free politics and the protection by law of the rights of individuals. Behind that lies the theoretical question about modern liberalism itself. What were the modern assumptions which at the same time exalted human freedom and encouraged the cybernetic mastery which now threatens freedom? (10)

"This," Grant avers, "questions modern liberalism at its theoretical heart" (12).

Thus Grant presents his project in Part I of *ESJ*. Part II is devoted to a trenchant critique of Harvard philosophy professor John Rawls' *A Theory of Justice*.[1] In this "book of six hundred pages about justice," Rawls "does not give any account of those theoretical positions about morals and politics which in the western world have stood as alternatives to our liberalism." As for Rawls' approach to classical political philosophy, "all that need be said . . . is that in a book on justice there are four times as many references to a certain Professor Arrow as there are to Plato" (95). These are egregious deficiencies in a book devoted to the meaning of justice. However, Grant wryly observes, "The advantage of this procrustean stance is that it allows Rawls to hold English-speaking liberalism before us for our individed attention" (95-96). As may be gathered from these few quotations, Grant's dissection of Rawls' reasoning proceeds with his customary relish.

Rawls posits human beings as shrewd calculators who enter into and observe contracts on the basis of narrow self-interest, and who derive the principles of justice from those contracts. He is thus an exemplar of modern liberalism. *A Theory of Justice* is "the attempt to make clear the nature of that social contract (a) in light of the new conditions of advanced technological society and (b) in terms acceptable to modern analytical philosophers" (16). As regards the first task, Grant lucidly demonstrates the inadequacy of Rawls' attempt; as regards the second, the inadequacy of the task itself. Suffice it to say it is Grant's intimate familiarity with those theoretical positions that have stood as alternatives to our liberalism—the spectrum from Marx to Nietzsche and Heidegger—that enables him to maintain his profound critical perspective on Rawls. He elucidates the superiority of the thinking of Rawls' avowed masters, Locke and Kant, to their Harvard student, and generally how what's good in Rawls isn't new, and what's new isn't good. The core of Rawls' problem is "the inability to state clearly what it is about human beings which makes them worthy of high political respect" (33). Typical of modern liberals, Rawls "mysteriously" or "sentimentally" relies on the word "person" to cover up this inability (33).

Part III of *ESJ* is devoted to the question, "Why is it that liberalism remains the dominating political morality of the English-speaking world, and yet is so little sustained by any foundational affirmations?" (48). The answers are (a) English-speaking liberalism's virtual immunity to philosophic critique because the last English-speaking philosophers of the first rank, Hobbes and Locke, were among the founders of modern liberalism, and (b) the deep influence of English-speaking Protestantism. "Modern European history brings forth the comparison: Germany with its philosophy and music, its political immaturities and extremities; England with its poverty in music and contemplation, its political moderation and judgment" (59-60). Only a great fool would be contemptuous of political moderation and judgment, and Grant is no fool. He believes, however, that the halcyon days of contemplative debility combined with political health are over for the English-speaking world.

Grant illustrates his argument in Part IV of *ESJ* with a discussion of the U.S. Supreme Court's decision on abortion in the case of *Roe v. Wade*. The decision "speaks modern liberalism in its pure contractual form" (70); nevertheless, it "raises the cup of poison to the lips of liberalism" (71). The "cup of poison" is the "unthought ontology" underlying the decision, which enabled the justices to distinguish between adult human beings and fetuses of the same species, and which, "unavoidably opens up the whole question of what our species is" (71). Should modern liberalism genuinely attempt to think its unthought ontology, it must end in abandonment of modern liberalism. Grant's analysis of *Roe* can be questioned on a number of grounds, and Clifford Orwin did so forcefully in a masterful review of *ESJ*, shortly after its Canadian publication, in the *University of Toronto Law Journal.*[2] But Grant uses his analysis to raise profound questions that must not be ignored. Grant writes of how Nietzsche, "more than a hundred years ago . . . laid down with incomparable lucidity that which is now publicly open: what is given about the whole in technological science cannot be thought together with what is given us concerning justice and truth, reverence and beauty, from our tradition" (77). Following Nietzsche, Grant reserves his contempt for those "who want to maintain a content to 'justice' and 'truth' and 'goodness' out of the corpse that they helped to make a corpse" (77), those modern liberals who celebrate "God is dead" but want to retain His Ten Commandments (oh, well, sort of.)

For Christians such as Grant, the darkness that surrounds the question of justice in our era is merely a theoretical, not a practical concern. But Grant is a thinker, and will not rest with practical light and theoretical darkness. Grant calls for the "undoubtable core of truth which has come out of technology"—the great theoretical achievements of modernity: quantum physics, evolutionary biology, modern logic—"to be thought in harmony with the conception of justice as what we are fitted for" (86-87), if this is possible. Be there any "Canadianists" among us who wish to ignore Grant's plea, they stand convicted of helping to fulfill his ominous concluding prophecy: "it is improbable that the transcendence of justice over technology will be lived among English-speaking people" (89).

Notes

This chapter, a review of George Parkin Grant, *English-Speaking Justice* (Notre Dame, Ind.: University of Notre Dame Press, 1985), was originally published in the *American Review of Canadian Studies 15* (1985). Reprinted with permission.

1. John Rawls, *A Theory of Justice* (Cambridge, Mass.: Harvard University Press, 1971).

2. Clifford Orwin, "On George Grant, *English-Speaking Justice*," *The University of Toronto Law Journal 30* (1980): 106-15.

Chapter 12

On Allan Bloom's
The Closing of the American Mind

In preparing my remarks for today, I have tried to remember that brevity is the soul of wit. I was asked to speak at this symposium because I know Allan Bloom personally, and I have been urged to be anecdotal, so I shall introduce Mr. Bloom to you, so to speak, with some personal reminiscences. One of the astonishing things—astonishing to me, at least—that occurred to me in preparing these remarks, is that I have known, and admired, and loved Allan Bloom for half my lifetime; and I am almost the age, now, that Allan Bloom was when I met him.

So, I should state clearly from the outset that I came here today to praise Allan Bloom, not to bury him: My motive is a kind of filial piety. I am sensitive to the degree of respect accorded piety of any kind in state universities these days, and it is with corresponding confidence that I hazard my remarks. I should also make clear, when I speak personally about Allan Bloom, that while I was one of the "inner circle" of his Toronto students during the early 1970s, I was not one of his closest or his best students.

I arrived at the University of Toronto in 1971, a teenager, having little idea what to expect, but desperately hoping it would not be four more years of high school, from which I had been suspended many times, even expelled once, and which I had loathed. In retrospect, I realize I had loathed it, in part, not so much because I was usually smarter than my teachers (as they, themselves, on occasion, confided to me), but because they seemed to know nothing important that I did not already know (which they were also apt to confess). I realize, in retrospect, that they were victims, in their own college education, of the kind of thing Allan Bloom excoriates in *The Closing of the American Mind*.[1]

So, I arrived on that Tuesday after Labor Day, my first year in college, my first day in college—as I recollect it, my first class in college—and a very large, very Jewish-looking man, a kind of hybrid of Orson Welles and Carl Reiner, stormed into the room, furiously sucking on a cigarette, panted his name, the title of the course—Introduction to Political Philosophy—and asked if there were any questions about the reading list, which his graduate assistants were hastily distributing.

I remember vividly one of the exchanges from that first class. The reading list began with Machiavelli, went back to Plato, and then proceeded, more or less chronologically, through, among others, Shakespeare, Hobbes, Swift, Rousseau, Tocqueville, Flaubert, and Nietzsche: it was a six-credit course. Anyway, a young woman complained that the most "up-to-date" author we were to read that year had died at the turn of the century; were we not going to read any authors who were "relevant" today? (The young woman was insufficiently "up-to-date," herself, for she had failed to add, as she surely would today, that they were *all* men.) I can still picture the scene: Bloom stepped from behind the lectern and approached the front row of the lecture hall (the young woman was seated in about the third row, which put them at eye level with each other).

"Tell me," he asked, "What do you think of your mother's views about sex?"

Silence.

"You know, what would you say about your mother's views on premarital sex, marriage, abortion?"

"Well," the student blurted out, "I think they're kind of out of touch with today's values."

"Ah," said Bloom, half under his breath as he returned to the lectern, "no college education."

"No," the student protested, "as a matter of fact, my mother graduated from *this* university!"

Bloom smiled. "Well," he said, "it appears that she got an education that was 'relevant' in 1950, but it's not 1950 any more! Perhaps you would like an education that will still be 'relevant' when *your* daughter comes here; if so, stick around!"

This exchange prompted another student to query concerning Bloom's "values." Bloom allowed as he had none (only later did I come to understand what he meant); what were the student's? Prominent among these were "sincerity" and "commitment."

"I myself have always kind of preferred," Bloom dryly responded, "insincere and half-hearted Nazis to sincere and committed ones."

Well, before the hour was out, I had no doubt that I was no longer in high school, and before the year was out, my world had changed. Sophomore year saw a working-class kid from an uneducated family who could not, or more correctly, *would* not learn French or bother with plane geometry in high school, doing well in his study of classical Greek and tackling treatises such as Jacob Klein's *Greek Mathematical Thought and the Origin of Algebra*[2] for leisure reading. Why? Because he had now been given a *reason* to study. He was getting an inkling, for the first time, of what was *relevant* about liberal education.

I had Allan Bloom as a teacher for only half of that first year; just before the second semester was to begin, he suffered a massive heart attack, and did not return to the lecture hall until the last week of classes, greeted by a standing ovation from about a hundred students. That was, at the time, the largest class in the Department of Political Science at the University of Toronto. Before I left three years later, enrollment had climbed to more than six hundred and the class had been moved to an amphitheater.

Bloom's heart attack brings me, ironically, to another thing that always amazed me about him: his incredible vitality. It enabled him, for example, to keep that class of six hundred in the palm of his hand: They would gasp when he wanted them to gasp, laugh when he wanted them to laugh, and stop breathing when he held his breath. But I remember especially his graduate seminars, which were always scheduled Friday afternoons from one to four o'clock. I was a student in those seminars in my junior and senior years. I don't think that one ever ended before 5:30, about six o'clock was usual, and I remember occasionally being there at seven! I don't recollect students leaving, or even grumbling afterward. These were courses in which we would spend the entire academic year reading one book, or at most two, virtually sentence by sentence. Nor did the academic year have clear limits: I remember my senior year when we had not finished reading the one book we had begun in September by the end of the second semester. Without mentioning the university calendar, Bloom simply announced the reading assignment for the next week, and the next week the seminar met. And the week after, and the week after that, even though the grades had been submitted, and I had, in fact, graduated. (I don't recall a decline in attendance.)

My most recent experience of Mr. Bloom's vitality outside the classroom was when I was one of about two dozen guests at a party in his new post-fame-and-wealth apartment in Chicago. A friend and I were the first to leave, about one o'clock in the morning. I heard the next day that the last guests left close to five o'clock, which was normal for the Bloom parties I had attended as an undergraduate. After my return to Orono, a student asked if I had seen Bloom interviewed on television, on "This Week with David Brinkley," on Sunday morning. No, but I had seen him late Saturday night. I was surprised, as I thought the Brinkley program was live. The point of the story, of course, is that it was.

Bloom's parties were always as interesting, too, as they were long. They usually began as a sort of seminar with a special guest from out of town making an informal presentation, followed by questions from Bloom and the other guests, followed by general discussion; eventually, as the alcohol and conviviality took effect, the event would turn into what would normally be called a party. Being one of the few undergraduates invited to attend (and deeply insecure), I usually made a contribution only to the drinking stage (at which I excelled). But I enjoyed it all immensely. Where else could a working-class kid get to sit on a sofa and dish, so to speak, with the likes of Hans Georg Gadamer, George Parkin Grant, or Eric Voegelin? And listen to amusing stories about what Gadamer heard Hannah Arendt say about Leo Strauss to Karl Jaspers some time in the 1930s? I remember 1973, when Gershom Scholem, the world's greatest authority on Jewish mysticism, was visiting Toronto, but had to leave abruptly to return to Israel because the October War broke out during his visit.

In thinking about Allan Bloom, and those heady days (for me), I am always reminded of an aphorism of Nietzsche: "Whoever is a teacher from the ground up takes all things seriously only in relation to his pupils—even himself" (*Beyond Good and Evil*, Aphorism No. 63).

Now, if we turn to Mr. Bloom's book, I am reminded of another aphorism of Nietzsche: "When a philosopher these days lets it be known that he is not a skeptic . . . everyone is annoyed" (*Beyond Good and Evil*, Aphorism No. 208).

There is much in *The Closing of the American Mind* that is annoying. Some of it is certainly annoying to a divorced father of two young children. But it was Allan Bloom from whom I first heard of Aristotle's assertion that while he loved Plato, he loved the truth more. And in reading Bloom's book, I believe our problem is frequently that our self-love gets in the way of our love of the truth. Loving the truth more than oneself is, of course, perhaps the hardest thing there is for a human being to do; so it cannot surprise if most of us are unable to do it most of the time, and if none of us is able to do it all of the time. Yet I believe the startling success of Mr. Bloom's book derives in part from the fact that it rings true with so many parents, even if they are pained by what it says. Ah, one might ask, but are Bloom's assertions supported by current research in the social sciences? Well, I don't know. But I strongly suspect that the book's indifference to that kind of "research"—the "data" and "analyses" of "social scientists"— goes a long way toward explaining its great appeal to ordinary people. And that indifference is well deserved, in my opinion: Social scientists qua social scientists too frequently seem to pride themselves on nothing so much as "proving scientifically" what most intelligent twelve-year-old kids already know, or refusing to accept as "true" what cannot be accounted for by their quantitative analyses.

The Closing of the American Mind is the fruit of decades-long meditation on the human soul, the very existence of which the social sciences officially deny, and for which they certainly cannot account even when they do not deny it. Bloom spent decades pondering every word, and preparing definitive English translations of Plato's *Republic; or On the Just*, and Rousseau's *Emile; or On Education*. The former needs, of course, no introduction, nor should the latter, but for those who may not be familiar with it, I have heard it aptly described by a prominent contemporary political theorist (Judith Shklar of Harvard) as Hegel's *Phenomenology of Spirit* masquerading as Dr. Spock. In short, the books on which Allan Bloom is among the world's leading authorities are not just *any* old books, but among the few greatest books ever written on the nature of the human soul and on the nurture it requires in order to fully realize its nature.

Now, Mr. Bloom's own book began as a piece of journalism, and it is really little more than an extended piece of journalism. I do not *here* intend "journalism" as a pejorative. There is journalism of a very high order: the *Federalist Papers*, for example, were daily newspaper articles (which, in itself, speaks volumes about the effect that two centuries of increasingly "accessible" universal education has had on American journalism, not to mention the reading public!). Now, *liberal* education (almost by definition at odds with "universal" education), how it is dying a slow death in American universities, and why, and what that portends for the American regime, but, more importantly, for the souls of perhaps generations of America's young—this is what Allan Bloom's book is all about.

The book contains a chapter, "From Socrates' *Apology* to Heidegger's *Rektoratsrede*," which traces the steady socialization, even domestication, of philosophy in the west, which reached a kind of symbolic nadir in Martin Heidegger's "Inaugural Address" as rector of the University of Freiburg in 1933. In that notorious lecture, Heidegger uttered, among other things, that Hitler's National Socialism was the unity of politics and philosophy and deserved the support of all thoughtful people. We are all, I am sure, justly appalled at such sentiments. Yet virtually every university president in 1987 asserts that the *appropriate* role of the university is "to serve the needs and reflect the values of society," and what administrator would dare *oppose* the "values" of the taxpaying public and its elected representatives? Our universities have become increasingly absorbed into the system of public opinion and public utility. The prevailing dogma is that the university should promote certain socially acceptable views—"equality," for example—and prohibit certain socially unacceptable ones—"elitism" and "sexism," for example. *We are growing afraid even to ask certain questions lest we be accused of these "crimes."* Bloom's concern, and mine, is what this fusion of "popular" politics and "pop" philosophy augurs for the increasingly meaningless idea of "academic freedom," and what that portends for *liberal* education: education, that is, that *liberates* one from "serving the needs and reflecting the values of society."

Now, I have not the same breadth of university experience as Allan Bloom, but I have personally experienced some of the dire effects of which he writes. For doing nothing more than teaching book 5 of Plato's *Republic* with an open mind, for example, and asking questions—to be sure, I admit, *provocative* questions; that is, questions meant to *provoke* thinking—I was charged by a politically active student with using the classroom to promote incest. Did I spend an hour and a half in my office sincerely attempting to allay the student's concerns on this point? Yes. I was nevertheless later "indicted" on this charge, complete with a little "trial." In the course of the "trial," the student eventually had to admit that there was no ground whatsoever for the accusation. At that point, in the midst of the final meeting concerning this matter (which was the culmination of proceedings that had consumed almost an entire semester), the charge was abruptly changed: I was homophobic! (This charge, by the way, some of my closest friends, even family members—not to mention Allan Bloom—would find especially laughable.) When I turned in utter disbelief to the administrators in the room, who were there, purportedly, to see justice done, neither so much as batted an eye! In any event, when the "trial" was over and all charges were dropped for lack of even a shred of supporting evidence, I was nevertheless handed a packet of "literature," which I was sternly admonished to "study," in order to improve the "chilly climate" in my classroom. And this, when I had been found innocent! Of course, to this particular "vanguard of the proletariat," *all* are guilty who have yet to attend reeducation camp. (Within twenty-four hours, by the way, various colleagues from around the university were commenting to me upon the outcome of this "confidential" investigation.)

At a recent honors program lecture on existentialism, in which the lecturer was expressing enthusiasm for the insights of Martin Heidegger, the philosophic core of that movement, and Jean-Paul Sartre, its greatest popularizer, I politely asked whether the facts that the former spent his brief political career as a Nazi, while the latter was an apologist for the worst atrocities of Stalinism, did not give the lecturer pause. When the question was evaded, I simply repeated it. This prompted one of my fellow instructors to turn around and angrily inform me that even Christians had committed crimes during the Second World War (thereby demonstrating that the point of my question had been entirely missed), and to storm out of the room—I hope, to this day, because of a previous engagement.

The attempt to get Heidegger onto the reading list in first-year honors (and keep him there)—he *is* arguably the most important philosopher of the twentieth century, notwithstanding his Nazism—has, by the way, failed. Why? As best as I can tell, because some of the faculty did not *like* reading him. And if that's not a sufficient objection, a number of the students did not *like* it, either. I can just hear them over in the physics department: "Well, no more of this quantum mechanics stuff, some of the students don't *like* it!" I have heard the same complaint made about Nietzsche in some faculty meetings—to be replaced by whom, one shudders even to guess.

In conclusion, I have not named names in these remarks, not only to protect my dwindling prospects for tenure, but more importantly, from justice: I sincerely believe that most of my colleagues are decent, well-intentioned people, with whom I simply strongly disagree; besides, we all have bad moments. I want it to be perfectly clear, too, that I do not believe that the University of Maine is worse than average in these respects. I do, however, find it to be an institution in which any distinction between "higher" education and "further" education has been blurred out of existence, all at the expense of the former. And I do think that many of the problems even of the honors program are the result of an apparently endemic inability in this university to distinguish between "liberal" studies and "illiberal" ones. And it does seem to me that the aspiration to *excellence*, avowed in the current "Service: Excellence: Efficiency" slogan of this institution, has all too often meant nothing more than improving the *efficiency* of our *service*. Finally, I do believe that Socrates would be put to death, or the current equivalent, more quickly at an American university than he was in the city of Athens, and that this is the result of many of the things that Allan Bloom writes about in *The Closing of the American Mind*.

In sum, I believe that what was said by a certain "gadfly"—Allan Bloom's own mentor, Leo Strauss—more than a generation ago, concerning the American political science profession, of which I am a member, applies today to our universities, at least in so far as liberal education is concerned. They are not diabolic institutions; they have none of the attributes peculiar to fallen angels. Nor are they Machiavellian; Machiavelli's teaching was at least graceful, subtle, and colorful. They are not even Neronian; nevertheless, one may say of them that they are fiddling while Rome burns. They are excused by two facts: they do not know that they are fiddling, and they do not know that Rome is burning.

Notes

This chapter was originally published as a portion of "*The Closing of the American Mind, Political Philosophy, and American Political Science,*" in *The Maine Scholar 10* (1997). It is the written version of remarks I delivered at a University of Maine Honors Program symposium on Bloom's book, held in November 1987. Reprinted with permission.

    1. Allan Bloom, *The Closing of the American Mind: How Higher Education Has Failed Democracy and Impoverished the Souls of Today's Students* (New York: Simon and Schuster, 1987).

    2. Jacob Klein, *Greek Mathematical Thought and the Origin of Algebra*, trans. Eva Brann (Cambridge: Massachusetts Institute of Technology Press, 1968).

Index